Country House Hotels of BRITAIN and IRELAND

Also published by Christopher Helm:

Europe's Historic Castle and Palace Hotels
Carole Chester

Country House Hotels of BRITAIN and IRELAND

CAROLE CHESTER

CHRISTOPHER HELM
London

Line illustrations by Isabel Lovering
Maps by Graham Douglas
Christopher Helm (Publishers) Ltd, Imperial House,
21–25 North Street, Bromley, Kent BR1 1SD

ISBN 0-7470-0425-0 (UK)

A CIP catalogue record for this book
is available from the British Library

First published in North America by
Hunter Publishing Inc.
300 Raritan Center Parkway
CN 94, Edison, N.J. 08818, USA
Tel. 201 225 171 4

ISBN 1-55650-172-2 (US)

Typeset by Tradespools Ltd., Frome, Somerset
Printed and bound in Spain.
by Gráficas Estella, S.A. Navarra.

Contents

Key to Symbols

Information is given on each hotel concerning the facilities, situation, price, and so on. The following system of symbols has been used:

3	Number of rooms
🏨	Opening dates
✕	Cuisine
✳	Ambience
𝒫	Recreation
♫	Entertainment
★	Sights in the vicinity
🚗	Situation
£/$	Price (Graded from A — the most expensive — to E)

INTRODUCTION

What is a country house hotel? The term suggests out-of-town accommodation, but different people interpret it in different ways. Some maintain it must be small and personal; others, regardless of the size, look to a setting for rural pursuits. Some consider a hotel with a drawing-room (not a guest-lounge) butler service rather than bar is traditional country-house style. Others feel that swimming pools and TVs are important, whatever the location.

The connoisseur won't put a strict definition on his or her choice but considers all the aspects: comfort, cuisine, character, décor, value for money. The choice therefore might be a converted manor house, a historic coaching inn, a cosy lodge or a country complex which features sports. It could even be a private home which accepts only a handful of paying guests, not a hotel *per se*.

This is where I point out that some of the accommodation mentioned in this book is indeed to be found in private homes — members of an excellent consortium known as Wolsey Lodges. Their owners have asked me to stress the fact that as they are not hotels, they do not provide the services one might justifiably expect of the latter, such as room service, laundry and restaurant choice. Also, most Wolsey Lodges do not take credit cards. On the other hand, they are a far cry from the average B and B or seaside boarding house.

All the entries selected have been chosen on the basis of personal knowledge and/or recommendation by respected colleagues; they are not paid-for listings. We welcome comments and further suggestions about all or any of them, favourable or not.

Sadly, because of our times, I have not felt inspired to show a strong representation in Northern Ireland.

1 Abingworth Hall
2 Alexander House
3 Anstey Hall
4 Armathwaite Hall
5 The Arundell Arms
6 Ashen Clough
7 Ayton Hall
8 Bailiffscourt
9 Beechfield House
10 The Bell Inn
11 Belstead Brook
12 Bilbrough Manor
13 Billesley Manor
14 Bishopstrow House
15 Boscundle Manor
15 Bourne Eau House
17 Bredon Manor
18 Brockencote Hall
19 The Brookhouse Inn
20 Buckland Manor
21 Buckland-Tout-Saints
22 Bunwell Manor
23 Burghope Manor
24 Calcot Manor
25 Cavendish Hotel
26 Charingworth manor
27 Chedington Court
28 Chewton Glen
29 Chilston Park
30 Cliveden
31 Combe Grove Manor
32 Combe House Hotel
33 Congham Hall
34 Coniston Sun Hotel
35 The Cotswold House
36 Crabwell Manor
37 Crayke Castle
38 Crosby Lodge
39 Crugsillick Manor
40 The Devonshire Arms
41 Dormy House
42 The Dragon House
43 Eastwell Manor
44 Elcot Park
45 The Elms
46 Fairfield Manor
47 Fairwater Head Hotel
48 Fallowfields
49 Farlam Hall
50 Farthings
51 The Feathers
52 Fifehead Manor
53 Fox's Earth
54 Fulford House
55 Gidleigh Park
56 Gilpin Lodge
57 The Glebe
58 Goodwood Park
59 Grafton Manor
60 Gravetye Manor
61 Great Fosters
62 The Greenway
63 Grinkle Park
64 Grove House
65 Hambleton Hall
66 Hatton Court
67 Headlam Hall
68 Hintlesham Hall
69 Holne Chase
70 Homewood Park
71 Hope End

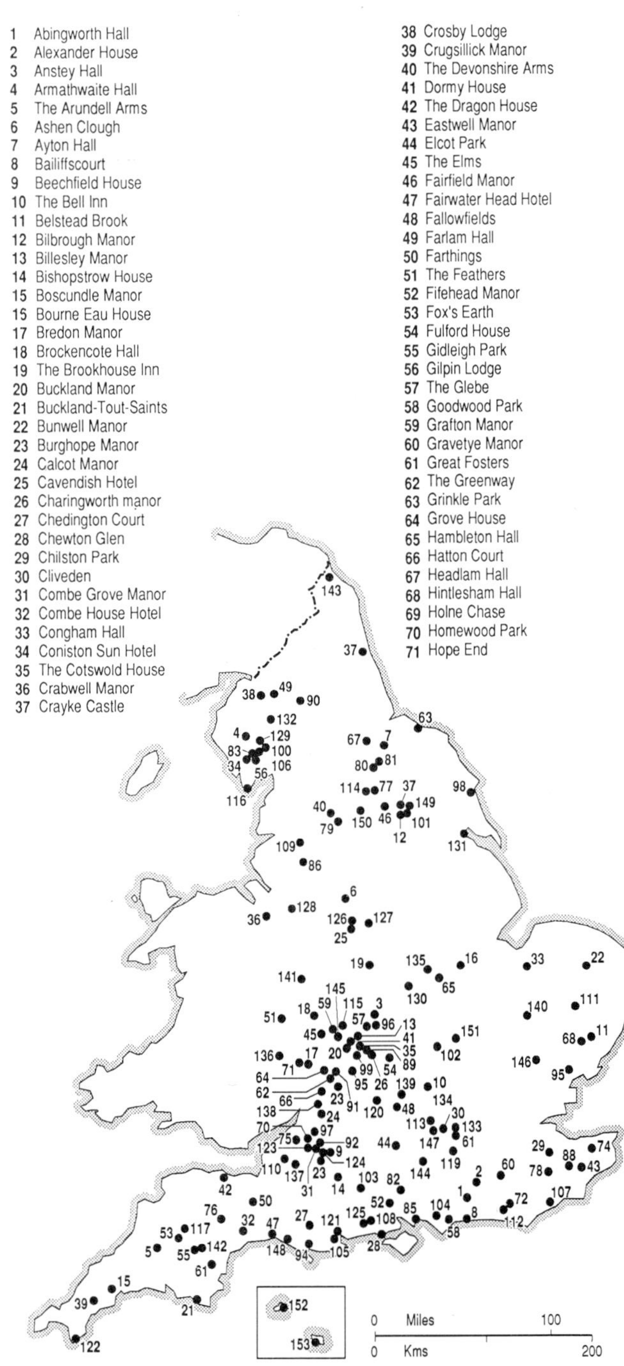

ENGLAND

The English country-house hotel scene is a flourishing one with new ones appearing all the time. The Elms (p. 60) was one of the first of its kind, but these days almost all the hotels have glamour attached: that of a former stately home or manor house, a celebrity owner, antique and/or expensive furnishings and fitments, highly rated food and an air of exclusivity. Rates therefore are not inclined to be cheap, but the concept is one of alternative accommodation to the boxy, impersonal, hotel kind.

Not every worthwhile English country establishment belongs to a marketing group, but three consortia exist which are worth mentioning for the high calibre of their members: Relais & Chateaux, Prestige, and Pride of Britain.

In keeping with the trend for more personalised service, the upmarket B & B is also flourishing, offering guests the chance to stay in a home rather than a hotel, but without the domestic chores attached.

72 Horsted Place
73 Hotel de la Bere
74 Howfield Manor
75 Hunstrete House
76 Huntsham Court
77 Jervaulx Hall
78 Kennel Holt
79 Kildwick Hall
80 Kirkby Fleetham Hall
81 Kirby Sigston Manor
82 Lainston House
83 Langdale Chase
84 Langley
85 Langrish House
86 Last Drop Village
87 Linden Hall
88 Little Hodgeham
89 Longdon Manor
90 Lovelady Shield
91 Lower Slaughter Manor
92 Lucknam Park
93 The Lygon Arms
94 Maiden Newton House
95 Maison Talbooth
96 Mallory Court
97 The Manor House
98 The Manor House
99 Manor House Hotel
100 Michael's Nook
101 Middlethorpe Hall
102 Mill House
103 The Mill House
104 The Millstream
105 Mortons House
106 Nanny Brow
107 Netherfield Place
108 New Park Manor
109 Northcote Manor
110 The Oak House
111 Oaksmere
112 Ockendon Manor
113 Ye Olde Bell
114 The Old Hall
115 The Old Rectory
116 The Old Vicarage
117 The Oxenham Arms
118 Parkhill Hotel
119 Pennyhill Park
120 The Plough
121 Plumber Manor
122 Polurrian
123 The Priory
124 Priory Steps
125 Red Lion
126 Riber Hall
127 Riverside Country House
128 Rookery Hall
129 Rothay Manor
130 Rothley Court
131 Rowley Manor
132 Sharrow Bay
133 Sir Christopher Wren's
134 The Springs
135 Stapleford Park
136 The Steppes
137 Ston Easton
138 Stonehouse Court
139 Studley Priory
140 Swynford Paddocks
141 The Talbot Inn
142 Teignworthy
143 Tillmouth Park
144 Tylney Hall
145 Upton House
146 Whitehall
147 The White Hart
148 The White House
149 Whitewell Hall
150 Wood Hall
151 Woodlands Manor
152 Le Fregate (Guernsey)
153 Longueville Manor (Jersey)

Abingworth Hall

During the 17th and 18th centuries this property was owned by the Mellersh family and was flanked by the Warminghurst estate, owned by William Penn from 1676 to 1702. The Penns and the Mellershes were great friends and often worshipped together at the Quaker Meeting House.

The present Hall was built in 1910 after a fire had destroyed the previous one, and the first to occupy the new house was Sir Oswald Mosley, whose grandson became such a political celebrity in the 1930s.

Surrounded by 8 acres (3 ha) of grounds, the hotel has superb views of the South Downs. In the garden there are an ornamental lake with two islands and plenty of quiet corners.

Thakeham Road, Storrington, West Sussex RH20 3EF. ✆ (07983) 3636

22 (Each with en suite bathroom, colour TV, hair dryer.) Rates include full English breakfast, early-morning tea and newspaper. Breaks available

Year round

✕ French nouvelle influenced plus traditional English dishes. The hotel makes baked items on the premises and its own sorbets, ice creams and preserves. Comprehensive wine list, mostly French

✻ Restful

All-weather tennis court, pitch and putt course, croquet lawn, bowls. Golf nearby

♫ No

★ Wisley Gardens, Petworth House, Arundel Castle. Brighton and Glyndebourne are within easy reach

2 miles (3 km) north of Storrington. From London take the Brighton road M23/A23 to the A272 signed Billingshurst. Turn left off A272 at Coolham onto B2139. The hotel is on the left, 4 miles (6 km) from Coolham

£/$ C

Alexander House

Sydney looks very much the part of the English butler in his black bow tie and frock coat, distinguished thatch of white hair and welcoming, but not obtrusive, manner. He is in fact the concierge at the newest hotel in the Gatwick airport area — Alexander House. And he also drives the burgundy Daimler that can be summoned on request to pick you up from the airport.

Alexander House, sometime 19th-century mansion home to Shelley, home of the Governor of the Bank of England and retirement home for the clergy, is named for Earl Alexander of Tunis, whose famous father commanded the Eight Army before Field Marshal Montgomery in World War II. However, don't be misled into thinking you've come to a lordly-owned house to take tea with the titled. A picture of Earl Alexander and family graces a table in reception, but His Grace is generally elsewhere.

Those who are there, the staff, are young, friendly but courteous, greet you with a smile (and sometimes a handshake) and are trained to remember your name (British formal fashion — none of the 'Hi Dave!'). They appear willing to act on your every whim, carry out your every demand. And that'll do nicely, thank you!

The gracious service makes up for the 'over' tasteful décor, which has stuffed so many antiques into drawing and reception rooms that the beauty of the some of the pieces cannot really be appreciated. There's so much ormulu and gilt you'd think it was ersatz, but this kitsch is genuine all right, including the caged birds in the hall (though not the stuffed variety in the library). It's a simple case of the owning-company chairman's love of works of art. Last year, for instance, he was among those to snap up a Noel Coward painting from Christies (though he bought by phone). It cost £48,000 — but it was for Alexander House. He spent even more on a bed once owned by Napoleon, a gilded and canopied four-poster, now quilted in blood red, the highlight of the Imperial Suite.

Five of the 12 rooms are, indeed, suites with spacious bathrooms, though few of them boast a shower. They are all named and they all feature the niceties one has come to expect from an upmarket country house hotel: wooden fitments around the wash basin and bath, wooden toilet seats; terry dressing gowns to match the towels; Floris toiletries; cotton wool balls and tissues in fabric pouches; hair dryers, colour TVs and bottles of Ashbourne water.

There are several lounges for guest or private-function use on the ground floor, but the library (yes, the books are real) is the place to relax with a drink. A vintage armagnac perhaps, poured from a bottle on a trolley at armchair's side (no bar stools in this 'bar'), or a glass of champagne in a crystal flute.

I am always pleased to find fine china in an establishment like this — Alexander House uses Royal Worcester (for its ash trays too) and sets the tables in the pastel dining room with shining silver. At breakfast time the toast arrives in silver racks, the orange juice is freshly squeezed, and the ketchup, jam and butter are not bottled, potted or wrapped — a true Englishman wouldn't have it any other way. A word of warning when it comes to dinner: the chef is keen on sauces (albeit nouvelle cuisine style) so if you like your food on the plainer side, request the sauce be served separately or opt for a grill. They'll be sure to oblige.

Turners Hill, West Sussex RH10 4QD. ✆ (0342) 714914

12 (including 5 suites; all spacious, and each with en suite bathroom, colour TV, luxurious fitments)

Year round

✕ Exotic combinations of fresh foods, a little heavy on the sauce side though plain grills available. Well-stocked wine cellars. A la carte and table d'hôte

✳ 'Overstuffed' antiquey

Tennis, croquet; nearby local golf courses and fishing. Health club with pool planned

♫ Piano music

★ Brighton beach is about 25 miles (40 km) away. Visits may easily be made to the Bluebell Railway, Sheffield Park, Springhill Wildlife Park and Bolebrook Castle.

9 miles (14 km) from Gatwick Airport, 45 miles (72 km) from Heathrow. Turners Hill is 6 miles (10 km) from the M23 motorway (leading to Gatwick) and 15 miles (24 km) from the M25.

£/$ A

Anstey Hall

Built in 1678, this charming redbrick Caroline house is one of those hideaway hotels you may not have heard about. Immaculately styled and furnished (pinks and peaches are the favoured colours here) with spacious public rooms, Anstey Hall projects a refined, uncluttered aura.

The hall overlooks its own 8 acres (3¼ ha) of gardens with farmland beyond. Some of the produce which helps towards the imaginative menus is grown in the hall's walled garden. Anstey also prides itself on its selection of vintage ports, cognacs and malt whiskies for after-dinner consumption.

Anstey, nr. Coventry, Warwickshire CV7 9HZ.
✆ (0203) 612222

13	(Each with en suite bathroom, colour TV, radio, trouser press, hair dryer, fresh flowers and mineral water.) Rates include newspaper and early-morning tea
🏨	Year round
✕	Modern English. Sample starter: smoked salmon consomme garnished with brunoise of fresh vegetables. Sample main dish: caramelised duck, glazed in honey, leg wrapped in filo pastry, on a rhubarb and white wine sauce. Wine list 200-strong including classics and lesser known. Good selection of vintage ports and cognacs. Table d'hôte and à la carte
✻	Chic
🎾	No
♫	No
★	Coventry Cathedral
🚗	On the edge of Anstey village, 2 minutes drive from Junction 2 of the M6/69 motorways on the B4065
£/$	C

Armathwaite Hall Hotel

This formerly the house of Benedictine nuns was frequently plundered during the Middle Ages, dissolved during the Reformation, and only later became a private house. It was converted into a hotel in 1930.

Today it is filled with antiques and bric-à-brac and offers a variety of facilities. Extensive wood panelling and hunting trophies help preserve its old-world associations. A wide range of liqueurs and malt whiskies are a speciality in the bar with its open fire. A la carte French and English cuisine is served in the wood-panelled restaurant looking out to Bassenthwaite Lake and the surrounding Skiddaw Mountains. Modernised bedrooms also provide good views of the 133 acres (54 ha) of deer park that encircle Armathwaite.

Bassenthwaite Lake, Keswick, Cumbria CA12 4RE.
✆ (059681) 551

42 (Including suites and four-posters, most with view of lake or park; each with en suite bathroom, colour TV, in-house video, hair dryer.) Rates include breakfast. Breaks available

Year round

✕ French and English in the à la carte restaurant

✳ Mod cons in manor setting

In the leisure club a heated indoor pool, jacuzzi, sauna and solarium, trimnasium and beauty salon. Also on the premises a games room, outdoor tennis court, pitch and putt, antique squash court, croquet, golf, boating on the lake. Riding nearby

♫ No

★ All the joys of the Lake District within easy reach

From the M6 to Penrith, leave the motorway at Junction 40. From the A66 to Keswick roundabout, take the A591 signed Carlisle. After 7 miles

The Arundell Arms

The Arundell Arms is definitely a fisherman's hotel. Well, owner Conrad Voss-Bark knows enough about the sport to be an accredited writer on fishing for *The Times*, and his wife Anne (looking far younger than her years), was a former Woman Hotelier of the Year winner. Put them together with a young English chef in a previous coaching inn close to the uplands of Dartmoor and you have the hostelry answer to a sportsman's dreams.

Four rivers — the Lyd, Carey, Wolf and Thrushel (which rise on the peaks of Dartmoor) join the Tamar (the frontier river which divides Devon from Cornwall) about a mile (1½ km) or so from the hotel. Between them, they provide the Arundell with 20 miles (32 km) of private fishing — for salmon, sea trout and brown trout. Lake trout is for the catching on the hotel's own 3-acre (1¼ ha) Tinhay Lake. Enthusiasts generally take packed lunches with them — forms for these are provided the night before in the dining room.

You may, of course, bring everything you need with you, but if not, The Arundell's bailiff and assistant not only issue the water authority licences, but also beat-books, maps of the salmon pools and free advice. The hotel's tackle shop is well stocked with the latest fishing equipment and local flies, and you can hire thigh or hip waders on the spot. (There's a drying room to cope with the odd drenching!)

If fishing is a new hobby you're only beginning to appreciate, you may want to take a course — three or four-day courses are given throughout the year for beginners and the more advanced. You'll find instructor Roy Buckingham in the Rod Room every morning at 9 a.m. or evening at 7 p.m. It used to be the old cockpit (one of the few left in England), albeit with a new roof. Cock fighting was made illegal in Victorian times but was said to have continued in country districts for a long time after it had ceased in towns. The original parts of the hotel (from the present office and part of the lounge through the cocktail bar to the Lyd Room and TV room, are slightly older than the cockpit (250–300 years), though it is suspected there was an even earlier inn on the site. Certainly, a William Arundell brought the then White Horse Inn in 1815 and changed its name to his own, though it is said he gambled it away in 1850. At that time The Arundell Arms boasted seven bedrooms, three parlours, a bar and stables.

Today the guest rooms have en suite bathrooms and colour TV, fresh flowers and a decanter of port awaits guests in the cosy sitting room overlooking the garden. Across and around the quadrangle of the car park there's a games room, skittle alley and a second bar for those who like darts and pool. Fish remain important: stuffed, in pictures, written about in magazines on the lounge's coffee table — and to be eaten. Kippers and trout are matter of fact for breakfast, and dinner might include Tamar salmon in some exquisite sauce.

Shooting and stalking are two other pursuits that may be followed here. There are four-day shoots for driven snipe every week from mid-November to the end of January; driven pheasant and duck shoots on nearby estate from mid-October and deer stalking in season.

Lifton, Devon PL16 0AA. ✆ (0566) 84666

29 — 5 of which in annexe (All but two with en suite bathrooms, and each with colour TV, tea/coffee facility.) Rates include English breakfast. Breaks and course rates

Year round

✕ Traditional English and French dishes with the emphasis on seafood; considered exceptional. A la carte, but also special-occasion fixed-price menus

✻ Fisherman's must

20 miles (32 km) of private fishing water on the Tamar and four of its tributaries. Instruction and fishing courses for beginners and the more advanced; tackle shop. Deer-stalking and shooting for duck, pheasant and snipe

♫ No

★ Surfing beaches of the north Cornish coast, the ruins of Tintagel Castle, fishing villages of Boscastle and Port Isaac where boats may be hired. Also the famous houses and gardens of Cotehele and Lanhydrock.

On the A30 road to Cornwall, midway between Dartmoor and Bodmin Moor, 38 miles (61 km) from Exeter, 25 miles (40 km) from Plymouth

£/$ C

Ashen Clough

Ashen Clough is a private home, once a 16th-century yeoman's house now modernised, in an acre (½ ha) of garden mid the hills of the Peak District National Park. Your host Norman Salisbury is a vet who farms the land and keeps sheep when he's not lending a helping hand to his wife Isobel, a cordon bleu cook. Dinner must be ordered in advance (as is usual at a Wolsey Lodge) but is worth doing so for Isobel prepares some interesting dishes, and both Salisbury's dine with their guests. Ashen Clough is also licensed, so no worries there.

Family furniture and antiques decorate the bedrooms, two of which have their own bathrooms. Located in the Heart of the England, the house could be a good stopover for those travelling north or south.

Chinley, Derbyshire SK12 6AH. ✆ (0663) 50311

3 (2 with en suite bathrooms). Rates include full English breakfast

🏨 Year round

✕ Fixed-price menu using home-grown and local fruit, fresh vegetables, fish and meat

❋ Cottage style

🎾 No

♫ No

★ Chatsworth, Haddon Hall, Hardwick Hall. Close to Chester, the Crown Derby Factory and the Potteries

🚗 Within easy reach of the M1 and M6, 40 minutes from Ringway Airport. Chinley is approached from the A6, by A624 or B6062.

£/$ E

Ayton Hall

Melvin and Marian Rhodes's home is a Grade II-listed builing built on 13th-century foundations. Indeed, the 13th-century cellars now house some 1,500 bottles of wine for your selection.

The Shottowe family from Norfolk inherited the place in the 18th century and it was Thomas Shottowe's family who employed James Cook Senior at Airyholme Farm. During this time, Captain James Cook (then a boy) became a frequent visitor to the house, and what is now a private lounge commemorates the fact, decorated with original watercolours and points of interest on the Captain Cook Heritage Trail.

As a hotel Ayton Hall is very personalised and quite small, with only five letting bedrooms and a 50-seater restaurant plus an intimate cocktail bar decorated in Moroccan style.

Low Green, Great Ayton, North Yorkshire TS9 6PS.
✆ (0642) 723595

7 including suites and four-poster; (Each with private bathroom, colour TV, video, radio, trouser press, hair dryer and plenty of niceties.) No children under 10. Rates include newspaper and English breakfast

Year round

✕ Table d'hôte and à la carte.

✻ Very personal

Hard tennis court; trap shooting, archery and croquet on request. Nearby golf, pony-trekking and fishing

♫ No

★ The coastal towns of Whitby and Saltburn are a 15-minute drive away

In the centre of the village of Great Ayton at the entry of the North Yorkshire moors; 16 miles (26 km) from Teeside airport, 20 miles (32 km) from Darlington station

£/$ C

Bailiffscourt

Bailiffscourt was built this century, but the mass of tawny Somerset stone is a replica of Sir Roger de Montgomery's 13th-century courthouse originally tended by bailiff monks, and once you have walked through the front door you will have left the 20th century behind. It is designed medieval fashion in the shape of a large, hollow square with a court in the centre overlooked by the inner windows, and is only two storeys high. What is fascinating is that each stone, window and doorway comes from the original period, for in the 1930s Lord and Lady Moyne searched the south of England for authentic items with which to refashion their house, now such a unique country house hotel.

Huge tapestries hang on the walls; there is a liberal scattering of antique furniture, and spiral stone stairways lead to picturesque beamed bedrooms. In the dining room, for example, there are stone mullioned windows, a magnificent ceiling of moulded oak beams and a 16th-century fireplace. The oak ceiling in the Long West Room was once part of a rectory; the door to the entrance hall used to belong to South Wanborough Church in Somerset, and the archways were once part of Holditch Priory.

Several of the individually decorated bedrooms have four-poster beds; there are several lounges to choose from and a welcoming bar.

Climping, Littlehampton, West Sussex BN17 5RW.
✆ (0903) 723511

20 (12 twins or doubles, 4 singles, 2 suites and two cottage apartments in the grounds; 8 rooms with four-posters. Each individually decorated and with en suite bathroom and colour TV.) Rates include early-morning tea, newspaper and English breakfast. No children under 8, but dogs welcome for small fee

Year round

Fixed-price menu. Sample starter: chicken and asparagus terrine with pistachio nuts, served with marmalade pickle. Sample main course: grilled monkfish on a tomato and brandy cream sauce with green peppercorns and chives

Medieval eclectic

Sauna and exercise rooms. In the grounds a swimming pool, tennis courts, croquet lawn and golf practice area. Riding can be arranged in Arundel and golf at three local clubs. Climping Beach is fine for windsurfing

No

★ Winchester Cathedral, Arundel Castle, Goodwood and the Brighton coast

Within easy driving distance of Portsmouth, midway between Southampton and Eastbourne. From London take the Kingston By-pass, turning left on the A24 as far as Beare Green to the south of Dorking, then the A29 through Billingshurst and Pulborough. Carry on to the roundabout below Arundel, then take the route marked Ford and Climping; 3 miles (5 km) on turn right at the junction of the A259 Littlehampton to Bognor road. Bailiffscourt is a few hundred yards (metres) down the first turning to the left

£/$ A

Beechfield House

Built in 1878 of ochre Bath stone, this Victorian-style house was the family home of a successful family of brewers for a century before becoming a praiseworthy small hotel. Great attention has been given to the decor — pretty papers and colours, an antique piece here and there. A restful drawing room and a blue colour-schemed restaurant overlooking the gardens are both most attractive and the food is exceptionally good. The dinner starts with canapés to accompany your aperitif and ends with petits fours with the coffee.

Each of the bedrooms is named for a species of tree — 'Cedar' is the one with the antique four-poster. Eight of the rooms are in the main house and eight in the adjacent coach house which overlooks garden and swimming pool. Good value for this calibre.

Beanacre, Melksham, Wiltshire SN12 7PU.
✆ (0225) 703700

16 (8 in the main house, 8 in coach house, including four-poster; each individually decorated, with en suite bathroom, colour TV, radio, trouser press, hair dryer, fruit, mineral water, toiletries etc.) Rates include early-morning tea, newspaper, English breakfast

Year round

✕ Table d'hôte and à la carte modern English

✳ Enchanting

Outdoor pool, tennis, croquet. Fishing on the River Avon

♫ No

★ The National Trust village of Lacock, Bowood House, Roman Bath

On the A530 Melksham/Chippenham road, 2 miles (3 km) north of Melksham. Leave M4 at Junction 17

£/$ C

The Bell Inn

No coach and horses outside The Bell today, but it does continue to offer rest and refreshment to travellers as it did when it was a staging post for the Duke of Buckingham between his seat at Stowe and his palace on The Mall, back in the 17th century. In 1650 Mrs Raffald's 'drunken loaf' was a speciality on the menu — perhaps that's where the tipsy cake evolved from. In any case, meals are the mainstay of The Bell today, served à la carte (except for Saturday dinner) in an exceptionally lovely room furnished with leather chairs and well-spaced mahogany tables.

The current owner is particularly knowledgeable about wine, but then his father was always interested in it, so much so that it grew into a business of its own. The hotel's wine shop continues on the same site, enlarged and flourishing — buying, shipping and bottling a wide range under the Gerard Harris label.

Aston Clinton, Buckinghamshire HP22 5HP.
✆ (0296) 630252

21	(6 in main house, 15 in courtyard; each with en suite bathroom, colour TV, radio, hair dryer, robes, niceties.) Rates include continental breakfast
🏨	Year round
✕	French style à la carte, except Saturday night with six-course fixed-price menu with choices. Good wine list
✻	Coaching inn
🎣	Nearby fishing
♫	No
★	National Trust properties include Waddesdon Manor, Ascott and Claydon House
🚗	On A41, 4 miles (6 km) southeast of Aylesbury (leave M1 by junction 8)
£/$	C

Belstead Brook

A Saxon hall originally stood on this site with two principal rooms, each with a large fireplace on either side of what is the present house's old front door. During Jacobean times a new wing was added, and oak panelling installed as well as the then fashionable herringbone brickwork on the stairs leading up to the first dining room. More recently, two end wings were added, now housing the Reception and library.

In addition to the regular single and twin rooms, six luxury garden suites are offered, twice the size of the standard rooms, each with a separate sitting room and French windows opening onto a patio and the garden, plus whirlpool bath in the bathroom. There are also eight executive suites, double-bedded rooms larger than standard, whose bathrooms feature therapeutic air baths.

Belstead Road, Ipswich, Suffolk IP2 9HB.
✆ (0473) 684241

30 (Including 6 garden suites, 8 executive suites and a four-poster; each with en suite bathroom, some with spa or therapeutic air baths, trouser press, colour TV, tea/coffee facility and radio.) Suites have hair dryers

Year round

✕ Table d'hôte and à la carte English traditional

✻ Much modernised Tudor

No

♫ No

★ Woodbridge with 18th-century tide mill, the wool town of Kersey, Gainsborough's house in Sudbury, the castles at Orford and Framlingham

From Ipswich station, if you are facing it, turn left and fork immediately right up to Willoughby Road, turn right to Belstead Road. The hotel is ½ mile (800 m) on the right

£/$ C

Bilbrough Manor

An attractive manor house hotel in a lovely Yorkshire village, Bilbrough first appeared on the map as Byleburgh in 1284. The most famous family to own the property was the Fairfax family — the first Lord Fairfax being Thomas, born in 1560 and whose subsequent successors remained in residence until 1716 when Bilbrough was sold for £7,523 17s 6d (£7,523.75) to Admiral Robert Fairfax. The building you see today was built by his descendant Guy Thomas Fairfax in 1901.

Bilbrough also enjoys an American connection: in the 17th century another Thomas (the fifth Lord) married American heiress Catherine Culpepper. Six subsequent Lords Fairfax were American, and in 1743 George Washington's brother Lawrence Washington married Anne Fairfax.

Your hosts today, Colin and Susan Bell, do not have such a claim to fame, but they have skilfully converted the manor into an enchanting hotel.

Bilbrough, York Y02 3PH. ✆ (0937) 834002

12 double (Each with en suite bathroom and colour TV, hair dryer, trouser press; one with four-poster bed.) Rates include full English breakfast. No children under 12. Breaks available

Year round

New classical French. Jacket and tie requested

American connections

Croquet. Shooting may be arranged. Golf courses and horse racing at York.

No

York and the spa town of Harrogate

On the edge of the village of Bilbrough, a half-mile (800 m) from the York to Leeds road, route A64, 5 miles (8 km) from the centre of York

£/$ A

Billesley Manor

In the heart of Shakespeare country, Billesley Manor is a traditional English country house hotel with a history that goes back ten centuries. It was originally known as Billesley Hall, an estate which became the property of the Trussel family thanks to a grant from William I. Not all the Trussels were good and true — when Thomas Trussel was convicted of highway robbery and sentenced to death, the Crown confiscated the family lands in 1588.

Much of the fine woodwork and oak panelling that enhances today's hotel was done for Sir Robert Lee, Lord Mayor of London, who bought the estate towards the end of Elizabeth I's time. Some of the large oak doors still bear the fine steel box-locks he had installed, made by the Flemish armourer who crafted those for the Tower of London.

The Manor, outbuildings and chapel, are all that remain of what was in fact a village, a village which suffered vastly from the Black Death and again when the success of the northern wool mills diminished its own prosperity from sheep farming. The village of Billesley finally disappeared, though you can still spot its foundations in dry weather. The house itself was left to decay until early this century when the first Hon. Charles Hanbury-Tracy, later Lord Sudley, began restoration work.

What better place for visiting Stratford-upon-Avon, 3 miles (5 km) away, especially when you realise Shakespeare himself used the library here and his granddaughter Elizabeth Nash married her second husband in the chapel. Its conversion to a quality hotel has left it the superb carved wood and fireplaces, but added an indoor pool and sauna. Drawing rooms, where log fires blaze in winter, are spacious and handsomely appointed — just the place for a distinguished port from what is a very fine cellar. And traditional English fare is served in oak-walled restaurants.

Billesley, Alcester, Warwickshire B49 6NF.
✆ (0789) 763737

41 (All luxuriously decorated including 3 four-posters, 5 suites, some period, some modern décor; each with en suite bathroom, colour TV, trouser press). Rates include full English breakfast. Weekend breaks

Year round

✕ A la carte in both oak-panelled French and English restaurants. Jacket and tie for dinner

✻ Traditional English

Indoor heated pool, sauna; croquet on the lawn, tennis courts in the grounds. Fishing may be arranged.

♫ No

★ The Royal Shakespeare Theatre, Warwick Castle, Ann Hathaway's Cottage and all the Cotswold villages

3 miles (5 km) from Stratford-upon-Avon, off the A422.

£/$ C

Bishopstrow House

Classically Georgian, decidedly opulent, Bishopstrow House is a member of the prestigious Relais & Chateaux consortium. Designed by John Pinch of Bath, built in 1817, it is surrounded by 25 acres (10 km) of superbly maintained parkland.

Public rooms are elegant, with English and French antiques, 19th-century oil paintings and Persian carpets. The light conservatory-style dining room is designed in two sections: a large room with plenty of space between the tables overlooking the garden, and the small conservatory which has its own garden atmosphere. Food, as befits a Relais member is on the 'light' side, to be accompanied by a wide selection of wines stored in the original cellars beneath the house.

Bishopstrow, Warminster, Wiltshire BA12 9HH.
✆ (0985) 212312

26	(15 in the main house including suites; each with en suite bathroom, some with whirpool baths, a few with private safes.) No children under 3
🏨	Year round
✕	The emphasis is on seasonal and local ingredients
✻	Posh
⚲	Indoor and outdoor heated pools, sauna and solarium; indoor and outdoor tennis court. Free fishing from the hotel's bank of the River Wylye.
♫	No
★	Stately homes Longleat and Wilton. Also Lacock Abbey, where Fox Talbot invented photography. Stonehenge and Salisbury Cathedral a short drive away
🚗	A couple of miles (3 km) from Warminster. By car the most direct route is via the M3, exit near Basingstoke onto the A 303 toward Exeter, then on to the A36 at Wylye towards Warminster
£/$	B

Boscundle Manor

Andrew and Mary Flint refer to their 18th-century manor house turned hotel as a 'restaurant with rooms' and now run it as a private home. When they first purchased the property they employed both chef and manager — now Mary supervises dinners and Andrew, the breakfasts and front of house.

Don't expect a glossy place nor practised service. The house is a jumble of assorted objects, including antiques Furniture, like plushy velvet armchairs, are designed for comfort rather than impression since the Flints prefer to keep the atmosphere informal. That goes for the garden too, which they love, having revived it from former wilderness without 'manicuring' it. It offers many a sheltered corner for the escapist plus an outdoor heated pool for the more energetic.

Next to the top of the property is land once the site of the Wheal Eliza tin mine which started operations in 1620. When it ceased operation it was planted with pine trees which have now been cleared to highlight the remains of the old tin workings, and replanted with broad-leaved trees. The Flints have improved walkways and have created a short practice golf course, and will eventually have some fish in the new lake in this part of the property.

Boscundle Manor has ceased to accept functions and does close in winter to enable their family-style operation to work more smoothly. They have a large collection of maps and booklets which they're happy to lend, and children of all ages are welcome.

Breakfast is served in the private dining room or conservatory. Residents who don't wish for a full fixed-price dinner may request a snack, and on Sundays there is normally a roast or barbecue by the pool in good weather.

Tregrehan, St Austell, Cornwall PL25 3RL.
✆ (072681) 3557

11 (9 in the main house, 2 in the cottage at the top of the garden; each with en suite bathroom, colour TV, some with spa baths.) Rates include full English breakfast

Mid-Feb to mid-Dec

✕ Fixed-price 3-course menu and coffee with several choices for each course. Wine list of 150. Sample main dishes: baked salmon with hollandaise, grilled Dover sole, pork Normandy

✻ Informal eclectic

Heated outdoor pool, practice golf course, small exercise room. Golf, riding and fishing nearby.

♫ No

★ Notable villages nearby include Charlestown, Mevagissey and Fowey and also the picturesque Roseland Peninsula

2 miles (3 km) east of St Austell on the A390, where you will find a small turning marked 'Tregrehan' almost opposite the St Austell Garden Centre. The manor is about 100 yards (90 m) up this road

£/$ C

Bourne Eau House

The Bourne Eau is a stretch of water where geese and swans swim by, a natural border between the gardens of this privately owned B & B and the 12th-century abbey and Hereward the Wake's castle ruins. The house is a 17-room, listed country home for Dr and Mrs Bishop, a piece of award-winning restoration that combines modern comforts with 16th-century oak beams and inglenooks.

There are six magnificent reception rooms at Bourne Eau: a Jacobean sitting room with log fire; a Georgian drawing room; Elizabethan dining room with inglenook; a music room and a library. In keeping with Wolsey Lodge policy, the Bishops provide dinner on request and will cater to individual diet needs.

30 South St, Bourne, Lincolnshire PE10 9LY.
✆ (0778) 423621

5	(Including master suite with dressing room, 3 with en suite bathrooms; each has colour TV and coffee/tea facility.) Rates include full English breakfast
🏛	Year round
✕	Fixed-price dinner, lunch by arrangement
✻	Friendly personal
🎾	No, but nearby golf and riding
♫	No
★	Ideal for exploring central England — Lincoln Cathedral, Oxford and Nottingham. Burghley House, famous for its horse trials, and Spalding noted for its flower festival
🚗	Bourne is signposted on the A1. Two hundred yards (183 m) from the traffic lights in the centre of the town is the concealed entrance directly opposite the cenotaph in the park
£/$	D

Bredon Manor

Guests speak of this tiny Cotswold hotel in glowing terms: 'Superb home' ... 'Lovely, friendly atmosphere' ... 'Truly English'. The Whittinghams make a great effort to ensure that their guests do consider Bredon as 'home' if only for one night, providing dinner round one large table and asking them not to choose from a menu but what they don't like to eat.

The hotel name is a combination of the ancient Celtic word for hill — *bre* and *dun* or down, an Anglo-Saxon word for the same thing. The earliest part of the manor, facing out across the River Avon valley, was built around 1455, probably on the site of an earlier monastery. Much of what you see today was added in local stone in the 18th century.

Until the Civil War in the 17th century, the manor, farm, tithe barn, rectory and church were all in the hands of the Bishops of Worcester. When Parliament forces took Worcester in 1651, deposing Bishop Prideaux, all links were broken with the church, but the 'Churchgate' and monks' fishpond remain in use today.

Guests are free to linger in the drawing room or use the bar as they would in their own home, and there is space inside for a game of darts or billiards as well as an outdoor tennis court, croquet and minature putting course. Personal attention is the key here as befits a Wolsey Lodge member, this one with four rooms. The master suite, for example, has its own dressing room and overlooks the rose garden while The Elizabethan is a two-roomed suite.

Bredon Manor is surrounded by 12 acres (5 ha), four (1½ ha) of which are cultivated with a large number of unusual plants and shrubs. Guests are encouraged to enjoy the gardens, including the water garden where seating is available under a weeping willow tree.

Bredon, Tewkesbury, Gloucestershire GL20 7EG.
✆ (0684) 72293

4 (Including 1 four-poster; each with en suite bathroom.) Rates include full English breakfast. No children under 12. Breaks available

Year round

Dinner by request served family style, no choice at fixed time. Most vegetables come from the manor's walled garden; main courses might be fresh salmon or roast lamb; starters: smoked trout or homemade soup. Breakfasts are cooked to order at a time to suit

Private house personal

Hard tennis court, outdoor pool, putting, croquet and coarse fishing

No

★ Stratford-upon-Avon, Broadway, Worcester, Cheltenham, Gloucester and Malvern all within easy reach. Warwick and Bath not far away

Well located for exploring the Heart of England, with easy access from London via the M40 or A40 to Cheltenham; the North via the M6 or M5 and South Wales via the M50. The Manor is at the entrance of the village of Bredon on the B4080, 3 miles (5 km) from Tewkesbury

£/$ C

Brockencote Hall

Brockencote Hall is a gracious white-faced house surrounded by a 70-acre (28 ha) estate whose grounds are manicured and landscaped, incorporating a 2-acre (¾ ha) lake. The estate has been in existence for over 300 years, still with its gatehouse, half-timbered dovecote and prime examples of European and North American trees. The present Hall, until recently a private home, is probably around 150 years old, architected in a classical style.

As a hotel you will find the interior bright, airy and modern with an emphasis on pastel colours, and pine and maple panelling for the bar. Some period furniture has been chosen for the bedrooms, each different. Chandeliers and flowers enhance the spacious restaurant where food is 'French inspired'.

Chaddesley Corbett, nr Kidderminster, Worcestershire DY10 4PY. ✆ (0562) 83876

9 (Each with en suite facilities, including four-poster, colour TV and magnificent views.) Rates include continental breakfast

Late Jan to Dec 26

French-inspired table d'hôte and à la carte

Typically English manor home

No

♫ No

★ The Clent and Lickey Hills a short distance away. Also Harvington Hall (moated Tudor manor), Worcester Cathedral and the Vale of Evesham

On the A448 at Chaddesley Corbett between Bromsgrove and Kidderminster. 30-minute drive from Birmingham Airport within easy reach of the M5 (Junction 4) and M42 (Junction 1)

£/$ C

The Brookhouse Inn

This William and Mary Grade II-listed building of great architectural appeal, is the home of Bill and Deirdre Mellis. The beds are all antique, original works of art hang on the walls and the curtains and bed linen are trimmed with Nottingham lace.

Tables in the beamed dining room are also antique so are left uncovered by cloths, but are set with silver, crystal, candles and fresh flowers. The Mellises pride themselves that the food they serve is just that little bit different and it is all cooked to order.

Located in one of Staffordshire's most attractive villages, The Brookhouse has been sympathetically renovated to provide a homely atmosphere.

Rolleston-on-Dove, Burton-on-Trent, Staffordshire DE13 9AA. ✆ (0283) 814188

16 (Including four-posters and half-testers; each individually styled and with en suite bathroom and colour TV.) Rates include newspaper and English breakfast. No children under 12. Special breaks available

Year round

✕ Fresh food cooked to order. Wine list includes rare varieties

✻ Homely

No

♫ No

★ Historic houses of Chatsworth, Sudbury Hall and Haddon Hall. Also within easy reach of Alton Towers amusement park, the Staffordshire Potteries and the Derbyshire Dales

Set in a country garden by a brook just north of Burton-on-Trent, off the A38 and A50. Convenient to East Midlands and Birmingham Airports

£/$ C

Buckland Manor

There are so many favourable reports about this pedigree Cotswold manor house hotel that it would be unthinkable to leave it out of this guide, although it is located in an area which boasts many equally lovely country house properties.

Part of Buckland dates from the 13th century, but 20th-century amenities are very evident today under the watchful eyes of the Bermans. Although their career background was not in the hotel industry they have proved most successful in appealing to a well-heeled clientele who delight in public rooms with antiques and fresh flowers, and bedrooms with deep-pile carpets.

Compliments go to the food and service and to the setting — 10 acres (4 ha) of gardens and grounds with water and rose gardens, tennis court, croquet and putting green. It is hard to believe that touristy Broadway is only 2 miles (3 km) away. Barry and Adrienne Berman are amenable and talkative, happy to help with anything you need to know.

Buckland, nr. Broadway, Gloucestershire WR12 7LY. ✆ (0386) 852626

10	(Including suite and four-posters; each with en suite spring-fed bathroom, and colour TV.) No children under 12. Rates include breakfast. Breaks available
🏨	Year round except 3 weeks Jan/Feb
✕	Excellent à la carte and wine list
✳	Expensively restful
🎾	Tennis, croquet, putting green
♫	No
★	Cotswold villages and attractions
🚗	1½ miles (2½ km) southwest of Broadway, east of the A46
£/$	A

Buckland-Tout-Saints

An elegant Queen Anne manor house, Buckland-Tout-Saints was part of a large estate when it was built in 1690 by Sir John Southcote, and is now a hotel personally owned and managed by the Shepherd family.

Decorated with finesse, its oak-panelled lounges are adorned by paintings and fresh flowers — log fires for winter warmth. English and French-style food is served in the panelled Queen Anne dining room, complemented by wines from around the world.

Bedrooms as one might expect are all different: the Buckland Room features a hand-carved four-poster bed made in mahogany to match the existing antique furniture. Smaller rooms on the second floor are decorated in Provence style with shuttered windows which, when open, look out onto the surrounding countryside. The house itself is located in 27 acres (11 ha) of parkland.

Goveton, Kingsbridge, South Devon TQ7 2DS.
✆ (0548) 3055

12 (Each with en suite bathroom, colour TV, hair dryer and trouser press; each individually decorated, including 1 four-poster.) Rates include early-morning tea, newspaper and English breakfast. No children under 8. Special breaks available

🏨 Year round

✕ Modern English and French. International wine list

✻ Quiet manorly

⛳ Croquet lawn and putting green

♫ No

★ Plymouth, Dartmoor, Dartington Glass factory, Dartmouth Naval College

🚗 20 miles from the city of Plymouth and a half-hour's drive from the A38 dual carriageway that links directly with the M5 motorway at Exeter

£/$ C

Bunwell Manor

Bunwell Manor in the heart of Norfolk farmland originally dates from the 16th century. This is a small, simply furnished country house with attractive gardens where snacks and drinks are served in clement weather. And in winter you can sit in the upstairs lounge by a log fire over a chess or backgammon board.

Pre-dinner drinks may be taken in the bar or terrace while you peruse the à la carte menu. I can certainly promise the wine selection will be a good one, for when I first met Carolyn Meunier (one of the owners) she was in the wine business with her father. She continues to use French growers she's known for years, and personally tastes and chooses what's on the list. Non wine-drinkers might like to know Bunwell also specialises in real ale.

It is nice to know that though small (only 11 bedrooms), room service is provided until midnight and that breakfast is served in your room until 11 a.m.

Bunwell, Norfolk NR16 1QU. ✆ (095389) 8304

10 (Each with en suite bathroom, colour TV)
Year round
A la carte country French
Off the beaten track
Croquet, nearby golf
No
Newmarket race course, Melford Hall, Banham Zoo
From the A11 going north, turn right at Spooner Row, just after Attleborough. Cross the railway line, turn right at Three Boars pub. Follow the road for 3 miles (5 km) into Bunwell
£/$ E

Burghope Manor

Burghope Manor is a classic example of a medieval Cotswold stone manor house, dating in parts to the 13th century, and John and Elizabeth Denning are classic examples of English country gentility. They are the founders of the Heritage Circle — a group of landed gentry who have opened their homes to tourists as a means of survival. For the tourists, a stay is a delight for the stately homes are full of history, and their owners charming and interesting hosts.

Not only is Burghope studded with antiques, it *is* one as you'll see from its arched Tudor doorways, priest's hole and old mosaic-style hall floor tiles, not to mention the enormous fireplaces like the one in the morning room. The faint Latin inscription engraved on this one is thought to have been inscribed by Thomas Cranmer, archbishop to Henry VIII. Translated, it reads: 'Remember the Sabbath and All that's holy. Six days shalt thou labour...' — the opening words of Cranmer's Church of England prayer book commissioned by the king.

There is another huge stone fireplace in the dining room where up to ten people may be seated around the handsome table. Because this is a family home, paying guests sit and mingle with invited guests and dinner becomes an occasion. What is interesting here is that the fixed-price, fixed-menu meal includes aperitifs, wines and after-dinner liqueurs usually taken in the pink-carpeted and spacious, 15th-century drawing room. All very social.

The guest rooms, like the rest of the house, are light and elegant. The one at the top of the stairs is huge, with traceried windows and a walk-through wardrobe to reach the bathroom. Breakfast is served to guests as and when they drift down.

Winsley, nr Bradford-on-Avon, Wiltshire BA15 2LA.
✆ (022122) 3557

5 (Doubles with en suite bathrooms.) Rates include English breakfast

Mid-April to Oct

✕ Fixed-price, no-choice menu includes pre-dinner drinks, wine with meal and liqueurs. Served family style

✻ Gracious, private home

No

♫ No

★ Berkeley Castle, Beaulieu Abbey, Farleigh Castle, Great Chalfield Manor and Wilton House. Bath, Cheddar Gorge and Caves are also both near

2½ miles (4 km) from Bradford-on-Avon — take the B3108 a turning off the Bath road to Winsley village. After passing the War Memorial, an 'S' bend, the Seven Stars public house you will come to Sutcliffe School. About 80 yards (73 m) further on, take the next right marked 'Except for Access'. 5 miles (8 km) from Bath — take the A36 Warminster road.

£/$ C

Calcot Manor

Calcot Manor, until 1983, was a farmhouse, the kind you wish you'd bought — what with its 15th-century main house, its stables (now timbered suites) and its old stone barns, among them one of the oldest tithe barns in England. It was built originally in the 14th century by Cistercian monks from nearby Kingswood Abbey, damaged by lightning in 1728 but rebuilt the following year. Visitors from Cincinnati, Ohio, should have a certain affection for the place for in 1927 the barn's roof beams and slates were sold to Mariemont, where they now roof the Mariemont church.

The Ball family who now run this golden-coloured Cotswold property as a hotel, have converted it with care. In keeping with the rural surrounds, décor is strictly soft pastel with abundant use of wallpapers and fabrics. Antiques and ornaments are scattered throughout but not overdone.

As country house hotels go this one isn't large, but you can count on luxury appointments. Bedrooms all have a sitting area; fully tiled bathrooms match the colour scheme — three of them featuring whirlpool baths. Each has its own personality: the Chiltern Room, for example, is decorated with hedgerow wallpaper, matching fabrics and bramble-patterned bathroom tiles. The Cotswold Room features handcrafted mirrors and flowery chintzes. Highlighted feature of the Master Room is its draped and canopied four-poster bed.

Meals are served in the not-too-formal apricot and green dining room overlooking green countryside (lunch or drinks on the terrace in fine weather.) Michelin starred food is accompanied by choice wines from a comprehensive list.

Calcot is definitely a place to relax even in winter when log fires blaze away. All windows overlook the South Cotswold countryside or the hotel's own landscaped courtyard and grounds, where you'll find a herb garden and small arboretum as well as large lawn and shrubbery, and in a secluded section, an open-air heated pool.

Nr Tetbury, Gloucestershire GL8 8YJ. ✆ (066689) 355

12 (All double or twin, including four-poster; each with en suite bathroom, colour TV. Individually decorated, 3 with whirlpool baths.) No children under 12. Rates include early-morning tea and newspaper plus English breakfast

Year round

✕ Based on classical English and French. Fixed-price lunch and dinner menus. Sample dishes: smoked loin of veal stuffed with cabbage and bacon, served with a light artichoke mousse and dark veal sauce. Hot passion fruit soufflé in filo pastry on milk chocolate sauce. Comprehensive wine list. No smoking dining room

✻ Relaxed rural

Crouqet on the lawn, outdoor heated pool. Clay pigeon shooting may be arranged on the grounds. Fishing and riding nearby

♫ No

★ Easy journeys may be made to Cotswold villages like Broadway or The Slaughters and to the old Roman capital, Cirencester. Also National Trust property, Dyrham Park, Berkeley Castle, Cotswold Wildlife Park and Malmesbury Abbey

Tetbury is the nearest town, though train-travelling guests will be met at Kemble station. By road, Calcot is located a 20-minute drive off the M4 or M5

£/$ C

Cavendish Hotel

On the edge of the Duke and Duchess of Devonshire's Chatsworth estate the Cavendish shows plenty of Mitford evidence (the Duchess is one of the famous Mitford sisters). The ten newer rooms, for example are named after members of her family.

There has been an inn on this site for so long that no one seems completely sure of its exact history. Certainly, it was the famous Peacock Inn in the 1780s, property of the Duke of Rutland and serving the turnpike between industrial Chesterfield and the spa town of Buxton. It became the Duke of Devonshire's property around 1830, rebuilt and restored in 1975.

All of the bedrooms overlook the estate. The Paxton Room Restaurant also has a perfect view, serving somewhat ambitious dishes on Wedgwood china accompanied by Sheffield silver. This hotel provides breakfast any time of the morning and lunch, either formally, in the bar or garden casually, or as a picnic.

Baslow, Bakewell, Derbyshire DE4 1SP.
✆ (024688) 2311

23 (Each with en suite bathroom, colour TV, clock radio, coffee/tea facility, fridge bar, travel pack, bathrobes.) Breaks available

Year round

✕ Ambitious dishes based on homemade and local produce

✻ Ducal influence

Putting green and golf driving net, fishing in the Rivers Derwent and Wye

♫ No

★ Chatsworth House, Hardwick and Haddon Hall, Pennine Way

2½ hours from London via the M1, leave at Junction 29. Nearest railway station at Chesterfield

£/$ C

Charingworth Manor

The Manor of Charingworth is new to the country house hotel scene but was first mentioned in the Domesday Book of 1086, recorded then as Chevringworth. Even much of what you see today dates to the early 14th century — the beams showing their original medieval decoration can still clearly be seen.

Bedrooms here, with their beams, and in some cases, heavy wood four-posters, have atmospheric appeal. They are all named after previous owners of the estate, although the T.S. Eliot Suite is named to commemorate his frequent visits to the manor in the 1930s.

Charingworth, nr Chipping Campden, Gloucestershire GL55 6NS ✆ (038678) 555

8 (Including suites and four-posters, each with en suite bathroom, colour TV, video, radio, trouser press, hair dryer and room safe; individually named and decorated.) No children under 12. Rates include early-morning tea, newspaper and English breakfast. Breaks available

Year round

✕ Sophisticated but unpretentious restaurant; should be first class.

* Sophisticated Cotswold

No

♫ No

★ Stratford and the rest of the Cotswolds, Cheltenham, Hidcote Gardens, Warwick Castle

3 miles (5 km) from Chipping Campden, 24 (39 km) from Cheltenham. From Chipping Campden take the B4035 towards Shipston-on-Stour. Ignore signs for Charingworth, instead carry on until you reach the Manor entrance, about 3 miles (5 km) on left

£/$ A

Chedington Court

Read the history books and you'll discover the manor of Chedington has had many a 'pious' owner since the time of Elizabeth I. During her reign the rector of Shepton Beauchamp was a co-owner with local parish rector Christopher Minterne. Ousley bought out his partner's interests, and on his death in 1629 left the estate to his descendants. A new purchase in 1650 still found a rector, Richard Hody of Odcombe in Somerset, whose grandson left it to a relative, the Rev. William Cox. The latter's great grandson built Chedington Court as you see it now, in 1840. Mind you, the estate today is not the size it was then, but the lovely Jacobean-style house, now a hotel, warrants its membership in Relais du Silence as a peaceful getaway.

Chedington Court is very 'traditional English', run by the steady, solid hands of Philip and Hilary Chapman. Hilary does the cooking in a no-messing-about way, offering a no-choice menu (though there is appetiser and dessert selection) based on what fresh produce is available that day. Dinner is served at a precise time in a formal, but not dramatic, dining room whose leaded windows look out onto the garden. Wines from Philip's well-stocked cellar are especially strong on riojas.

Drinks and coffee may be taken in the drawing room or library and afterwards, the billiard room which has its own small self-service bar, offers some diversion. Handsome woodwork, oriental rugs and velvety furnishings are to be found throughout the house, but it's not full of paintings and fancy fabrics. A pleasant place to sit is the conservatory, a veritable greenhouse planted with plumbago, mimosa and passion flowers.

Some of the more solid pieces of furniture were bought from the state rooms of the Queen Mary, and all the bedrooms are named for flowers or places, such as spacious twin-bedded Rhododendron or the Thomas Hardy double. (The village of Chedington is of course in the region that Hardy loved and knew so well.)

The gardens — 10 acres (4 ha) of them — are a major feature: sweeping lawns and shaded terraces, a summerhouse for those who care for a snooze in the sun, a water garden and greens for clock golf and croquet.

Chedington, Beaminster, Dorset DT8 3HY.
✆ (093589) 265

10 (Double or twin, including one four-poster; each with en suite bathroom, colour TV and niceties like bath foam and mineral water.) Rates are half board

Year round

✕ Table d'hôte dinners cooked with finesse including creamy dessert choice. Good wine list, strong on riojas

* Formal house run friendly fashion

Billiard room. Putting, clock golf and croquet in the grounds. Coarse and trout fishing can be arranged

♫ No

★ Sherborne Castle and Butterfly Centre, Thomas Wildlife Park, Hardy's Cottage, Montacute House and Glastonbury

In the Dorset Hills, just off the A356 Crewkerne to Dorchester Rd at Winyard's Cap with commanding views of the Somerset, Devon and Dorset countryside

£/$ A but half board

Chewton Glen

Located on the fringe of the New Forest, Chewton Glen is a handsome old Georgian manor house set in beautifully manicured gardens and parkland which boast a swimming pool, croquet lawn, tennis court and nine-hole golf course. It all looks well tended — and it is — and this is one of the reasons (though not the only one) why it has received countless accolades from industry specialists and private individuals. It is also one of the reasons why the titled and famous (King Hussein, Lady Chalfont, to name but two) often choose it as a place to relax or for a top-level business meet.

Red, the predominant colour of the Marryat Bar, gives a comforting rosy glow to proceedings even before a bottle of well-chilled champagne or rich brown cognac adds to them. The bar is named for Captain Frederick Marryat who write his best-known work. *The Children of the New Forest* here whilst staying with his brother George in 1846. The house, which was probably originally built in the 1730s, was George Marryat's home from 1837 to 1855. His novelist brother loved the area and often stayed at Chewton, gathering material for that most famous last book.

The 1857 watercolour and photograph done for the subsequent owner, Alexander Elphinstone, and displayed in the hotel, show a stuccoed frontage; but in the first decade of this century, when Colonel Edward Tinker took up residence, the facades were remodelled in brick, and the bar to the left of today's main entrance was a vinery.

After World War II Chewton Glen became a hotel, albeit with only two bedrooms when the Skan family purchased the property in

1966 and embarked on an enormous modernisation plan. I first met proprietor Martin Skan well over a decade ago. In the interim staff have changed — though deputy general manager Joe Simonini claims over 20 years service, as does François Rossi who heads up the bar team — more rooms have been added, and décor changed. But Martin's boyish charm and enthusiasm haven't diminished at all, and he still enjoys presiding over things when he can.

He often dines in the restaurant, for whilst Chewton Glen doesn't rely on nearby neon or disco music to enhance its reputation, its kitchen is a matter of pride. Head chef Patrick Gaillard mixes tastes and textures whilst accentuating fresh produce. Vegetables here are cooked French style (crisp) and meat, pink, but guests' preference for slightly longer-on-the-burner is just as warmly acceded to. And the menu in a matter-of-fact and useful way points out that as all dishes are cooked to order, some delay is inevitable. Prime wines — 260 bins to choose from and Lanson the 'house' champagne — are other favourable features.

New Milton, Hampshire BH25 6QS. ✆ (04252) 5341

33 — 11 suites (Each named for a Capt. Marryat character, individually decorated, with en suite bathroom, colour TV, basket of toiletries, complimentary sherry.)

Year round. Xmas and other special packages. No children under 7

✕ Modern-ish, plain grills on request, vegetables prepared to individual taste. A la carte and table d'hôte. Silver service, elegant setting, jacket and tie necessary, no pipes or cigars in dining room. Noted, justifiable reputation

✻ Upmarket, somewhat formal

Outdoor pool, tennis, croquet, snooker, golf. Arrangements for other sports, e.g. riding, fishing, readily made. Own helipad

♫ Piano music

★ Stately homes like Broadlands (home of the late Earl of Mountbatten), Wilton House (home of the Earl of Pembroke) and Lord Montagu's Beaulieu. Also Kingston Lacy (superb example of 17th-century architecture), Henry VIII's flagship, *The Mary Rose*

1½ miles (2½ km) from New Milton Station, 5 miles (8 km) from Hurn Airport, 20 miles (32 km) from Southampton. About a half-hour's drive from Bournemouth. By motorway from London, the M3 and A33, turning before Southampton onto the M27 (signposted to Bournemouth). Then the A337 to Lyndhurst and the one-way system onto the A35 for about 10 miles (17 km). Turn left at the Walkford and Highcliffe sign, go through Walkford and take the second on the left, which is Chewton Farm Road.

£/$ A

Chilston Park

The owners of this fine, restored mansion publish an antiques guide, so while it is rare to find them in residence here the house is a treasure trove of their selected buys. Guests will find original oils and water colours decorating the walls of their rooms — and a mini catalogue of the antiques it may contain.

There are more works of art in the public rooms: a large, pillared reception hall lit by a chandelier, filled with beautiful pieces of wood, decorated with family portraits. Leather sofas, objets d'art and plenty of flowers enhance the drawing room, a quiet retreat after an active day. Books line the shelves of the music room, and display cabinets show off items of porcelain almost everywhere.

In addition to the guest rooms in the main house (named to suit their décor so that here it might be the Tulip Room, and there the Regency), there are converted cottage and stable rooms — umbrellas provided. In winter you can be sure of a traditional woollen-covered hot-water bottle to take any chill away. 'Butlers' and 'maids', suitably dressed are on hand to help with the unpacking or sort out valet services.

This Grade I listed, 17th-century country house hotel overlooks 250 acres (101 ha) of Lord Chilston's original estate, which includes a natural spring lake, one of the sources of the River Stour.

Sandway, Nr Maidstone, Kent ME17 2BE.
✆ (0622) 859803

40 (25 in the main house, the rest in cottage and stable area; each individually furnished and named, with en suite bathroom and colour TV.) Rates include full English breakfast. Breaks available

Year round

✕ 5-course fixed-price menu. Emphasis on English and French, including hams, baron of beef and lamb

✻ Impersonal grandeur

Tennis, hot-air ballooning, clay pigeon shooting, fishing in the lake, croquet, punting, riding in the park

♫ No

★ Leeds Castle and all the pleasures of the 'Garden of England' on the doorstep

A few miles (km) off the A20 between Maidstone and Ashford. Within 30 miles (48 km) of the Channel ports and 40-minutes' drive of Gatwick

£/$ A

Cliveden

No country house connoisseur would omit a stay at Cliveden if budget permits, for it is after all not only a stately home of note but the only National Trust property so far to have been converted into a hotel. Perhaps the Great Hall, so carefully and expensively restored, with its portraits of previous owners including Sargent's famous one of Nancy Astor, and its imposing stone fireplace, does prove too dark and oppressive for my own tastes, but no one can fault the architectural and decorative work that went into turning Cliveden into an exclusive stopover.

The house (home of a Prince of Wales, three dukes and the Astor family) has known such a colourful history, always at the centre of Britain's social and political life, is irresistible — whether or not the service and cuisine is as faultless as it claims.

The first house was built here in 1666 by the 2nd Duke of Buckingham, wealthy courtier and politician. The next owner was the Earl of Orkney, one of the Duke of Marlborough's most trusted generals, who was given the tapestries in the Great Hall by the Duke to celebrate the latter's Blenheim victory. Many of the gardens were laid out during his time in the 18th century. When his daughter inherited the property, she let it to Frederick, Prince of Wales, who used it as an escape hatch until his death in 1751.

Two subsequent disastrous fires resulted in the present building designed by Sir Charles Barry for the then owners, the Duke and Duchess of Sutherland (1849–69), an era when Queen Victoria was a frequent visitor. The last private purchaser of Cliveden was William Waldorf Astor in 1893, to be succeeded here by two generations of the same family. Among the Astors, Nancy has become practically legendary — her former writing room is now the pretty blue, Adam style morning room called simply The Boudoir.

Bedrooms at Cliveden, as one would expect, are named for previous owners and opulent in their own right. A few like the Rudyard Kipling room are a little 'heavy', but thank goodness, the Lady Astor room's original dark wood panelling has been considerably lightened. The original frieze along with a fireplace surround and mantlepiece was discovered in an antique shop and restored to the room. This suite overlooks the parterre and has its own private terrace.

As befits a private-house atmosphere, guests will find drinks trays with decanters in their rooms (not complimentary). To discourage the odd disappearance of items, decanters, enamel boxes and bath robes all created for the hotel, are available for sale. So is the soap, a 'Cliveden fragrance' designed by Floris. Private-house niceties like butler and footman service for tea, drinks or unpacking service are part and parcel of the Cliveden concept. (There is no bar, reception desk or cashier.)

The hotel's superb surrounding 375 acres (152 ha) of woods and gardens, studded with statuary, are open to the general public at specific times, though not the celebrated outdoor pool, nor the exclusive *Suzy Ann* riverboat which may be hired or chartered.

Taplow, Berkshire SL6 0JF. ✆ (06286) 68561

25 (including 8 suites but mostly twin or double; each with en suite bathroom, colour TV, drinks tray and luxury niceties.) Rates include full English breakfast. Special packages available

Year round

Table d'hôte and à la carte. Sample dishes: saddle of rabbit with garlic with mustard sauce; fillet of lamb with wild mushrooms in tarragon cream sauce

Opulent

Outdoor heated pool and croquet in own walled garden. Indoor card and billiards rooms, exercise room, Turkish bath, sauna, massage, squash; indoor and outdoor tennis. Riding and golf arrangements can be made

No

The grounds themselves are worth exploring. Nearby are Windsor, Bray and Marlow, also Henley, famous for the Royal Regatta

A 20-minute drive from Heathrow, 45 minutes from central London. From the M4 leave at Junction 7, turn left onto the A4 and after ½ mile (800 m), at a roundabout, turn right, signed Burnham. Follow this road for 2½ miles (4 km) as far as the 'T' junction. The gates of Cliveden are directly opposite

£/$ A

Combe Grove Manor

Combe Grove Manor is just the right looking 18th-century mansion to be located so near to Bath, surrounded by 68 acres (28 ha) of formal gardens and woodland. Extensive refurbishment over the last couple of years have brought it up to the highest standards of luxury. Built in 1781, the estate was used more than once by John Wesley for his sermons.

The gardens are of particular interest. A 19th-century pond is built of Bath stone and surrounded by a crazystone path and a rock garden merging into a larger water garden, stocked with 500 goldfish. Nearer the house is the Green Arch, a fascinating example of 18th-century taste.

Brassknocker Hill, Monkton Combe, Bath BA2 7HS.
✆ (0225) 834644

10 (Individually designed including suites and four-posters; each with en suite bathrooms, some with jacuzzis, colour TV, mini bar. Half are non-smoking rooms.) Rates include full English breakfast

Year round

✕ Fixed-price dinner. Dishes frequently change but always include an interesting fish dish. Jacket and tie requested

✳ Intimate glamour

Jogging tracks, nature trails, outdoor pool and spa bath, 4 tennis courts, squash courts, five-hole par 3 golf course and two-tiered, 17-station, 300-yard driving range. Also complete fitness centre

♫ No

★ Bath Spa, Chippenham, Wells Cathedral, Longleat

2 miles (3 km) from Bath, 12 miles (19 km) from Junction 18 on the M4. Located southeast of Bath on Brassknocker Hill, between Combe Down and Monkton Combe

£/$ B

Combe House Hotel

A stately Elizabethan mansion, parts of which date to the 15th century, Combe House stands at the head of a secluded valley near Honiton and commands views over the Blackmore Hills as far as Exmoor. The grandeur of the entrance hall with its carved pine Caroline panelling and its massive mouldings repeated round the stone fireplace was created by a 17th-century owner, Sir Thomas Putt. The ceiling was remodelled in the 18th century.

Combe features a fine panelled drawing room hung with 18th-century portraits; a cosy bar adorned by hunting and coaching prints and photographs of racing triumphs (current owner John Boswell's hobby is horseracing); and a smaller drawing room. Therese Boswell not only supervises the cooking but is responsible for the murals in the dining room, where you'll also notice a handsome Italian fireplace.

Therese is a trained Cordon Bleu cook and now works with a team of young staff to ensure the food is first class, though she promises they'll cook any dish as plainly as you like.

Gittisham, nr Honiton, Devon EX14 0AD.
✆ (0404) 2756

13	(Individually designed, including 1 suite. Each with en suite bathroom and colour TV.) Rates include full English breakfast
🏨	End Feb–to mid-Jan
✕	Table d'hôte and à la carte. Sample main dishes: pan fried Scottish beef in a mustard sauce; salmon filled with fish mousse wrapped in filo pastry, on white wine sauce. No young children in the dining room
✕	Intimate but stately
✻	Croquet. Nearby fishing, golf and riding. Shooting can be arranged
♫	No
★	Bradley Manor, Compton Castle, also Sidmouth
🚗	Under 2 miles (3 km) from the main A30 London to Exeter road in 3,000 acres (1,214 ha) of parkland
£/$	C

Congham Hall

Congham Hall is a charming white Georgian house that was until 1982 the home of Lady Meriel Howarth and is still surrounded by 44 acres (18 ha) of gorgeous grounds that include their own cricket pitch with thatched pavilion, a small swimming pool and tennis court, as well as flower gardens, a herb garden and orchards.

Cuisine is high on the list of consideration at this hotel, served in a Regency pink-and-gold dining room. It has won Congham much praise in the past, but since the chef has very recently changed I cannot attest to current possibilities, only the reputation. The new British chef, Robert Harrison, I am assured, has an enthusiasm for fine English cooking, featuring fresh local produce and vegetables, fruits and herbs from the estate.

Pretty fabrics and period furnishings are to be found in the foyer lounge and drawing room, and drinks are taken in the cane-furnished bar. A handsome staircase leads to traditionally decorated bedrooms.

Grimston, King's Lynn, Norfolk PE32 1AH. ✆ (0485) 600250

11 (Each in period style with en suite bathroom, including four-poster suite, colour TV, fresh fruit, hair dryer, books.) Rates include light breakfast. No children under 12. Breaks available

Early Jan to Dec 24

✕ Said to be memorable and imaginative

✻ Stylish

Swimming pool, tennis court, cricket pitch. Riding may be arranged

♫ No

★ Sandringham, Oxborough Hall, Holkham Hall

Just off the King's Lynn to Fakenham road towards the village of Grimston

£/$ B

Coniston Sun Hotel

This Victorian house, built onto the original Pack Horse Inn, was Donald Campbell's base during his attempt on the world water-speed record on Coniston Water.

It is a cosy place to stay with traditional 'inn' appeal, decorated in what the proprietors call 'soft country house style'. Guests are encourage to feel at home by the side of a log fire (on chillier days) with a book or board game.

Dinner is at 8 p.m., a fixed-price meal with no choice except for dessert, though if there is a part of the menu that is not to your liking, let the Farmers know in advance and they'll provide a substitute dish, including vegetarian if required. Guests help themselves to coffee and mints in the lounge afterwards. As an alternative, the attached 16th-century, slate-floored, black-beamed inn serves homemade bar food and real ale.

Coniston, Lake District, Cumbria LA21 8HQ.
✆ (0966) 41248

11 (Individually decorated, including 2 four-posters; each with en suite bathroom, colour TV, electric blankets, tea/coffee facility.) Rates include English breakfast. Breaks available

Year round

Fixed-price 4-course menu

Cosily traditional

Detailed series of walks are provided for guests' benefit so they can get away from main routes and enjoy the area's best scenery. Golf, fishing, squash, riding and shooting can be arranged

♫ No

★ 'Old Man of Coniston', Grizedale Forest, good walking country

1 mile (1½ km) from Coniston Water, on the fringe of the village in grounds that run down to the beck. Reached via the A593 or B5285

£/$ E

The Cotswold House

How lovely to find The Cotswold House restored in the way it should be, an improvement even on the way it was when it was the residence of textile merchant Richard Greville in 1810.

There is a lounge bar and a courtyard for fine-weather eating and drinking. In winter the lounge and sitting room are warmed by open log fires. The main dining rooms manages to be elegant without being stuffy.

Greenstocks' All Day Eaterie is part of the hotel but it is also its own entity with a large non-residential clientele. Breakfast, lunch, snacks, tea and supper are all served here along with cocktails and other beverages.

Chipping Campden itself is a picturesque village with many antique shops.

Chipping Campden, Gloucestershire GL55 6AN.
✆ (0386) 840330

15 (Mostly twin or double, all individually and luxuriously decorated; each with en suite bathroom, colour TV.) Rates include full English breakfast. Breaks available

Year round

✕ Interestingly English, e.g. roast beef on oyster mushrooms in Madeira and cream sauce, but not fussy. No-smoking dining room. All-day eating until 10.30 p.m. in Greenstocks Eaterie, but main dining room open evenings only except for Sunday lunch

✳ Tastefully comfortable

No

♫ No

★ Some of the Cotswolds' loveliest villages, e.g. Broadway, Stow-on-the-Wold, Stratford-upon-Avon, Blenheim Palace and Warwick Castle

90 miles (145 km) from London. Direct trains to Cheltenham

£/$ C

Crabwell Manor

The castellated frontage gives a castle-like impression to Crabwell Manor, a new, luxury country house hotel. It was added in 1600 to what was probably a Tudor farmhouse. Crabwell's acreage has seen many a skirmish between cavalier and roundhead, and a manor was recorded long before that, in the Domesday Book. What you see today is the third (Grade II) listed building to stand on the site.

Inside, décor is Georgian style with plenty of light chintzy fabrics — log fires for winter weather. Individually designed bedrooms are spacious, with breakfast tables, easy chairs or sofas and usually a desk.

The restaurant, with smoking and non-smoking section, overlooks the gardens and woodland, and the menu changes seasonally, using free-range poultry and organically grown vegetables when possible.

Millington, Chester CH1 6NE. ✆ (0244) 851666

32 (Individually designed, including 6 suites; each with en suite bathroom, colour TV, in-house video, trouser press, hair dryer.) No children under 5. Breaks available

Year round

✕ Modern French à la carte

✻ Posh, but unstuffy

No, but nearby

♫ No

★ Chester itself. North Wales within easy reach

Off the A540 Chester/Parkgate Road, a few minutes drive from the city. Easily accessible from London and the Midlands via the M1, M6 and M56. 40 minutes from Manchester Airport

£/$ A

Crayke Castle

Don't be misled by the 'castle' name as this is a private home (and Wolsey Lodge member). But it *is* a Grade I listed building, erected in 1430 as a safe refuge for the Bishop of Durham and now lovingly restored by Peter and Belle Hepworth, who bought it a couple of years ago.

Crayke's history is almost as long as York's itself — the remnants of the 12th-century castle once visited by King John, Henry III and three Edwards, still stand close by in the grounds. Within the castle's 5-foot (1½ m) thick walls there are well-proportioned rooms with beamed ceilings. The enormous stone-vaulted undercroft now serves as the kitchen — where guests may choose to eat more informally if they don't opt for the formal and impressive dining room.

Though accommodation is limited, it is of luxury standard.

Crayke, York YO6 4TA. ✆ (0347) 22285

3 (Individually decorated, including four-posters; each with en suite bathroom, colour TV, radio, tea/coffee facility, hair dryer and niceties like sewing kit and sherry.) Rates include breakfast. Breaks available

Year round

Fixed-price dinner

Historic

No, but plans call for tennis court

No

York Minster and Jorvik Museum. Wensleydale, Wharfedale and the northern moors all within easy reach. Also Castle Howard and Newby Hall

About 12 miles (19 km) north of York, just off the A19 York–Thirsk road. Leave the main road at Easingwold, signposted Crayke 2½ miles (4 km)

£/$ C

Crosby Lodge

Crosby Lodge certainly looks what it is — a baronial Victorian mansion whose castellated exterior gives it a grandiose air. Victorian room dimensions mean that reception rooms are spacious and airy, comfortably uncrowded, but the staff and service is pleasantly friendly.

From the beamed-ceilinged dining room there are views through long windows of the surrounding tree-lined parkland. Proprietor Michael Sedgwick is in charge of the kitchen — fixed-price menus offer a wide choice. Various period styles have been adopted for bedroom décor, though they all have modern conveniences.

It is a place in a pastoral setting but with easy accessibility, worth investigating.

Crosby-on-Eden, Carlisle, Cumbria CA6 4QZ.
✆ (022873) 618

11 (All individually styled and each with en suite bathroom, colour TV, hair dryer). Rates include English breakfast

Jan 24 to Dec 24

✕ Table d'hôte and à la carte

✳ Country baronial

No

♫ No

★ Hadrian's Wall is close by, as is the Lake District. Carlisle's own castle and cathedral are worth seeing, also the Solway Firth

4 miles (6 km) from the M6 and Carlisle

£/$ C

Crugsillick Manor

Jeremy and Diana Lloyd have refurbished this Grade II listed manor house, giving it the comfort and detail that has led guests to write in the visitors book 'Words aren't enough. English country ambience, gracious hospitality, wonderful cooking.'

As a Wolsey Lodge, Crugsillick Manor offers unpretentious luxury in a private home dotted with Persian rugs and objets d'art, paintings and silver. The Lloyds have always loved entertaining, and they keep lists of menus they have served guests, so that on repeat visits the same food is never served.

The house is one of the most historic in Cornwall, at one time the home of the Kemp family. It was Admiral of the Fleet Arthur Kemp who travelled the world with Captain Cook, and was at the storming of the Heights in Quebec City with General Wolfe.

Ruan High Lanes, Truro, Cornwall TR2 5LJ.
✆ (0872) 501214

2 (Twin, furnished with period antiques; one with en suite bathroom, one with adjacent bathroom; additional single room available as part of a booking for 3 or 5) Rates include breakfast

Year round except Xmas

✕ Home-cooked four-course dinners with advance notice

✳ Genteel family home

Shark fishing can be arranged given notice

♫ No

★ Many attractive fishing coves and harbours on the Roseland Peninsula. St Mawes, a picturesque Cornwall village is a 15-minute drive away

Nearest train station is St Austell (a 4-hour train ride from Paddington). Nearest airport is Newquay, a half-hour's drive away

£/$ D

The Devonshire Arms

The Devonshire Arms is a sister hotel to the Cavendish Hotel (p 00) i.e. it belongs to the Devonshire family trust and shows that same unmistakable aristocratic influence. Originally, it was a coaching inn though the exact date of its founding is unknown. Through Georgian and Victorian times it was enlarged, and in this decade has been further extended and refurbished under the personal supervision of the Duchess of Devonshire.

From the pleasant restaurant there are views over the parkland. Light lunches and simple dinner food is served here as well as the more complicated and continental.

In some of the older rooms, trellises act as bedheads, gingham curtains decorate the windows and some beds are of brass. The newer bedrooms are lighter and brighter. You may be pleased to note that there are telephones in the bathrooms!

Bolton Abbey, Skipton, North Yorkshire BD23 6AJ.
✆ (075671) 441

38 (Including four-posters; each with en suite bathroom, colour TV, radio, tea/coffee tray.) Rates include breakfast

Year round

✕ Features local game in season. A la carte English and continental. Good wine list

✻ Yorkshire hospitality, ducal style

5 miles (8 km) of fishing rights on the Wharfe, well stocked with trout and grayling

♫ No

★ Bolton Abbey, Harrogate, Yorkshire Dales

In the Yorkshire Dales National Park on the A59 Skipton to Harrogate road, at the junction with the B6160 in the heart of Wharfedale

£/$ C

Dormy House

Dormy House still has the appearance of its 17th-century farmhouse origins, with its mellow stone walls, exposed beams and open log fires. Twentieth-century enhancements have been chosen to blend in well: some antiques here and there, mirrors in wooden frames.

Several rooms of the original farmhouse have been combined to create a restaurant so that instead of being large and impersonal, it is still intimate for 60 diners. In the adjoining bars drinks for all occasions are served, including real ale.

Some of the bedrooms have French windows opening on to small walled gardens where guests can sit and enjoy the summer floral display or watch the sun setting behind the Malvern Hills. Rooms are light and fairly modern in décor with all the expected amenities. Morning tea arrives at a pre-requested time, part of the hotel's personal service.

Willersey Hill, Broadway, Worcestershire WR12 7LF.
✆ (0386) 852711

49 (Including four-posters, each with en suite bathroom, colour TV and trouser press.) Rates include breakfast. Breaks available

Open: Year round, except Xmas

✕ Table d'hôte and à la carte, highly praised

✻ Cotswold country appeal

No

♫ No

★ Willersey Hill Camp, built by the Celts, Chipping Campden, Burford and Evesham. Also Stratford

Car: 2 miles (3 km) from Broadway. Leave the M5 at Junction 9, take the A435 to Toddington roundabout and follow the A438 signed to Broadway

£/$ C

The Dragon House

A pretty little country house hotel, The Dragon House dates from 1704. It used to be a smugglers' drinking den for many years with a reputation for riotous merrymaking on contraband liquor. By way of sharp contrast, it later became a Methodist preaching house!

No preaching here now and no contraband, though there might still be some evening merrymaking in the cosy lounge bar beside its brick-surround fireplace. Excellent snacks are served here too. There is an attractive small lounge and simply furnished dining room plus ten bedrooms with light décor. The Dragon House is well maintained and spotlessly clean, set in a pretty garden alongside the A39, and is good value for money.

Bilbrook, nr Minehead, Somerset TA24 6HQ.
✆ (0984) 40215

- 10 (Each with en suite bathroom, colour TV, radio, tea/coffee facility) Rates are half board
- Year round
- 4-course table d'hôte
- Simple and restful
- Own stables; nearby fishing. Hunting and shooting can be arranged
- ♫ No
- ★ Quantock Hills and the Brendon Hills, Exmoor
- Between the coast and Exmoor National Park on the A39
- £/$ C half board

Eastwell Manor

A really impressive-looking, regal-style mansion surrounded by 62 of its own acres (25 ha) and part of a 3,000 acre (1,214 ha) estate in the 'Garden of England', Eastwell Manor is permeated by grandeur. Spacious reception rooms feature decorative high ceilings, majestic fireplaces and wood panelling.

The panelling is a highlight of most rooms including the billiards room, meeting room and twinned dining rooms overlooking the garden. Eastwell Manor refers to its cuisine as a 'subtle choice of English and French dishes', and its cellars are certainly outstanding with 15,000 bottles to choose from, including the hotel's exclusive champagne, Blanc de Noir.

Bedrooms here are all named and individual, so you could find yourself in the gold-toned Robert Curtoys Room, the mushroom-pink dominated Earl of Northumberland Suite or the Countess of Midleton Suite with its Edwardian bathroom.

All guests are free to walk about the estate, which includes a two-mile (3 km) stretch of the Pilgrims' Way, the historic route to Canterbury Cathedral.

Eastwell Park, Ashford, Kent TN25 4HR.
✆ (0233) 35751

20	(Individually furnished, and each with en suite bathroom, colour TV and radio)	♫	No
🏨	Year round	★	Canterbury Cathedral, coastal resorts like Margate, Royal Tunbridge Wells
✕	English and French. Home-baked bread. Excellent cellars — 15,000 wines, heavy on French	🚗	30-minutes drive from European ferry ports of Dover, Folkestone and Ramsgate, and within easy reach of the M2 and M20
✻	Grand		
🎾	Tennis, croquet, billiards	£/$	B

Elcot Park

Elcot Park is a handsome, 17th-century manor house in the lush and rolling countryside of the Kennet Valley. The original residence was constructed in 1678 on this high ground that commands such superb views of the valley and the Coombe Hills. In 1848 Sir William Paxton, the royal gardener, planned and set out the 16-acre (6 ha) park with its rare trees and shrubs.

Modern features have been added to Elcot, but it retains its period elegance by tasteful decoration and furnishings in its public and guest rooms. Log fires burn in handsome fireplaces on chillier nights, and though the house is sizeable enough for spacious accommodation, it is not too large to lose the family atmosphere projected by its hosts.

There have been varied reports about Elcot, with niggles about cuisine but not about service. And the bedrooms, both in the main building and the converted mews, are fitted to a high standard.

Nr Newbury, Berkshire RG16 8NJ. ✆ (0488) 58100

37 (Including suites and four-posters; each with en suite bathroom, radio, colour TV, tea/coffee facility, Malvern water, fresh fruit, biscuit barrel, sherry.) Rates include full English breakfast. Breaks available

Year round

✕ Table d'hôte and à la carte — nouvelle style

✻ Tranquil

Tennis, croquet, woodland walks

♫ No

★ Oxford, Windsor, Ascot, Salisbury, Winchester and the New Forest, Newbury Racecourse

Just north of the A4 London to Bath road, 5 miles (8 km) west of Newbury

£/$ C

The Elms

One of the first of the luxury country house breed, The Elms is a grand Queen Anne house with two additional wings sympathetically added. Happily, reception rooms have been left with their original proportions and furnished to that style. The Library Bar, for example still has its old mantlepiece and fine mahogany bookcases. The three lounges, scattered with antiques, open onto the garden patio; and the Regency dining room sets just the right mood for dinner *à deux*.

An array of niceties are to be found in the guest rooms, though those on the top floor are somewhat small. For the best views, pick those at the back, where you can see over the 13 acres (5 ha) of formal gardens and park. The Elms's herb garden is considered one of the best.

When I first stayed at The Elms it was owner-managed; since it has passed out of single ownership it has lost some of the personal touch, though not the charm of setting.

Abberley, nr Worcester WR6 6AT. ✆ (029921) 666

27 (Including suites and four-posters, 9 in annexe; each with en suite bathroom and colour TV.) Rates include breakfast

Year round

✕ English and continental

Croquet, putting, tennis court

♫ No

★ Convenient for the Wye Valley, Wales and the Cotswolds. Harvington Hall, Hartlebury Castle, Burford House, Worcester Cathedral

On the A443, 12 miles (19 km) from Worcester. Leave M4 at Junction 5 at Droitwich

£/$ C

Fairfield Manor

An early Georgian mansion that prides itself on Yorkshire hospitality, Fairfield Manor holds its traditions dear. In Lord Nelson's time, by the time Londoners got here they were 199 miles (320 km) from home — a milestone marks the spot where those wishing to avoid the tollgate just up the road at Skelton, turned off by the field track to go round by Skelton Landing.

Earl de Grey purchased the estate in 1874 for his kinsman, Captain Robert de Grey Vyner. All the comforts of the era were installed including a laundry to take care of starching quality linen. The elaborate oak panelling on the staircase and reception area seen today reflects that monied era.

The Prince of Wales, later Edward VII, was a frequent visitor, and even after the house passed into the hands of Countess of Rosslyn, the royal connection continued — after her engagement, Princess May of Teck (the future Queen Mary) came to stay here.

Shipton Road, Skelton, York YO3 6XW.
✆ (0904) 625621

25 (Each with en suite bathroom, colour TV, radio, tea/coffee facility, including four-poster.) Rates include full English breakfast

🏨 Year round

✕ International table d'hôte and à la carte

✻ Traditional Yorkshire

⚲ No

♫ No

★ The cathedral city of York, Harrogate, Wetherby, Ripon and Thirsk. The North York Moors National Park and the Dales, Jervaulx Abbey, Brontës' Haworth and Herriot country

🚗 Set back from the A19, 3 miles (5 km) from York on the outskirts of the village of Skelton

£/$ C

Fairwater Head Hotel

This delightful country establishment above the Axe Valley was given its name by a young Bengal Staff Corps widow, Harrietta Briscoe, who chose the site for her home in the late 19th century. The Fairwater stream flows strongly at the foot of the hill, and water for her new house (which she designed) was 'rammed' back up the hill into enormous chambers under the kitchens. Hence the name, 'Fairwater Head', the source of the stream.

Built of local stone, Fairwater continues to preserve its peaceful, casually comfortable image (though as a hotel modern bedside lights have replaced spitting oil lamps): wall-to-wall carpeting, linoleum and refrigeration, Calor gas. Harrietta was a talented artisan — her workshop is now the morning room — a lasting example of her skill can be seen over the fireplace in the hall, the carved message: 'East or West, Home is Best'.

For the past five years this hotel has been owned by the Austin family, so the atmosphere is friendly and hospitable. One of the favourite places for coffee or drink is the pine-roofed Garden Lounge, which is a superb place to watch the Devon sunsets. From the dining room there are views of the gardens, and the cooking is very much home style, using free-range eggs from a nearby farm and fresh seafood from a local Lyme Regis fisherman.

Those gardens are a delight from spring on with their succession of blooms and their unusual shrubs and trees. Birds are easily spotted here; sheep and cattle continue to graze contentedly in adjacent meadows, and since the hotel terrace is a sun trap, the sheltered seats couldn't be better for an afternoon nap.

Expanded accommodation at Fairwater now includes four luxury bedrooms in a garden wing, a few steps from the main entrance with panoramic views across the gardens and Axe Valley.

Hawkchurch, Axminster, Devon EX13 5TX.
✆ (02977) 349

18 (Including 4 in the Garden Wing; each with en suite bathroom, colour TV, coffee/tea facility that includes fresh Devon milk.) Rates include afternoon tea and baked cakes on arrival plus English breakfast. Special packages available.

Mar to Dec

Home-style cooking concentrating on Scotch beef, venison and pheasant from Exmoor, fresh vegetables and fruit, crab and lobster from Lyme Regis. A la carte and table d'hôte. Light lunches available in the Garden Lounge and bar

Family friendly

Billiard room, croquet. Nearby sports including special rates at Lyme Regis Golf Club

Sat evening, piano music

★ Famous houses and gardens nearby include Montacute, Killerton, Forde Abbey, Sherborne Castle (built by Sir Walter Raleigh). Also Cricket St Thomas Wildlife Park and Parnham House or Abbotsbury's swannery and subtropical gardens. Within easy reach are the Fleet Air Arm Museum and the Tank Museum at Pecorama Pleasure Gardens

Tucked into tiny Hawkchurch Village on the borders of Devon and Dorset, close to the famous market town of Axminster, 5 miles (8 km) away

£/$ C

Fallowfields

Praise comes from several quarters for this establishment. The house, Gothic styled, is interesting itself and was the home of the Begum Aga Khan before her marriage. The hostess too is a colourful character, who has spent a varied life before removing herself to the country and accepting paying guests, which she has been doing at Fallowfields for over ten years.

By all means borrow the books in the sitting room, says Mrs Crowther, but return them before you leave. Her personal treasures and antiques are expected to stay where they are, however. As usual in a personalised, small establishment like Fallowfields, dinner is booked in advance and menu selection made by 6.30 p.m.

You'll find all three bedrooms comfortably furnished with pretty linen and ample wardrobe space.

In the 12 acres (5 ha) of well-kept grounds there are a swimming pool and tennis court for guests' use. Croquet and table tennis are also available on the premises.

Southmoor, Abingdon, Oxfordshire OX13 5BH.
✆ (0865) 820416

3 (Each with en suite bathroom, one with four-poster, coffee/tea facility). No children under 10. Rates include breakfast

Easter to Sept

✕ Fixed-price dinner on advance booking. Excellent vegetarian meals available on request. First-class sweet trolley. Not available Wed night

✻ Private home attention

Croquet, table tennis, swimming pool, tennis all on premises. Riding school 5 mins away. Water sports available at Stanton Harcourt Leisure Centre, 5 miles (8 km) away

♫ No

★ Oxford colleges, Vale of the White Horse, Berkshire Downs, Cotswold country, Bath

On the A420, 8 miles (13 km) from Oxford, 6 miles (10 km) from Abingdon

£/$ E

Farlam Hall

This fine old creeper-clad house looks the way it always as, now being a listed building. Dating from the late 17th century, it was enlarged to its present form in Victorian times. John Wesley was allowed to use a cottage in the grounds for services, and George and Robert Stephenson of steam engine fame stayed here.

The house is surrounded by 4½ acres (2 ha) of lawns with mature trees and shrubs and a stream which feeds an ornamental lake.

The public rooms reflect the Victorian elements of the house with a smattering of antiques. The pretty bedrooms on the first floor with Virginia creeper fringing their windows have a certain Georgian feel. Other bedrooms are grander, like The Garden Room which has a six-foot (1.8 m) four-poster bed and sitting area, or Caroline, a twin room with sitting area and jacuzzi bathroom. Views from some of them extend as far as 20 miles (32 km) on a clear day. Meals are served in the spacious rooms overlooking the garden, notable for their full-height windows and ornamental ceilings.

Brampton, Cumbria CA8 2NG. ✆ (06976) 234

- 13 — (Each different, including a four-poster; each with en suite facilities and colour TV.) No children under 5. Rates are half board
- Mar to Jan
- × Four-course dinner menu is based on fresh local ingredients. A soup is followed by Lancashire quail or local beef, for example
- * Friendly and down to earth, family-run
- Croquet. Golf courses are nearby
- ♫ No
- ★ Hadrian's Wall is 4 miles (6 km) away. The Lake District, Yorkshire Dales and Solway coast all accessible
- Located 11 miles (18 km) east of Carlisle and the M6, 2½ miles (4 km) from Brampton on the A689 to Hallbankgate and Alston
- £/$ A but half board

Farthings

A delightful Georgian country house hotel in an idyllic position for anyone planning to tour the Cornish peninsula, Farthings was built in 1805 and stands in 3 acres (1¼ ha) of lovely gardens. It is in a quiet village location but Hatch Beauchamp is readily accessible via London and Midland routes.

George and Clair Cooper have imprinted their own personalities on what is a house with character, giving Farthings an easy-going atmosphere. Clair is responsible for the cooking, preparing food to order, which is served in a simply decorated restaurant. If there is a wait, it will be worth it — ask any of the locals.

Guest rooms here are named for trees such as Willow, a twin, or Sandalwood, which has a double bed. One of the rooms features a handsome, hand-carved spiral staircase leading to a luxury bathroom. All rooms look out onto the gardens and wooded countryside.

Hatch Beauchamp, nr Taunton, Somerset TA3 6SG.
✆ (0823) 480664

6 (Each with en suite facilities and colour TV, individually styled.) Rates include early-morning tea, newspaper and English breakfast. Breaks available. Unsuitable for children

Year round

Four-course, fixed-price dinners cooked to order. Sample main courses: baked brill with a herb crust or breast of chicken stuffed with crab mousse. Interesting home-made ice-creams

Rural retreat

Not on site, but golf, polo, riding etc. nearby

No

Exmoor's National Park, the Quantock and Blackdown Hills

Convenient to the main arteries of the southwest, the hotel is situated 4 miles (6 km) from the A303 and the same distance from the M5 (Junction 25). Equidistant from the Somerset and Devon coasts

£/$ C

The Feathers

Without doubt, The Feathers looks every inch a traditional olde worlde English inn, with its spectacular half-timbered black and white frontage, its crooked stairs, its carved mantlepieces and ornate plaster ceilings, panelling and original fireplaces.

A certain Rees Jones, whose initials are carved into the heavy entrance door, leased this property in 1609, later buying the freehold. It became an inn in 1656, named in honour of James I's son Prince Charles. The town declined during William and Mary's reign, but was reopened in 1752 by Samuel Corne with stabling for 60 horses.

Since then its fortunes have risen and fallen under a series of owners, including the Tanner Family in the 1920s when you might have had a dinner for two with champagne for less than £1. Not so nowadays I'm afraid. Nor will you find meals in the Richard III Restaurant (once the inn's kitchen) with an original fireplace, quite as gourmet as you may have hoped.

Although I recently found some of the standard rooms rather small and in need of redecoration, for 17th-century atmosphere in the heart of Ludlow though, The Feathers is hard to resist.

Bull Ring, Ludlow, Shropshire SY8 1AA. ✆ (0584) 5261

37 (Including suites, family rooms and some four-posters; each with en suite bathroom, colour TV, trouser press and hair dryer.) Breaks available

Year round

✕ Lacks imagination, somewhat standard

✳ 17th-century atmosphere

No

♫ No

★ Attingham Park, Benthall Hall, Wilderhope Manor

In the centre of Ludlow, reached via the A49 from Hereford or Shrewsbury

£/$ C

Fifehead Manor

Only the Anglo-Saxons could dream up a name like *Wallop*, a word believed to mean 'stream on the hillside' or 'place of the Ancient Briton'. Wallop was part of the Wessex estates owned by Saxon Earl Harold whose wife Godiva (yes, Coventry's one and the same), lived where Fifehead Manor stands today. (Their son, who became King Harold, to die in the Battle of Hastings, owned the adjoining Manor in Over Wallop.) Of the original Royal Manor listed in the Domesday Book, then about 2,640 acres (1,068 ha), only the Manor House and 17 acres (7 ha) now remain, but its owner retains a traditional right to call himself The Lord of the Manor. US President, George Washington, was a direct descendant of a 15th-century Lord of the Manor of Wallop Fifehead.

The hotel's dining room is thought to have been the Main Hall in the 11th century — you can still see traces of a minstrel's gallery, and priests used a ledge inside the Elizabethan chimney stack for concealment during Henry VIII's reformation. The mullioned windows are mid-15th century, and the small fireplace Jacobean, but the rest of the house is comparatively new.

Middle Wallop, Stockbridge, Hampshire SO20 8EG.
✆ (0264) 781565

15 (The more modern are largest; each has en suite bathroom and colour TV). Rates include breakfast

🏨 Year round except for Xmas

✕ Table d'hôte and à la carte

✻ Pleasant but not opulent

🏇 Nearby riding and fishing

♫ No

★ Salisbury and Winchester Cathedrals, Romsey Abbey

🚗 From Heathrow or Gatwick leave the M3 at Junction 8 for the A303 to Andover, then exit for A343 to Wallop and Salisbury. The hotel is 70 miles (113 km) from London, 20 miles (32 km) from Southampton

£/$ C

Fox's Earth

Ornate ceilings, panelling and carvings enhance this 17th-century manor house, home of the Baring-Gould family since 1626. Leaded windows and huge working fireplaces are features of all the public rooms, along with deep comfortable chairs and period paintings.

Once you have passed through the wrought-iron gates and into the gardens leading to the front door, you know you have found a safe haven. The grounds comprise 11 acres (4½ ha) of gardens and woodland plus a 2-acre (¾ ha) lake stocked with trout and fed by a 60-foot (18 m) waterfall. Surrounding the grounds is the 1,000-acre (505 ha) Lewtrenchard Estate, where you are welcome to wander peacefully at will; and Dartmoor itself is only minutes away.

An American couple, Greg Shriver and Mary Ellen Keys, now live in this historic house and run it with great enthusiasm.

Lewtrenchard Manor, Lewdown, Okehampton, Devon EX20 4PN. ✆ (056683) 256

10 (All with character and views to the gardens, some with four-posters, each with en suite bathroom and colour TV.) Rates include early-morning tea and breakfast. Breaks available

🏨 Year round

✕ Award-winning food. Locally grown produce and fresh seafood always on the menu

✻ Intimate getaway

🎣 Fishing

♫ No

★ Cornish fishing villages are an easy drive. Plymouth less than an hour away. Dartmoor and Land's End within an easy drive

🚗 In a lush valley just off the northwest corner of Dartmoor. Reached via the A30 from Exeter

£/$ C

Fulford House

Fulford House is another hot favourite when it comes to private homes accepting paying guests. This is another Wolsey Lodge, with your hosts Stephen and Mary Pen Wills giving warm personalised attention.

The mellow, golden Northamptonshire stone house itself is a Grade II listed building, and Stephen tells me the earliest part dates from the 1600s when it was probably a farmhouse, though certainly later additions have been made. The Wills are especially proud of their gardens, which are laid out on three levels, and from the top level you can see over several miles of rolling farmlands.

As a place to stay, you'll find Fulford comfortably furnished with country antiques, and the gregarious Wills usually join their guests for dinner by candlelight around their rare, circular early-Georgian mahogany dining table — for dinner is considered a social occasion.

The Green, Culworth, Banbury, Oxfordshire OX17 2BB.
✆ (029576) 355

3 (Each with en suite bathroom, colour TV, coffee/tea facility.) No children under 7. Rates include breakfast

Year round

✕ French country style cooked by your hostess, for dinner, which must be arranged in advance

✻ Horsey/country

Croquet in the garden; nearby golf

♫ No

★ Many nearby notable houses and gardens like Sulgrave Manor, George Washington's ancestral home. Oxford and Stratford are within easy reach. Also Silverstone and Towcester race courses

The nearest town is Banbury, from which you take the A442/B4525 Northampton road. Turn left 1½ miles (2½ km) after passing Thorpe Mandeville and follow the road into Culworth, passing the church, to the village green. At the top of the green, turn right.

£/$ E

Gidleigh Park

Gidleigh Park was built for an Australian shipping magnate as his country retreat, and was started as a hotel in 1977 by an American couple, Kay and Paul Henderson. It is a particularly beautiful, black-and-white timbered house with a marvellous view over the Teign valley and set in 40 acres (16 ha) beside Dartmoor National Park. It is a British member of the exclusive Relais & Chateau group, and its restaurant has won accolades of the highest nature.

Within a wine list composed of 400 plus 250 bin ends, it is not surprising that Paul asks guests to give special orders before 5 p.m. to allow him time to find them! And he is not being immodest when he suggests Gidleigh Park has one of the best lists of digestifs in the country. Exotic concoctions on the menu are complemented by an excellent British farmhouse cheese board and home-baked croissants and brioches.

The interior is luxurious without being ostentatious: plenty of panelled walls, pretty chintzes, sink-in armchairs, fresh flowers everywhere and log fires for cold weather. The bar opens onto a small terrace where afternoon tea is served in fine weather. Brown and pink shades predominate in this home-away-from-home for the affluent.

Twelve of the 14 delightful bedrooms are in the main house — a few at the back with balconies, facing Dartmoor, some of the best on the first floor facing front. The other two rooms are in a converted chapel annexe (but umbrellas are provided).

The Hendersons have restored the elaborate water garden in their grounds, which also boast two croquet lawns, a tennis court, a herb garden and well-stocked vegetable garden. The energetic are encouraged to walk the moors, but the rest of us merely sit back and enjoy it.

Chagford, Devon TQ13 8HH. ✆ (06473) 2367

14 (Double, each individually furnished with en suite bathroom, colour TV, clock radio, hair dryer, towelling bathrobe; 12 in the main house, 2 in annexe.) Rates are half board (continental breakfast) and include early-morning tea

Year round

Table d'hôte and à la carte. Imaginative main dishes as well as plainer roasts. Excellent sauces

For the affluent connoisseur

Croquet, tennis. Swimming in the river and walking the moors. Golf, riding, fishing nearby

No

★ Dartmoor National Park is the biggest attraction.

A 3½-hour train journey from Paddington to Exeter, or by motorway, the M4, M5, A30 to Whiddon Down from London. By road, the approach is from Chagford, not Gidleigh. In Chagford Square, facing Webbers with Lloyds Bank on your right, turn right into Mill Street. After 150 yards, fork right, go downhill to Factory Crossroad. Travel straight across into Holy Street and follow the lane 1½ miles (2½ km) to the end.

£/$ A but half board

Gilpin Lodge

Gilpin Lodge is a tiny, very personal country house on the private side, but operating as a hotel for about four years. Furnished harmoniously with picture-lined walls and pretty table dressing in its restaurant, lots of fresh flowers and floral fabrics, it is a quiet retreat from the stress of modern living — tucked away in 20 acres (8 ha) of garden and woodland.

Though each bedroom has its own character, a favourite is the four-poster suite with lounge area and superb views across the valleys. Here too, a spacious bathroom with sunken tub to ease away any of the day's exertions.

Lake Windermere is only a couple of miles (km) down the road — a mecca for yachtsmen; or there's golf at the Windermere Club where a cordial reception awaits visitors.

Crook Road, Windermere, Cumbria LA23 3NE.
✆ (09662) 2295

6	(No two alike, including four-poster suite, each with en suite bathroom and colour TV.) Rates are half board
🏨	Year round
✕	Fixed-price menus. Samples: chicken liver parfait, fricassée of turbot, Norfolk duckling
✻	Warmly personal, but well organised
🎾	Yachting, golfing, riding, shooting — all nearby
♫	No
★	Lake District
🚗	On the B5284 about 2 miles (3 km) from Windermere, 6 miles (10 km) from Kendal
£/$	C half board

The Glebe at Barford

A Grade II listed Georgian house, The Glebe was previously the rectory next to a historic church in the centre of Barford. Dating from 1820, it stands in an acre (½ ha) of pleasant gardens where light meals and snacks are served in good weather, Mon to Sat. The restaurant also opens onto the lawns and is open every evening and for Sunday lunch when fare is typical English.

Officially a three-star hotel, The Glebe has been awarded four crowns by the English Tourist Board, and other reports commend it for food and service.

Barford, Warwick CV35 8BS. ✆ (0926) 624218

15	(Mostly en suite, each individually furnished and with colour TV.) Rates include breakfast. Breaks available	♫	No
🏨	Year round	★	Warwick and Kenilworth Castles, Stratford-upon-Avon and Cotswold country, Leamington Spa
✕	Table d'hôte international	🚗	Barford is on the A429, 3 miles (5 km) south of Warwick and Leamington Spa, close to the M42 and M6
✳	Quiet but convenient	£/$	D
🎾	No		

Goodwood Park Hotel

The attraction for Goodwood House as a conference venue led to the enlargement and refurbishment of the old Richmond Arms inn in is grounds, but that doesn't mean to say you have to be a conference delegate to stay here.

Standing as it does in the 12,000 acre (4,856 ha) Goodwood Estate, it has been owned by the Duke of Richmond for nearly 300 years — but don't expect the current Duke to welcome you at the front door. As far back as 1786 this property welcomed weary travellers and their horses — six of those former stables have now been converted into luxury bedrooms, each named after a famous racehorse. Some guests still prefer the rooms in the older part of the house.

A daily English menu plus an à la carte French-influenced one is available in The Duke's Restaurant, and the Richmond Arms bar serves a variety of ales and snack food.

Chichester, West Sussex PO18 0QB. ✆ (0243) 775537

89	(Including suites and four-poster; each with en suite bathroom and colour TV.) Rates include English breakfast. Breaks available
🏨	Year round
✕	English and French influenced
✻	Meetings orientated
🎾	Magnificent leisure club. 18-hole golf course opening August 1989
♫	No
★	Goodwood House, racecourse and airfield. Singleton Open Air Museum. Chichester
🚗	1 hour from Gatwick and 1 hour 15 mins from Heathrow. By car take the A3 through Guildford then the A286 via Haslemere and Midhurst
£/$	C

Grafton Manor

Grafton has a long and distinguished history from the time of William the Conqueror, when the original residence was given to his cousin. In the 16th century the house was turned into a lavish mansion by the Talbot family, one of England's most prominent Catholic families (it was rumoured that Sir John Talbot was one of the conspirators in The Gunpowder Plot).

Today all is peaceful in this stylish small hotel set in its 26 acres (11 ha) of superb Worcestershire countryside. The 18th-century dining room under the direction of chef proprietor John Morris is a focal point. Produce from the estate is used whenever possible, and all the herbs are grown in an extensive formal herb garden laid out in the form of a giant chessboard.

Grafton Lane, Bromsgrove, Worcestershire B61 7HA.
✆ (0527) 31525

8 (Individually decorated and furnished with antiques, some with open fires; each with en suite bathroom, colour TV, clock radio, trouser press and hair dryer.) Rates include continental breakfast. No children under 7

Year round

✕ Table d'hôte lunches and dinners offer imaginative dishes

✳ Tastefully relaxed

Coarse fishing in estate's own 2-acre (¾ ha) lake. Two 18-hole golf courses nearby

♫ No

★ Avoncroft Museum of Buildings, Worcester Cathedral, Stratford. The Royal Worcester Porcelain works and the Royal Brierly Crystal factory may also easily be visited

Close to the M5 and very accessible to Birmingham, Redditch, Droitwich and Kidderminster. One mile (1.5 km) south of Bromsgrove off the B4090.

£/$ C

Gravetye Manor

What a treat to step into a polished wood vestibule whose log fire puffs aromatically — a winter arrival at Gravetye Manor whose stone-mullioned windows look out into superb grounds — 30 acres (12 ha) of gardens bounded by a further 1,000 acres (405 ha) of Forestry Commission property. From spring to autumn you are greeted by a blaze of colour from primrose daffodils to brilliant rhododendrons and azaleas, from white, snowflake lilies to heavily scented roses.

The beauty of the grounds is thanks to the manor's most notable owner, William Robinson, who bought it in 1884 and spent his years creating and developing the 'English natural garden'. One of England's greatest gardeners, he planned, planted and landscaped what is still today a great asset to the hotel. It is only appropriate that the garden vegetables and fruit on the menu mostly come from the stone-walled, oval kitchen garden that Robinson built.

Robinson also used oak from the estate to panel the ground floor rooms at Gravetye, now drawing rooms and bar, as well as four of the bedrooms including the master one. Though Gravetye isn't stuffy or pretentious, it does have a slightly formal air as you'll see when you take the long drive that sweeps up to the front entrance. The interiors are not exactly Sotheby's but there are some very fine period pieces dating from the 16th century, to the 19th-century gilded wood-surround mirror in the main drawing room, and including the 17th-century cabriole-legged dresser opposite Reception.

Gravetye is an Elizabethan stone mansion built in 1598 by Richard Infield for his wife Katharine — their initials formed in stone are to be seen above the garden entrance and their portraits carved in oak are above the fireplace in the master bedroom. Guest rooms are named for English trees like Ash, which features a beautiful 17th-century chest of drawers, and Bay which boasts a little Elizabethan bible table, engraved with a cross. They all contain niceties like chilled sherry and a bedside flask of spring water, as well as courtesy toiletries and fluffy bath robes.

Many would say that this hotel's crowning glory is its food, served in an elegant, oak-panelled room candlelit at night, but perhaps you should see for yourself now that the proprietor's son, Leigh Herbert, is in charge of the kitchen. His approach is the 'light' touch, but he has plenty to work with for Gravetye has its own smoke house where salmon, duck breast and venison are prepared, as well as its own chickens (free-range variety) and spring water. What's more, there's a remarkable cellar rambling beneath the manor providing a list for thoughtful selection.

There is no discotheque nor in-house movies here at Gravetye (though there are TVs) and peace and quiet are its key. It wasn't always that way as 'Smugglers Lane' in the grounds, reminds you — the manor at one time was a smugglers' hideout. And at one time its furnace supplied the 12-pounder guns to Woolwich in the 18th century.

Nr East Grinstead, West Sussex RH19 4LJ.
✆ (0342) 810567

14 (Each with en suite bathroom, hair dryer, colour TV, books, toiletries, bathrobes; individually decorated.) No children under 7

Year round

✕ Fixed-price lunch but à la carte dinner. Sample light dish: steamed chicken breast with leek puree and chartreuse sauce. Home-smoked salmon, duck and venison. Homemade preserves and free-range eggs for breakfast. Jacket and tie for dinner.

✱ Comfortable sense of grandeur

Croquet, clock golf, fly fishing. Tennis, riding and golf nearby

♫ No

★ Wakehurst Gardens, Hever Castle, Petworth House plus Bodiam, Lewes and Arundel

30 miles (48 km) from London. Take A22 and about 7 miles (11 km) past Godstone at crossroads turn right on to B2028 to Turner's Hill. Or leave the M23 at Junction 10 for Crawley, turning east taking the A264 towards East Grinstead. At the roundabout by the 'Duke's Head' turn right on the B2028.

£/$ C

Great Fosters

Forget the purpose-built conference centre in the grounds, and what you have here is no ordinary hotel but a place of great character and atmosphere. Great Fosters is a Grade I listed building, once a Royal hunting lodge in the heart of Windsor Forest which for four centuries was the stately Elizabethan home of many notable families.

During the Middle Ages the area around Great Fosters was known as Imworth — it is known that the family de Imworth lived here in 1224. But the original core of the house as it is today was probably built in 1550 by Sir William Warham. The name no doubt is derived from 'foresters'. One of the most famous early inhabitants was Judge Dodderidge in the 17th century, nicknamed 'the Nodding Judge' because he always considered cases with his eyes shut. Later patrons have included the Prince of Wales, who danced here; Noel Coward, who gave Great Fosters a line in one of his plays; and Charlie Chaplin, who used the secret passage through the bottom of a cupboard in one of the bedrooms to say goodnight to his children.

Even as a hotel, Great Fosters remains an outstanding example of a red-brick, 16th-century house with a formal garden surrounded on three sides by a moat that probably pre-dates the house by a thousand years. All the windows are mullioned, and the nine different brick pinnacle chimneys (made unsafe during the last war) were replaced to exact pattern, winning the hotel a 1970s award.

You will step back in time the moment you enter the doorway, over which is the arms and initials of Elizabeth I and the date 1598, for the stout inner door admits only one person at a time, and its bolts and hinges are of very early ironwork. This hall has 17th-century pilastering and linenfold panelling, and at one end boasts a Jacobean, wood chimney piece, delicately carved and dating about 1620.

Through the hall to the left, the Anne Boleyn Room (now a sitting room) shows a remarkable plaster ceiling and stone chimney piece. A small room at the far end used to be a chapel with a priest's staircase that leads to the Tapestry Room above. The other way to get upstairs is by the superb oak staircase dated around 1600 which leads to the first and second floors, from where a small spiral staircase continues up to a tower room.

These days the Tapestry Room is one of the hotel's more famous bedchambers, adorned with tapestries of course, plus an ornate ceiling, and containing another remarkable chimney piece and stone mantlepiece that is carved with the story of Adam and Eve. To meet 20th-century comfort requirements, bathrooms have been added — in this case there are the remains of the secret staircase which emerges through a trapdoor in a cupboard in the Nursery Suite above.

Personally, I think it is a great shame that the added bathrooms lack even a trace of grandiose style to be found in the overwhelming bedrooms like this, and the Panel I and II rooms, the Queen Anne and the Italian bedrooms. The latter is almost overly regal with its damask walls, gilded Italianate furniture and plasterwork. All the walnut doors in the house, by the way, were made out of two great walnut trees which formerly stood in front of the house.

Dining at Great Fosters is also an experience — at least for the setting, either of the small Tudor dining room with its Mortlake tapestry, or the 15th-century Tithe Barn where Saturday evening dinner dances and medieval banquets are held.

For historic interest, yet modern conveniences and readily accessible location, this hotel comes tops.

Egham, Surrey TW20 9UR. ✆ (0784) 33822

44 (23 are in the main house including two four-posters, one canopied; many with antique furnishings and unusual character. All with en suite bathrooms.) Rates include English breakfast

Year round

✕ Table d'hôte and à la carte and typically English

✻ Antique 16th-century charm

Outdoor heated pool open May to Sept, tennis court, superb gardens. Several golf courses within 12-mile (19 km) radius; polo at Windsor Park, boating on the Thames. Windsurfing at Thorpe within walking distance and riding and squash nearby

♫ Sat evening dinner dances, medieval banquets

★ Runnymede, Savill & Valley Gardens, Windsor and Eton, Hampton Court, Wimbledon

Located midway between Egham and Virginia Water, signposted from both directions; 7 miles (11 km) from Heathrow, less than 20 (32 km) from London's West End. Within easy reach of all the major motorways

£/$ C

The Greenway

The Greenway takes its name from the 4,000-year-old walkway which runs beside the hotel up onto the Cotswolds. This walkway — the Green Way, was the original drovers' road through the lowlands, which were then marsh and forest inhabited only by wildlife.

The original house on the Shurdington estate was built in 1548 as a private home for the Laurence family (wealthy wool merchants). The house as you see it now is more Georgian, its coach house recently converted into additional bedrooms.

Spacious ground floor public rooms are exactly the kind you'd anticipate finding in a country house hotel. In winter a wood fire blazes in the 17th-century baroque fireplace of the entrance lounge. In better weather, summer sun streams in from the gardens to highlight the attractive drawing room, where you can sink into a plump armchair or sofa to read the papers or order a cocktail from the bar.

Superb food is served in the Conservatory Dining Room, a smallish, appealing room that looks out onto the sunken garden and lily pond. Each bedroom has its own character — one a domed ceiling, another a mixture of exposed beams and alcoves, and another a half-tester bed. The other accommodation is in the stable block, where brickwork has purposely been left exposed and decoration is in bright colours.

No longer a secret, The Greenway is a popular overnight stop with the cognoscenti exploring Cotswold country.

Shurdington, nr Cheltenham, Gloucestershire GL51 5UG.
✆ (0242) 862352

19 (12 in the main house, individually decorated in coordinated colour schemes; each with en suite bathroom and colour TV.) No children under 7. Rates include breakfast. Breaks available

Jan 4 to Dec 28

✕ French-style, fixed price menu. Jacket and tie necessary

✻ Refined rural

No, but four 18-hole golf courses within 6 miles (10 km) and other sports nearby

♫ No

★ Cheltenham, Roman Cirencester, Tewkesbury and Gloucester

2½ miles (2½ km) from Cheltenham, 8 (13 km) from Gloucester. On the A46 Cheltenham/Stroud road

£/$ A

Grinkle Park Hotel

For centuries the Grinkle Estate belonged to the Conyers-Middleton family, but the present country retreat, in 35 acres (14 ha) of parkland, was built in 1881 for one of the great industrialists, Sir Charles Mark Palmer.

In cool weather an open fire burns in the entrance hall, the place to take tea, or if you prefer, the garden-styled Camellia Room decorated in green and white, with Italian cane furniture, is an alternative spot for refreshments. The adjacent billiards room allows for a relaxing game of snooker after dinner in the restaurant and verandah room, overlooking the lawn.

All 20 bedrooms were totally refurbished a couple of years ago, each to an individual design. On the first floor they are named for local flora and place names, like Ingleby or Azalea, which has a four-poster bed. On the upper floor they are named for the species of birds indigenous to the surrounding moorland, like Merlin and Skylark.

Easington, Saltburn-by-the-Sea, Cleveland TS13 4UB.
✆ (0287) 40515

20 (Including four-poster, each has en suite facilities, colour TV, tea-making facility and trouser press; each room individually decorated.) Rates include English breakfast. Children and dogs welcome. Special breaks available

Year round

✕ Table d'hôte and à la carte with well balanced choice

✻ Friendly

Within a few miles of the hotel guests can find most sport facilities

♫ No

★ North York Moors National Park is easily reached

In the hinterland of Whitby and Robin Hood's Bay, between the coastline and the Cleveland Hills. By road from Whitby, the A171 and A169

£/$ C

Grove House

Where do you find the niceties of a country house hotel with the personalised touch of a private home? In my opinion, nowhere better than at Grove House, a mellow old farmhouse in 10 acres (4 ha) of grounds not far from the Malvern Hills. It is the home of Michael and Ellen Ross, who are old hands at catering and hotelkeeping. (Until recently Michael was the proprietor and manager of nearby Cottage-in-the-Wood Hotel, which is not included in this book because we don't yet have reports about it under its new ownership.)

Because it is a private home, it is filled with family possessions and antiques, its walls studded with pictures from family albums. As a member of the Wolsey Lodge consortium, it accepts paying guests on an overnight or weekly basis for bed and breakfast or with dinner included.

Thanks to the Ross's hotel background, Grove House has an edge over same-category competition. The guest rooms, for example, are not only charmingly furnished as you might expect, but also feature en suite bathrooms and colour TVs, more regularly associated with country house hotels. Tea and coffee-making facilities are provided, along with a tin of delicious butter cookies; and as an extra service, Ellen does a lightning turn-down service while you're dining, complete with hot water bottle if the weather warrants it.

The elegant guest drawing room matches that in the finest country manor and the guest dining room, with its oak and silver and open fire, is so inviting you may not want to leave it. But remember this is not a hotel, so don't expect a bar or a choice of dinner menu. Ellen prepares and serves a five-course evening meal for those wishing to dine in, starting with a soup, followed by terrine or fish course, a main course (often a casserole), sweet, cheese and coffee. Guests sit around one grand family table set with crystal and silver, at a selected time to suit the majority. Suit yourself as to breakfast time, as simply continental as liked, or as full as a platter of eggs, bacon, sausages, tomato, mushrooms and fried bread.

Overseas visitors particularly enjoy this type of accommodation because they're seeing a real Englishman's home without having to do the dishes (though paying guests often feel they should offer). Telephone calls aren't encouraged but you can always use the family phone if necessary, and an essential lift isn't out of the question.

In summer neighbours allow Grove House guests to use their swimming pool, and the house itself has a tennis court as well as stables. Both Michael and Ellen are keen riders and will give riding instructions to beginners.

Bromsberrow Heath, Ledbury, Herefordshire HR8 1TE.
✆ (053181) 584

4 (doubles; each with en suite bathroom, colour TV, coffee/tea-making facilities). Rates include full English breakfast

Mar to Dec

✕ Excellent home cooking. Dinner must be requested in advance

✻ Warm, hotel-minded hospitality

Riding, tennis, use of neighbour's pool

♫ No

★ Gloucester, Ledbury, Malvern Hills

Leave the M50 at Junction 2, follow signs to Ledbury. Take first turning left signed Bromsberrow Heath. In village turn right by post office, up the hill. The house is on your right

£/$ E

Hambleton Hall

In a spectacular setting on a peninsular in the middle of a lake, Hambleton Hall has been earning marks for excellence since it first opened in 1980. The sybarites who can afford to stay here admire the lake setting and the Nina Campbell décor, and can't wait for the mouth-watering, much lauded dinners.

The Rabelais motto inscribed above the main entrance reads: 'Do as you please' and was inscribed well before the house's origin in the 1880s and, say the Harts, who transformed the Victorian house into a hotel, that's just as applicable now.

Main scenic feature at Hambleton is its dramatic view over Rutland Water, one of the largest and most picturesque bodies of water in Great Britain. Main hotel feature is the cuisine, as of 1988 still in the sure hands of chef Nicholas Gill, who trained at Maxim's in Paris.

Interior designer Nina Campbell's stamp is of course impressed on the décor, but some of the bedroom furniture includes pieces from Stefa Hart's own collection. Leisure facilities in the 10 acres (4 ha) of grounds include tennis, sailing and fishing.

Hambleton, Oakham, Rutland LE15 8TH. ✆ (0572) 56991

15	(Each with en suite bathroom and colour TV; individually furnished.) Rates include continental breakfast
🏨	Year round
✕	Nouvellish
✻	Personalised excellence
🎾	Tennis court; sailing, fishing, riding and shooting by arrangement
♫	No
★	Burghley House, Rockingham Castle, Belvoir Castle, Belton House
🚗	Off A606 Stamford road, 1 mile (1½ km) east of Oakham
£/$	A

Hatton Court

Hatton Court is large — there is a new block of additional guest rooms almost next to the main (and pretty) house — and it favours the business market. But its décor, services and efficient operation, plus its convenience to Gloucester warrant its inclusion even if it is not everyone's dream of a country house hotel.

The original house is a 17th-century manor. The £2 million building and refurbishment programme in 1988 added a 30-bedroom Cotswold-stone extension. The reception area and cocktail lounge in the main manor have a new, elegant look (that does suit a country house), and Hatton Court is planning a leisure complex for completion sometime this year (1989).

Charringtons Restaurant is worthy of a country house label: decorated in soft pinks and greens, graced by chandeliers and Wedgwood china, and overlooking the Severn Valley. One feature of the restaurant is its 'wine shop' or display case to invite you to choose among 250 varieties.

Upton Hill, Upton St Leonards, Gloucester GL4 8DE.
✆ (0452) 617412

52 (Each with en suite bathroom, 15 with jacuzzi, colour TV, video, radio, trouser press, hair dryer.) Rates include newspaper and breakfast

Year round

✕ Modern French, 230 wines

✻ Pleasant old/new combination

Outdoor pool. Leisure complex planned

♫ No

★ Cheltenham Spa, Bath, Wye Valley and Forest of Dean

3 miles (5 km) from Gloucester. Leave the M5 at Junction 13, take the A419 to Stroud. Follow the A46 to Cheltenham, turn left onto the B4073 at Painswick to Upton St Leonards. The hotel is 4 miles (6 km) along on the left

£/$ C

Headlam Hall

Whether or not this small Jacobean mansion hotel will be considered 'a find' will have to be left to the individual. Some reports suggest organisation could be a little better and that the ambience is not 'genteel' (in the usual country house way), though the staff is friendly.

The house itself is a charmer: from the outside, whose creeper-clad front entrance clearly shows Jacobean origins to a magnificent interior. The entrance hall with its massive, carved-oak fireplace, Doric columns and open staircase is especially splendid, and thre is a handsome Georgian drawing room with grand piano as well as a small, wood-panelled dining room.

Each of the 11 rooms is named for a colour, and there are five suites: the Lyme with its own kitchen and the Garth and Poppy each with two bedrooms. Three acres (1¼ ha) of formal gardens are scattered with ancient yew and beech trees and the odd sundial and arch.

For 150 years Headlam Hall was the home of the well-known Brocket family, and more latterly that of Lord Gainford. Today it is a peaceful country hotel worth investigating.

Nr Gainford, Darlington DL2 3HA. ✆ (0325) 730238

16 (including one with four-poster; and 5 suites, each individually decorated with en suite bathroom and colour TV.) Rates include breakfast

Year round

✕ A la carte, French influenced

✳ Informal

Hard tennis court

♫ No

★ Beamish, Bowes Museum. The Lake District for day's excursion

Located in the hamlet of Headlam, 2 miles (3 km) north of Gainford, 7 miles (11 km) west of Darlington off A67 Darlington to Barnard Castle road

£/$ E

Hintlesham Hall

A member of the Relais group, Hintlesham Hall is tastefully decorated but not pretentious; the service is reported to be efficient and the food A1.

Hintlesham Hall is certainly a beautiful house, very classical when approached by the long drive to the front door, 18th-century grand.

Inside, more magnificence in the double-height hall and the first floor drawing room with its lovely carved ceiling. Hintlesham was renowned in the 1970s, when it was a restaurant owned by Robert Carrier. Its present form is the creation of Ruth and David Watson, who bought it in 1984 and have achieved first-class results ever since. Though they made their own changes, they left some of the original touches, such as drop blinds and carpet embellished with an 'H', and the Hintlesham apple-and-pear motif.

Little touches have made reports effusive: fruit, biscuits, chocolates and a mini bar in each room, along with turn-down service, and for once, good bathroom lighting. Candles in the drawing rooms and bar and plenty of board games for enthusiasts. A choice between Italian coffee or cafetière after dinner.

Hintlesham, nr Ipswich, Suffolk IP8 3NS.
✆ (047387) 268

17	(Each with en suite bathroom, colour TV, mini bar, books, fruit etc.) No children under 10. Rates include breakfast. Breaks available	✻	Graciously friendly
		♫	Tennis, croquet, billiards, riding, nearby golf
		♫	No
🏛	Year round	★	Melford Hall, Thorington Hall, also Cliff Plantation beauty spot
✕	Seasonal menu with regular specialities like toasted veal sweetbreads on apple coulis. First-class wine list	🚗	4 miles (6 km) west of Ipswich on the A1071
		£/$	A

Holne Chase Hotel

Originally, Holne Chase was an 11th-century hunting estate of Robert of Normandy, uncle of William, and used by the Reformation Abbots of Buckfast, at which time it was owned by the ancestors of the Bouchier-Wrey family. The present house was probably built around 1710, but the main frontage was added in 1832. When the Maitland-Dawsons purchased the property in 1876, they made the house the focal point of the estate and planted many of the unusual trees to be found in the grounds today.

As a country house hotel (which Holne Chase has been since 1934), it is located in a serene position on the southern slopes of Dartmoor National Park, and is indeed a member of the Relais du Silence consortium (which concentrates on peace and quiet). It is run by friendly proprietors — Kenneth Bromage and his wife — who ensure open fires in the main rooms are warming in cool weather, that there are plenty of books to borrow, and use vegetables from their own kitchen garden whenever possible.

Rooms are available in the main house plus The Stable Cottage, a three-bedroomed annexe. Perhaps considered the best is the East Dart Suite, which has a four-poster double bed and its own sitting room, facing the front. Set meals give a choice of four starters, a middle course, four main courses (of which one is fish and one vegetarian), a selection of desserts or cheeses and coffee. Light lunches are available in the bar.

Within the hotel grounds there is one mile (1½ km) of salmon fishing on the Dart, comprising five pools on the right bank upstream from Holne Bridge. The season for salmon and sea trout is from mid-February to September, and for brown trout, from April to September — an amenity that is free to resident guests.

Ashburton, Newton Abbot, Devon TQ13 7NS.
∅ (03643) 471

16 (Mostly double or twin; most with en suite facilities and each with colour TV. The East Dart Suite has a four-poster and mini bar.) Rates include full English breakfast, Dogs allowed at owners' discretion, but not in public rooms

Year round

✕ Set meals and à la carte. No smoking preferable — dining room non-air conditioned

✻ Comfy

The hotel has a salmon and sea trout beat on the River Dart. Trout fishing is available on Duchy of Cornwall water over much of Dartmoor. There are good walks in the surrounds and 12 golf courses within 25 miles (40 km)

♫ No

★ The seaside of Torbay, beauty spots of Widecombe, Dartington, Buckfast, Totnes and Princetown all within easy reach. The Buckfastleigh terminus of the Dart Valley Railway (steam) 3 miles (5 km) from hotel. In summer steamers run between Totnes and Dartmouth

On the southern slopes of Dartmoor National Park. Three miles (5 km) west of Ashburton on the Two Bridges road, the hotel is located in 9 acres (3½ ha) of grounds between the road and the River Dart; 10 miles (17 km) from Newton Abbot, 12 (19 km) from Totnes

£/$ C

Homewood Park

Homewood Park's excellent reputation is without doubt due to Stephen and Penny Ross, the couple who own and manage this shining example of a small country house hotel. You can be sure (well, as anyone can be sure) that the food will be superb, the service helpful, and the surrounding serene. Perfection is not 100% — it never is — but this pretty little hotel near Bath should prove a pleasing experience.

Architecturally, the house is unassuming. It used to be an abbot's house dating from the 18th century, with Victorian additions. Its park adjoins the 13th-century ruin of Hinton Priory. Tennis and croquet are possible in the 10 acres (4 ha) of grounds.

Décor is subtle, and bathrooms have wooden loo seats and bath panels. The Rosses believe their biggest credit is their kitchen — original and creative dishes served in a dining room that looks onto the gardens and hills beyond.

Hinton Charterhouse, Bath, Avon BA3 6BB.
✆ (022122) 3731

---

15 (All double or twin, and each with en suite bathroom and colour TV.) Rates include continental breakfast

🏨 Mid-Jan to mid-Dec

✕ Home-produced ingredients used in original dishes

✳ Plush but not too posh

🎾 Tennis court and croquet, nearby golf and riding

♫ No

★ Bath Spa, Wells and Salisbury cathedrals. Good location for exploring the Heart of England

🚗 Just off the A36 Salisbury road, 15 minutes from the centre of Bath

£/$ B

Hope End

Edward Moulton Barrett (father of Elizabeth Barrett Browning) bought the property in 1809 with money made in Jamaica, and converted the original Queen Anne house into a coach house, employing Scottish landscape designer J.S. Loudon to create a 'folly' in Turkish style. Elizabeth lived here for 23 years, and it was only in 1873 that the 'Turkish house' was demolished, except for a still-existing, single minaret and arched gatehouse.

Nowadays the owner is food-writer Patricia Hegarty. Her husband John grows 100 varieties of vegetables and 40 different apples in the 18th-century walled garden here — all organically.

This tiny country retreat set in 40 acres (16 ha) of Herefordshire parkland is what you might call 'the ultimate health hotel'. It has its own spring and uses local suppliers for cheeses and ham, offers daily-changing, five-course dinners and breakfasts that always feature homemade muesli and bread.

Hope End, Ledbury, Herefordshire HR8 1JQ.
✆ (0531) 3613

---

9 (7 in main house, plus Garden Cottage Suite next to the walled garden, and Minaret Suite across the courtyard, both in the grounds; each with en suite bathroom.) Rates half board. No children under 14. Breaks available

Mar to mid-Nov

✕ Country-style home cooking, healthy style. 5-course dinners

✻ Healthy, homely peaceful

The surrounding area is good for walking

♫ No

★ Hope End is at the centre of a triangle formed by the three cathedral cities of Hereford, Gloucester and Worcester, celebrated for the Three Choirs Festival and closely associated with Edward Elgar's music

Located 40 miles (64 km) east of Stratford near the Malvern Hills off the B4214

£/$ A but half board

Horsted Place

If readers haven't heard about Horsted Place it's about time they did, for it's a gem of a country house hotel with a young, fresh-faced staff who welcome you with a smile at a non-reception desk and escort you to a suite which has known royal guests.

Built in 1850 in Gothic Victorian style, until a couple of years ago it was the home of the late Lord Rupert Nevill, treasurer to Prince Philip. (The prince's very room is as you might expect named The Duke of Edinburgh Suite and is indeed exceptionally comfortable, though it does not comprise two separate rooms.) When the Queen visited, she used what is now The Windsor Suite, an extra large room with separate sleeping and sitting areas. The bathrooms, by the way, are recommendable — American-style showers that shower, not dribble, and wooden toilet seats. But you won't find mini bars, and should you wake up at 3 a.m. with a raging thirst, don't expect an answer from room service — the only place the call goes through is to the manager's flat!

Because there is no night porter, Horsted is listed as a three-star hotel, though its quality and price is anything but. Furnishings are regal without being pompous, and staff seem to materialise when you need them without having to be called for. There is no bar — drinks or afternoon tea are taken on the south terrace looking across the Sussex Downs, or in the antique rosewood-panelled library where a secret door leads to the courtyard garden (created by Lord Snowdon as a gift to Lady Nevill).

Royal lifestyle country fashion means there is a chauffeured limousine service; there is a 20-acre (8 ha) estate and formal gardens designed by Sir Geoffrey Jellicoe, Britain's foremost landscape architect; and there are silver toast racks on the breakfast table along with butter in a dish, not in plastic. Croquet may be played on the manicured lawn of the Hidden Garden set in a secluded grove of rhododendrons. Alternatively, there's a tennis court and indoor pool.

Very few of the antiques and paintings were actually Lord Nevill's possessions but have been so carefully selected and positioned that one would think they were, including in the dining room which was created practically from scratch. Dinner, though it comes at fixed price with no choice, is delicious, with a small portion for each course that results in the meal being just right.

Little Horsted, Uckfield, East Sussex TN22 5TS.
✆ (0825) 75581

17 (All suites, most with separate sitting rooms; each with luxury en suite bathroom, hairdryer, colour TV.) Rates include English breakfast. No children under 7

Mid-Jan to Dec

✕ Fixed-price, no-choice 5-course menu, e.g. chilled leek and potato soup with chives, salmon with dill, noisettes of lamb with basil, chocolate marquise, coffee with petits fours, à la carte

✳ Refreshingly friendly

Indoor pool, hard tennis court, croquet, golf, hunting, shooting and sailing can be arranged

♫ Resident pianist Mon to Thurs evenings

★ Leeds Castle, Chartwell, the spa town of Tunbridge Wells, Ascot, Glyndebourne

An hour's drive from Heathrow — take the M4 to M25, then south to M23, exit at East Grinstead, then A22 to Uckfield. Horsted is 1 mile (1½ km) south on the A26 to Brighton. 30 minutes from Gatwick Airport via the M23

£/$ A

Hotel De La Bere

Hotel de la Bere is an old Tudor manor that now also boasts a country club. It is thought to have first been constructed in 1485 by Thomas Goodman, then the King's Steward for the area. Certainly, Goodman's initials and unicorn crest are still to be seen carved above the original entrance door — now in the outer wall of the Great Hall, a splendid, oak-beamed and panelled room with a minstrels' gallery and log-burning fire, used for banquets and receptions.

The building was completed by Sir John Huddlestone, a knight who was a favourite of King Henry VII, in 1501. It became known as Southam De la Bere in 1546 when his daughter Eleanor inherited it, since her husband was Sir Kynard De la Bere and in whose hands it remained for three centuries — which is probably why it has been so well preserved.

The elaborate oak mantlepiece in the panelled dining room shows the coats of arms of many a noble family associated by marriage with the De la Beres. In the Anne Boleyn bedroom directly above, the Huddlestone shield features in Tudor stained glass in the window.

Southam, Cheltenham, Gloucestershire GL52 3NJ.
✆ (0242) 37771

- 60 — (Individually decorated and named after a king or queen, including 6 four-posters; each with en suite bathroom, colour TV, mini bar, radio, trouser press, coffee/tea facility.) Rates include continental breakfast
- Year round
- ✕ Table d'hôte and à la carte to suit all palates
- ❋ Large, but interesting
- Squash, indoor and outdoor tennis, badminton, outdoor heated pool, snooker, saunas, solarium; 18-hole golf course 1 mile (1½ km) away
- ♫ No
- ★ Bath Spa, Stratford, Oxford, Cheltenham Spa
- At the foot of Cleeve Hill, 2 miles (3 km) from Cheltenham, on the A46
- £/$ C

Howfield Manor

Family-run Howfield lies in the heart of Kent countryside, a comfortably relaxed establishment in 5 acres (2 ha) of landscaped grounds. On winter evenings logs burn in the inglenook fireplaces in the sitting room and in the unusual round iron fireplace in the library.

At the time of writing, the Manor was just completing a new extension, adding six new en suite bedrooms, new bar, kitchen, reception and restaurant. In the past, the hotel has used the honour system for pouring drinks. The new restaurant is the former kitchen and oldest part of the manor dating to 1181, when it was a chapel belonging to the Priory of St Gregory — the 11th-century monks' well is to be the centrepiece. This will be a change from the former style when guests were seated family style around one table by reservation only. Reports on the style-change welcomed. Breakfast, though, I'm sure will continue to feature freshly squeezed juice, local farm eggs and homemade jams and marmalade.

Chartham Hatch, Canterbury, Kent CT4 7HQ.
✆ (0227) 738294

13 (All with private facilities, new rooms with colour TV.) Rates include breakfast

🏛 Year round

✕ In new restaurant table d'hôte and à la carte, predominantly English

✻ Friendly

🎾 No

♫ No

★ Within easy reach of Sheerness, Ramsgate and Dover. Close by bird watching at Dungeness, the Pilgrim's Way, Howlett's Zoo Park and Port Lympne. Canterbury Cathedral and Leeds Castle

🚗 53 miles (85 km) from London, 2 miles (3 km) outside Canterbury on the A28 Ashford road

£/$ D

Hunstrete House

Visitors headed Bath or Bristol way but who don't care to stay in either couldn't make a better bet than Hunstrete House, in the good hands of the Dupays. Thea Dupay (an accomplished painter) picked the antiques which furnish the public rooms, all furnished in quiet good taste, including a library. There is a selection of dining rooms, again unostentatious but elegant — to allow for private functions as well as smokers.

The house, an 18th-century manor, is built on a historic estate and is surrounded by 90 acres (36 ha) of private parkland. Six of the guest rooms are in the 18th-century converted courtyard house, a few yards (metres) from the main one. In the grounds is a swimming pool and tennis court as well as a walled garden which produces fresh vegetables, fruit and flowers for the hotel. John Dupay's hobby is, in fact, gardening, but he's also a keen connoisseur of wine so you can also be sure of the good cellar here.

Chelwood, nr Bristol, Avon BS18 4NS. ✆ (07618) 578

21 (Including 2 suites, 6 rooms in Courtyard House; each with en suite bathroom and colour TV; individually decorated.) No children under 9. Rates include breakfast.

Year round

✕ Venison is the speciality in generous portions. Baked items are made on the premises and on Sunday lunch there's a special dessert menu with favourites like treacle tart and bread-and-butter pudding

✳ Snob value comfort

All-weather tennis court, outdoor heated pool, croquet. Riding stables in Hunstrete village, golf and fishing nearby

♫ No

★ Bowood, Corsham, Dodington, Dyrham Park, Lacock Abbey, Longleat, Montacute, Stourhead, Wilton House, Berkeley Castle and Sudeley Castle all within easy reach

A half-hour's drive from Bristol, two-hour drive from Heathrow. Located on the A368, 8 miles (13 km) southwest of Bath

£/$ A

Huntsham Court

Mogens Bolwig (who's Danish) used to be a travel agent, so one reckons he knew what he was doing when he bought the Gothic pile that is Huntsham Court. He and his Greek wife Andrea have turned it into a relaxed, if slightly eccentric place to stay, one which has received all kinds of praise from those in the know.

Eccentric? Well, for one thing the furniture is eclectic rather than fashionable — without conformity whatsoever. Here, for instance, a grand Victorian sideboard; there a 1930s armchair; and in the bedrooms, not a TV in sight but instead, a pre-war radio. There's no formal reception desk and the bar is operated on the honour principle, ie. you help yourself.

Huntsham, with its high-ceilinged, large-dimensioned rooms, is about as unlike a modern hotel as you can find. The Bolwigs expect you to treat it like home so you're free to pick out a book from the library, borrow a bicycle, use the chess or backgammon sets, help yourself to tea or coffee from the Butler's Pantry day or night, and play any of the records or cassettes.

There is a leaning to the musical here — 3,000 choices mostly classical. Even the guest rooms are named for composers — spacious rooms with no locks on the door and no direct dial telephone. That's not to say they're without amenities like the convenience of en suite bathrooms and central heating, as well as open log fires. Most of the tubs are the old free-standing, claw-footed variety — Beethoven Room has two, plus a seven-foot (2.1 m) wide bed and a piano.

To help the houseparty atmosphere, fixed-price dinner is served in the subdued-lit dining room round one large table, and afterwards coffee and liqueurs are offered either in the drawing room or in the Great Hall. Readers then head to the Library, music lovers to the Music Room, and the more active to the Billiards Room, the mini gym or sauna. It's all part of country living the way the Bolwigs like it in a secluded spot far from the noise of traffic, in countryside where wellingtons or gum boots may be a necessity.

Huntsham Valley, nr Tiverton, Devon EX16 7NA.
✆ (03986) 210

13 (Including a suite, all with en suite facilities, log fires and plenty of space.) Rates include good English breakfast. Breaks available

Year round, except Feb 1 to 14

Five-course fixed-price dinners served family style, complemented by interesting selection of wines

Extraordinaire

Billiards room, table tennis, mini gym, sauna, sunbeds. Indoor games available; cycles for free borrowing. 8-acre (3¼ ha) garden with croquet and tennis courts. Trout fishing available in private lake; riding, golf nearby

Your own — free use of Music Room

The surrounding area is notably scenic: moors, valleys, fishing villages, inland market towns and old mines

In the heart of the West Country, on the edge of a Devon village but within easy reach of the M5 (Junction 25 — Taunton). Nearest train station, Taunton or Tiverton

£/$ C

Jervaulx Hall

In the grounds of one of Yorkshire's most resplendant ruined abbeys, Jervaulx Hall is a solid, early Victorian hotel with the furniture to match. Only a fence separates the hall from the abbey. The hall's own sheltered gardens have a main lawn, grassed walks and woodland paths.

This small hotel on the edge of the Dales National Park has received many compliments for its friendly, homely atmosphere. Log fires are lit in the reception rooms as weather requires — large rooms scattered with antiques. Bedrooms too are most comfortable, and the peaceful location lends itself to a good night's sleep.

Not a place for frills and frippery, nor haute cuisine, Jervaulx Hall is a down-to-earth Yorkshire house offering balanced menus.

Jervaulx, Ripon, North Yorkshire HG4 4PH.
✆ (0677) 60235

8	(Doubles, each individually furnished with en suite bathroom and tea/coffee facility.) Rates are half board
🏨	Apr to mid-Nov
✕	Basic Yorkshire fare with local lamb and game in season. Dinner at 8 p.m. punctually; orders must be placed half an hour beforehand
✻	Solid, quiet comfort
🎾	No, but riding, fishing, golf nearby
♫	No
★	Middleham Castle, Castle Bolton, Fountains Abbey, Castle Howard, Harewood House, Newby Hall
🚗	Accessible from the A1, on the A6108, 12 miles (19 km) north of Ripon
£/$	C

Kennel Holt Hotel

This Elizabethan manor is actually only 300 yards (275 m) from the main road, but as it is situated at the end of a secluded lane, it looks everything a country house should be. It is certainly meticulously run by the Cliffs.

Ruth Cliff taught for 16 years at a Cordon Bleu residential college and now supervises the kitchen at Kennel Holt, so meals are a pleasure, served in the alcove dining room with its original exposed fireplace. Both of the beamed sitting rooms feature log fires, and the informal reception bar contributes to the relaxed and rural atmosphere.

Though there are no sport facilities on the grounds, except for croquet, the hotel has an arrangement with three local golf clubs, and there are two riding stables within a 5-mile (8 km) radius.

Cranbrook, Kent TN17 2PT. ✆ (0580) 712032

8 (6 double with en suite bathrooms, one a four-poster; 2 served by individual private bathrooms; each with colour TV and hairdryer.) No children under 6. Rates are half board and include early-morning tea, newspaper, and afternoon tea

Year round, except Jan 1 to 26, and Sun/Mon nights to Mar 16

✕ 5-course set menu that features praiseworthy desserts

✻ Picturesque

No, except croquet, but golf and fishing can be arranged

♫ No

★ Many castles, including Scotney (14th century) and Hever, once Ann Boleyn's home, also Leeds Castle. Penshurst houses an interesting picture and armour collection. Chartwell also close by

35 miles (56 km) from Gatwick, 50 (80 km) from London. Located 1½ (2½ km) miles northwest of Cranbrook on A262 between Goudhurst and Cranbrook

£/$ D half board. No credit cards

Kildwick Hall

Sumptuously Jacobean (with some parts reputed to be Elizabethan), Kildwick Hall has character in abundance, with its mullioned windows, embossed lead pipes, ornate plasterwork, lovely oak panelling. You'll find creaking floorboards and a unique throne toilet, beams and marvellous fireplaces. The detached pavilion, gateposts and vases you'll see are typical of the garden work done in England when William III was king.

At one time the Currer family owned this hall — Charlotte Brontë, who lived only 9 miles (14 km) away, borrowed the name as her *nom de plume*, 'Currer Bell'. Evidence of the marriage between the Currers and the Haworths is found in the coat of arms over the door of the Parsonage.

This is a quiet corner of Yorkshire without an impersonal complex of rooms. From the 3 acres (1¼ ha) of gardens and woodland there are views over the Aire Valley, and facilities for croquet and putting.

Kildwick, nr Keighley, West Yorkshire. ✆ (0535) 32244

11 (Each with private bathroom, colour TV and radio, including four-posters.) Rates include breakfast. Breaks available

Year round

✕ Fixed-price menu — cuisine moderne

✻ Fascinating

Croquet, putting, other sports nearby

♫ No

★ Bolton Abbey, Skipton Castle, Ilkley Moor, Ingleton Caves and Falls, Haworth Parsonage (home of the Brontës)

Off A629 between Skipton and Keighley. In Kildwick village turn off towards Silsden between 'The White Lion' and church, cross the canal and turn left at the top of the hill

£/$ C

Kirkby Fleetham Hall

This fine country house, Elizabethan in parts, was extensively remodelled in 1783 to give it its present Georgian appearance. As its name might suggest, there were originally two villages — Kirkby and Fleetham. Kirkby grew up around the Knights Templar church (where Templar knight, Sir Nicholas Stapleton was buried in 1290) and beside the church the manor house was built. When arrogant squire William Aislabie purchased the estate in 1783 he decided there wasn't enough privacy, so he sent Kirby inhabitants packing, down the road to Fleetham. Today's guests will therefore find the small hotel in a spot of splendid isolation in its own 30 acres (12 ha) of grounds.

Relaxed and competent hosts, David and Chris Grant run the place admirably and can advise on where to tour and which wine to choose from their enviable cellars. The dining room, overlooking the lake, is the setting for candelight dinners at polished mahogany tables laid with crystal stemware and Wedgwood china.

Kirkby Fleetham, Northallerton, North Yorkshire DL7 0SU.
✆ (0609) 748226

15 (Including four-poster, each with en suite bathroom, colour TV.)

Year round

✕ First class, but uncomplicated. Drinks served in the library

✻ Chatty at home

No

♫ No

★ Yorkshire moors and dales, historic York, Ripon and Richmond, Newby Hall and Castle Howard

2 miles (3 km) off the A1, 1 mile ($1\frac{1}{2}$ km) north of the village of Kirkby Fleetham

£/$ C

Kirby Sigston Manor

This is one of those 'finds' that is neither a hotel nor simply a B & B. Kirby Sigston Manor is a privately owned and beautifully furnished Georgian country house which is a member of the Wolsey Lodges consortium. You will feel you're a guest in a private home because you are, albeit a paying one.

Hugh Renwick and his wife Di went 'into the business' four years ago. They spend time chatting to guests and advising on sights in the area, though they don't eat with them. The lady of the house cooks — a proper English breakfast, and dinner if desired given advance notice. Meals are taken round a family table.

There is a private drawing room — TV if wanted — and a snooker room, but because this is not a hotel you will be surrounded by the family's own knick-knacks and possessions and be using their own period furniture.

Northallerton, North Yorkshire DL6 3RD.
✆ (0609) 775245

2 (1 twin, 1 double; private bathrooms but not en suite, tea/coffee facility.) Rates include full English breakfast

Year round except Xmas

✕ Whatever you want for breakfast at whatever time. No-choice menu for dinner

✻ Elegant and very friendly family home

No, but Hugh can organise fishing or riding for guests

♫ No

★ Well placed for York, the Dales, the Moors, Castle Howard and Herriot country

Located about half-way between London and Edinburgh, close to the main A19 route. From north, south and east, leave A19 at white sign to Kirby Sigston and Northallerton, turn left after 1½ miles (2½ km). From west, to Northallerton — leave town by Bullamoor Road, after 3 miles (5 km) turn right to Manor

£/$ E

Lainston House

The name 'Lainston' is said to have meant 'stone house', thus distinguishing the squire's abode from the more humble wattle and daub dwellings of the villagers. The first recorded owner was Simon de Winton, who died in 1316, but it was probably Cromwellian supporters, the Dawleys, who developed the property to its manorial status.

Today the 'William and Mary'-style house is a pleasantly gracious, 32-bedroomed hotel set in 63 acres (25½ ha) of glorious Hampshire parkland. Reception rooms, including a wood-panelled library bar, are quietly, unfussily tasteful; the restaurant, reasonably informal with views over the lawns; and the guest rooms, modern and individually designed.

Sparsholt, Winchester SO21 2LT. ✆ (0962) 63588

32 (Including suites, each individually decorated and with en suite bathroom, colour TV, private bar). 24-hour room service

Year round

✕ Table d 'hôte and à la carte

✳ Relaxed, gracious living

Tennis, lawn croquet, clay pigeon shooting; fishing, riding and golf can be arranged

♫ No

★ Winchester, the capital of ancient Wessex is 2 miles (3 km) away, and Romsey Abbey 10 miles (17 km), where Broadlands, the Mountbatten home, is open to the public from April to Sept, and the New Forest is within easy reach

Located 25 minutes from Southampton airport, 50 minutes from Heathrow or a 90-minute drive from London via the M3. Nearest train station is Winchester — 60 minutes on the Waterloo main line. Lainston is signposted off the A272 Winchester–Stockbridge road, at Sparsholt

£/$ A

Langdale Chase Hotel

Langdale Chase is one of those splendid Victorian mansions with that happy position of being set in spacious, landscaped gardens which border Lake Windermere and look across to the Langdale Pikes and hills. From the laying of the foundations in 1890, the structure of Brathay Blue stone, took five years to complete. It was the residence of Manchester businessman's widow Edna Howarth until 1914, during which time a staff of 16 maintained the inside and out, and many a large garden party or croquet tournament were held.

It was subsequent owners, the Willows, however, who brought many of the treasures you see today to Langdale: the fine old oak paintings and the china plates now displayed in the Hall. It first opened as a hotel in 1930, though when new kitchens were added seven years later the old ones became the dining room, and what used to be the Butler's Pantry and Servants' Hall have since become the cocktail bar.

For those who admire fine embellishments, Langdale has plenty. The oak fireplace in the hall, for example, bears the date 1664 and the inscription 'Nicholas Tufton, Earl of Thanet, and Elizabeth, Countess of Thanet'. Elizabeth was the daughter of Lady Anne Clifford (who held many titles and owned the castles of Appleby, Brough Brougham, Pendragon and Skipton, all of which had fallen into a state of decay, and all of which she helped to restore.) A Latin motto also inscribed into the fireplace translates to mean 'A bird flies by its own wings; Honour flies by the rewards of valour', but a correct interpretation of the carved scenes has not yet been traced.

The oak staircases and carving round the hall was the work of Cheshire man Arthur Jackson Smith. In the drawing room the original fireplace carved of Australian mahogany still remains; the former dining room's fireplace surround (now in a lounge) dates to 1892 and was carved by the Grasmere Hermit showing the crest of the Howarth family; the oak panelling is early Tudor. Another unusual fireplace is to be found in the private sitting room — a particularly fine, carved dark-oak Gothic piece.

By comparison, bedrooms are modern, including the Lakeland stone Garden Bungalow's six guest rooms. From most of the accommodation windows there are views of the lake, but a unique room is the one over the Boathouse. The latter, also built of Brathay Blue stone in 1896, with its two adjacent jetties, is considered the best on the lake's shores.

Langdale's 4½ acres (1¾ ha) of grounds slope down to the lake. Planned and laid out by distinguished landscape architect Thomas Henry Mawson, their stone balustrading around the upper terraces and the stone steps to the tennis courts show first-class workmanship. Whatever the season, you'll find the gardens ablaze with colour; and if you're wondering about the hotel's 'squirrel' emblem, it's because in 1930 there were so many 'tame' ones running around, it was felt appropriate.

Windermere, Cumbria LA23 1LW. ✆ (05394) 32201

29 + 6 in Garden Bungalow. (Each with colour TV, coffee/tea facility. Most with en suite bathrooms and views of lake.) Rates include breakfast

Year round

✕ Table d'hôte traditional English. Jacket and tie and no smoking requested

✻ Mellow Victorian

Tennis courts in the grounds; boating on the lake

♫ No

★ All the lakes in the Lake District

On the shores of Lake Windermere

£/$ C

Langley

Langley is a private house, not a hotel — the property of Richard and Janet Herring, who invite paying guests to enjoy their home for a short while. The part 17th-century golden Cotswold stone manor is set in beautifully laid-out gardens which have uninterrupted views of the Cotswold hills. You will find this house a joy to be in. The original charm of enormous stone fireplaces, mullioned windows and oak beams is still in evidence. Full English breakfast here include homemade preserves and free-range eggs, and the Herrings are happy to provide light lunches, afternoon teas and evening beverages if requested. This is not licensed accommodation but you may bring your own wine.

Langley Road, Winchcombe, Gloucestershire GL54 5AB.
✆ (0242) 603959

4 (1 double, 1 twin, 2 four-posters, each with en suite bathroom.) No children under 12. Rates include English breakfast

Year round

✕ Fixed-price dinner on request

✻ Refurbished private manor

Indoor pool and sauna, outdoor tennis and croquet; golf and riding nearby

♫ No

★ Berkeley and Sudeley Castles, Sulgrave Manor, Gloucester Cathedral, Charlecote Park, Hidcote Gardens

From Cheltenham take the A46 towards Winchcombe and Stratford through the village of Prestbury to the top of Cleeve Hill. After about ½-mile (800 m) descent, turn left on an unmarked road opposite the sign for Stratford–Cheltenham. Follow the lane for ½ mile (800 m) Langley is on the left

£/$ C

Langrish House

You would have seen sheep grazing on this site in Tudor times, for Langrish House is built around a 16th-century farmhouse — the double wool-pond is still seen in the grounds.

The house takes its name from a family — a John Langrish became Lord of the Manor in 1419, his descendants continuing to hold that office for many generations. It was William Langrish who extended the farmhouse in 1600 to create the present malmstone structure you see today.

During the Civil War the Langrish family supported Cromwell — captured Royalist prisoners were relegated to prison cells beneath the house, which they had to help construct after their capture at the Battle of Cheriton. What was a cellar is today the Cromwellian Restaurant, where a small à la carte menu is presented.

In the 18th century the manor changed hands until it belonged to John Waddington in 1842.

Pleasing rooms, pampered service, idyllic surrounds are some of the phrases used to describe a stay at Langrish.

Langrish, Petersfield, Hampshire GY32 1RN.
✆ (0730) 66941

14 (All with en suite bathroom, colour TV, tea/coffee facility) Rates include continental breakfast

Year round

✕ Limited à la carte with emphasis on seasonal produce

✻ Peacefully pampered

No, but sports nearby

♫ No

★ Close to Portsmouth, Winchester and Chichester

15 miles (24 km) from Winchester, 17 (27 km) from Portsmouth. On the A272

£/$ E

The Last Drop Village

The Last Drop Village is unique — an 18th-century farmhouse that has been imaginatively converted and extended to become a 'living village' complete with cottages, pub, craft workshops, teashops and leisure facilities.

When it first opened it was an exclusive restaurant where the original stone cow stalls were retained to provide a feeling of intimacy. It became so popular that soon a cobbled street with Georgian bow-fronted windows led the way to the cocktail bar (formerly a farm midden). Not surprisingly, guests wanted to overnight here so rooms were built in the courtyard. Then came the 'Drop In' pub whose country atmosphere was created with the huge use of stone pillars and oak beams. Next door is Stocks Restaurant with its arched ceiling and continental atmosphere. In the teashop freshly baked scones and cream teas are served on gingham-covered tables in an oak-panelled room with an open hearth, reminiscent of a bygone era.

Bromley Cross, Bolton, Lancashire BL7 9PZ.
✆ (0204) 591131

83 (All to the highest standard and each with en suite bathroom, colour TV, in-house movies, tea/coffee facility, hair dryer and trouser press.) Rates include English breakfast

Year round

✕ A la carte and table d 'hôte in both restaurants. Pub food in The Drop Inn, tea and cakes in the teashop

✻ Group orientated

Leisure complex with swimming pool, jacuzzi, squash courts, exercise room, saunas and solarium

♫ In the 'Drop Inn'

★ Chester, The Lakes, Yorkshire Dales

14 miles (23 km) from Manchester. From the M61, M62, M63, M6 follow Bolton A666 and turn right at the end of the motorway link

£/$ C

Linden Hall

A stone-built Georgian mansion designed in Greek revival style, Linden Hall was built in 1812 for Charles William Bigge, a local industrialist and banker. This stately Northumberland home is named for the Linden Burn, the stream which flows through its 300 acres (121 ha) of grounds, and is approached via a private drive flanked by linden trees.

Prominent local architect John Dobson worked with Sir Charles Monck on the house design, and both have lent their names to what are now the cocktail bar and restaurant. The soothing Monck Bar, taupe coloured, features a marble chimney piece and plaster ceiling with a deep frieze — on summer evenings drinks are served on the sheltered West Terrace. In the regency-style Dobson Restaurant with its striped paper walls, there is also an ornate ceiling, mahogany doors and prints of Dobson's architectural achievements. Some of the vegetables come from Linden's own garden as do the herbs used for flavouring.

From the stone-flagged front hall you enter an antique world with a sweeping main staircase, rooms with high ceilings and chandeliers. An eye-catching period piece in the front hall is the monumental 1872 clock made by Guimard of Paris. Marble sculptures in the reception rooms are as impressive as the enormous fireplaces, and some of the heavy mahogany doors have silver knobs made from the large silver watch cases prevalent in the last century.

The drawing room particularly retains many of its original features like the draperies and mirrors, complemented by a Donegal carpet. A display of cacti is visible in the marble-floored conservatory which adjoins a small library. Under the house the cellars have been refashioned into a games area. The old granary has also been skilfully restored using existing brickwork and natural stone — now The Linden Pub, offering a wide selection of Northumbrian fare and North Country ales. Barbecue facilities are located in the pub's courtyard along with traditional pub games like quoits, garden draughts and boule.

Children have not been forgotten at Linden Hall, which features a specially constructed Adventure Woodland Play Area in the grounds. Adults may care to take the Woodland Walk — it's flat — play tennis or putt on the green.

Longhorsley, Morpeth, Northumberland NE65 8XF.
✆ (0670) 56611

45 (Furnished in many individual styles, including four-posters, each with en suite bathroom, colour TV, radio, hair dryer.) Rates include early-morning tea, newspaper and English breakfast. Breaks available

Year round

✕ High-quality, using local produce like smoked fish. Comprehensive wine list with lesser-known wines as well as classics

✻ Rural seclusion

Tennis, putting green, croquet, pub games, indoor games room, sauna and solarium

♫ No

★ Cragside House and Country Park, Wallington House, also George Stephenson's birthplace

An hour's drive from Newcastle. Take the A697 north of Longhorsley

£/$ C

Little Hodgeham

Roses cascade around the doorway of this picturesque 500-year-old cottage that resembles almost everyone's idea of a 'place in the country'. But the picture-postcard reality of Little Hodgeham is due to Erica Wallace, a vivacious Australian ex-journalist in whose home you can enjoy the niceties of life and country air. Every meal around the oval table is a dinner party, albeit for paying guests. Erica provides the 'interesting home cooking', a nightly surprise unless you have mentioned diets or dislikes when you booked.

Little Hodgeham is one of those special B & Bs which many people love to return to. All the bedrooms boast matching wallpaper and curtains and delicately coloured, lace-and-ribbon-trimmed duvets. In the Peach Room, with its canopied double bed, the morning tea tray features a silver tea pot; in the twin-bedded room across the way, all is blue and lilac.

Also, this tiny guest house has its own swimming pool, adjacent to a patio decked out with white ironwork tables and chairs, ideal in a spot of English sun.

Bull Lane, Bethersden, Kent TN26 3HE.
✆ (023385) 323

3 (Each with private bathroom, coffee/tea facility, including four-poster.) Rates are half board

Mar to Oct

✕ Home cooking — dinner by request; no-choice menu. Licensed

✻ Homely and special

Swimming pool

♫ No

★ Canterbury Cathedral, Leeds Castle, Sissinghurst Castle garden. Folkestone and Dover also easily reached

A 2-hour drive from Gatwick Airport and an hour away from Folkestone or Dover; 15 minutes from Tenterden. 2 miles (3 km) off the A28

£/$ C half board

Longdon Manor

Janet Brabyn's Elizabethan manor house is not a hotel but a home, one in which she shares her time between family, guests and running the surrounding farm — when she's not organising monthly concerts in the hall, that is.

The present house dates to the 14th century when it would have been a hall. That hall still survives, but two floors were added over it in the 16th century while the dining room and kitchen are 17th century. You will find plenty of old oak furniture, faded rugs and polished flagstones, a fine Jacobean staircase and musical instruments everywhere. The library is a peaceful retreat.

Views from all the bedroom windows look across rolling farmland, grazing sheep and Longdon's own garden, where a 17th-century dovecote stands. In the surrounding fields are the remains of a deserted medieval village.

Shipston-on-Stour, Warwickshire CV36 4PW.
✆ (060882) 235

3	(Bathrooms en suite.) Rates include full English breakfast. No-smoking house
🏨	Apr to Nov
✕	Fixed-price dinner by advance booking. Organically grown, home produced
✻	Informal personal
🏇	No, but a friend organises riding treks
♫	No
★	Stratford, Oxford and the Cotswold villages
🚗	Take the B4035 for 1½ miles (2½ km) from Shipston-on-Stour in the direction of Chipping Campden. Cross A429, after another ½ mile (800 m), turn right towards Darlingscott. After 1 mile (1½ km) the road bends sharp right. For the manor, drive straight ahead
£/$	D

Lovelady Shield

This quiet country house hotel lies in a sheltered valley by the River Nent and is approached by a long, tree-lined drive. The present building dates from about 1830, built on earlier foundations against a wooded hillside. Together with its 2-acre (¾ ha) garden, it forms a gentle oasis mid the wild fells of the High Pennines.

It is perhaps a tempting discovery for anyone en route to Scotland or the Lakes, with an assured welcome from resident owners. You will find an intimate cocktail bar, small library, drawing room and a dining room where helpings are substantial. That includes breakfasts, when a Cumberland mixed grill or kedgeree are favourites. Dinners are six-course affairs, rounded off by an English cheeseboard which includes the not so familiar Cotherstone from near Barnard Castle, and smoked Tynedale, made locally.

Alston, Cumbria CA9 3LF. ✆ (0498) 81203

12 (Each with en suite facilities, colour TV and electric blankets). Rates include full English breakfast

Mid-Mar to mid-Dec

✕ Traditional English recipes. Fixed-price, 6-course dinners

✻ Quiet and homely

Hard tennis court and croquet

♫ No

★ Walking country of the Pennine Way, Hadrian's Wall. Country roads lead to Barnard Castle and the Bowes Museum, west to the Lake District, east and north to the Northumberland National Park

Just 2½ miles (4 km) from Alston, England's highest market town on the A689

£/$ D

Lower Slaughter Manor

A delightful manor in one of the Cotswolds' most enchanting villages, which takes its name from a Norman knight — Philipe de Sloitre, who was granted land here by William the Conqueror. In 1443 the house became a convent for nuns from the Order of Syon. After the dissolution the property returned to the Crown. In 1603, during James I's reign, it was granted to Sir George Whitmore, High Sheriff of Gloucestershire, in whose family it remained until 1964.

What you see today largely dates from the 17th century, when Valentine Strong, an important stonemason, was asked to construct the house. (Strong's son Thomas was the principal contractor employed by Wren in the building of St Paul's Cathedral.)

To the side of the manor, the stable block (1770) boasts a fine, central clock tower. Some of the 19th-century additions include a gazebo window on the staircase landing overlooking the gardens.

Lower Slaughter, Gloucestershire GL54 2HP.
✆ (0451) 20456

19	(Each with en suite bathroom, colour TV, trouser press and hair dryer; some four-posters.) No children under 8. Rates include newspaper and continental breakfast.
🏨	Year round
✕	English country cooking
❋	Cosily informal
🏌	Indoor heated pool with sauna and solarium; croquet lawn and all-weather tennis court. Anglers may use the hotel's own trout-fishing stream; nearby golf and riding
♫	No
★	Cheltenham and many picturesque Cotswold villages
🚗	In a lovely Cotswold village reached via the A40 from Cheltenham, then the A436
£/$	C

Lucknam Park

At the time of writing Lucknam Park was newly opened, so we welcome reports as to whether it lives up to expectations. Without doubt it is a magnificent Georgian country house set in 280 acres (113 ha) of extensive parkland, bound we think for success with a discerning clientele.

The water tower, a prominent feature today, was built by the Walmesley family in the 19th century, though it now lacks its original battlemented top from which the flag was flown. The rest of the house has a 1720 date, and is filled with paintings and antiques from the late Georgian and early Victorian periods.

A straight, mile-long (1½ km) driveway leads to the entrance, past beech trees and green fields. Public rooms are tastefully decorated.

Colerne, Wiltshire SN14 8AZ. ✆ (0225) 742777

39 (Including 9 suites; each with en suite bathroom, colour TV)

Year round

✕ Table d'hôte and à la carte classical French and English

✻ Glamorous

Leisure spa with indoor swimming pool, jacuzzi, steam room, solarium, gym, tennis courts, snooker and beauty rooms. Riding, shooting, fishing and hot air ballooning can be arranged

♫ No

★ Historic Castle Combe village and Lacock, the stately homes of Bowood House and Corsham Court. Also Bristol is easily reached, as is Bath itself

6 miles from Bath and 15 minutes from Junctions 17 and 18 of the M4 Motorway. From Bath take the A4 to Chippenham. At Batheaston (2 miles — 3 km) turn left for Colerne. Pass through the village and the hotel is on the left

£/$ A

The Lygon Arms

I'll have to be forgiven for including such an old stager as The Lygon, which continues to be a showplace hostelry in a showplace village. It's had a few ups and downs when it comes to service, and some people don't approve of the added bedrooms and conference space; but it is slick, busy and cheerful — and historic.

The Lygon has been a celebrated inn since the reign of Henry VIII, but is history dates further back than that. For centuries it was known as The White Hart, the badge of King Richard II who died in 1400 — a fireplace in one of the bedrooms is reputedly a 14th-century one.

King Charles I is thought to have met friends at the inn on one of his many visits to Broadway. The room named after him features its original oak panelling and a secret spiral staircase. It is also told that Oliver Cromwell slept in a first floor room before the Battle of Worcester in 1651. Today, The Cromwell Room (used as a private sitting room) looks much as it did then with a handsome hand-carved Elizabethan fireplace, an early 17th-century plaster-embellished ceiling and frieze, and some splendid antique furnishings.

The hotel takes its name from General Lygon (family name of Lord Beauchamp), who bought the estate after serving with Wellington at the Battle of Waterloo and arranged for his butler to take over the inn's management. That butler gave the name, and the Lygon family coat of arms, two lions passant, now forms an integral part of the hotel's sign.

Although the hotel now has over 60 bedrooms, its many, little, tucked-away lounges give it the intimate atmosphere of the 16th-century coaching inn that it is. The actual cocktail bar is also romantic, though the lounge areas and Great Hall used for dining are sizable. If you like historic ambience, as I do, ask for one of the guest rooms in the main house, not the Orchard Wing, some of which really do date back — one to 1530.

There is a tennis court in The Lygon's 2-acre (¾ ha) garden, and the management runs the popular wine bar next door to the hotel in the High Street.

Broadway, Worcestershire WR12 7DU.
✆ (0386) 852255

64	(Including suites and four-posters; each with en suite bathroom and colour TV.)
🏨	Year round
✕	Table d'hôte and à la carte; traditional English and French
✻	Historic but slick
🎾	Tennis
♫	No
★	Stratford-upon-Avon, Coventry Cathedral, Kenilworth and Warwick Castles, historic Compton Wynyate, Chastleton and Broughton Castle, Sulgrave Manor
🚗	In Broadway's High Street
£/$	A

Maiden Newton House

Elizabeth and Bryan Ferriss don't really like to refer to Maiden Newton as a hotel — they feel it's too small and personalised. So let's say it's a country hostelry well suited to 'doing nothing'.

The house you see, built of yellow local stone with mullioned windows, was erected in the early 1840s by the Rev, the Hon. William Scott, styled in the original 15th-century way as you will see from the chimney and moulding details. Until 1938 it was the village rectory, a house described briefly by Thomas Hardy in his novels *Tess of the d'Urbervilles* and *Interlopers at the Knapp*. (He also immortalised the village of Maiden Newton, which appeared as Chalk Newton.)

Much of the stone from the first medieval building was re-used for the newer house — an occasional piece is still unearthed in the garden — but unfortunately nothing else remains. Today, therefore, the interior of Maiden Newton House incorporates several periods from its oak-boarded hall with 17th-century furniture to its English country house drawing room. It is full of porcelain, paintings and other ornaments that the Ferrisses have collected over the years, as well as a variety of books for guests to read — including a random selection in the bedrooms.

Each of the bedrooms is named, but in addition each guest's own name is slotted into a frame when he/she comes to stay. The most luxurious room is the William Scott Suite, with a four-poster bed whose reading light is inside the drapes, views over the river, an extra large bathroom and a dressing room. The little touches, though, make all the rooms special: a bedside jar of homemade shortbread, supplies of mineral water, and in the bathroom an emergency kit containing toothbrush and paste, shaving cream and razor, comb, aspirin, plasters and emery boards.

Meals are served *en famille* with the hosts in attendance. Cooking is Elizabeth's hobby as her collection of 400 cookery books should point out, and she prepares the daily fixed menu using vegetables and fruit from the kitchen garden when possible. The dining table, like that in a well-to-do friend's home, is set with silver, cut crystal and Minton china and graced by candles and fresh flowers. Bryan's wine list is purposely short but he does encourage guests to sample different ones, encouraging them with a glass of Montbaziac to go with dessert.

Main rooms overlook a grassed terrace and lawn where croquet is played, across the river to the Dorset hills beyond. Some of the yew trees in the grounds are 400 years old, but the rose walk in the walled garden is newly planted.

Maiden Newton, nr Dorchester, Dorset DT2 0AA.
✆ (0300) 20336

---

7 (All individually decorated; twin or double, including 2 four-posters; each with en suite bathroom, colour TV, trouser press, hairdryer, tea/coffee making facility and other little extras.) Rates include morning newspaper and English breakfast

Feb to Dec

✕ 4-course set dinner and coffee. House specialities are West of England cheeses and baked cheesecakes. Sample menu: Lyme Bay scallops in white wine, roast haunch of venison with junipers and four fresh vegetables, chocolate and brandy syllabub. Short international wine list includes local Dorset variety

* Personalised, private house charm

Croquet on the lawn; river fishing

♫ No

★ Maiden Castle, Athelhampton, Montacute, Parnham House and Kingston Lacy. Also Abbotsbury Gardens and Clapton Court. Dorchester itself was founded by the Romans in 70 AD.

The village of Maiden Newton is on the A356 Dorchester to Crewkerne road, and the house is close to the church. The A356 is reached via the A37 Yeovil road from Dorchester

£/$ C

Maison Talbooth

This Victorian mansion, has the distinction of being a country house hotel for 20 years and continues to be family owned. The Victorian-style drawing room with its log fire, picture collection and grand piano opens onto 2 acres (¾ ha) of garden and croquet lawn.

Though breakfast and light snacks are provided at the hotel, you do have to venture outside for dinner — at Le Talbooth, just down the road, on the banks of the Stour. Its 16th-century picturesque appearance and internationally recognized cuisine are worth the effort. The name probably dates from 1786 when it literally was a tollbooth for horse-drawn and river traffic.

When the Milsom family discovered it in 1952 it was rather a neglected tea house, but since, the River Room and bar have been extended, using the 16th-century timbers, and in 1973 a new extension was added. Today guests delight in a five-course gourmet menu or alteratively opt for à la carte.

Dedham, Colchester, Essex CO7 6HN. ✆ (0206) 322367

10 (Mostly suites, some with sunken baths; each individually decorated and with en suite bathroom, colour TV and private bar.) Rates include continental breakfast

Year round

✕ Traditional English and French cooking at Le Talbooth restaurant, ¾ mile (1¼ km) away

✻ Stylish home, but not for those who want facilities under one roof

Croquet on the lawn; fishing and sailing can be arranged

♫ No

★ Cambridge and Newmarket are an hour away. Boats may be hired to travel down the Stour to see Constable's famed Flatford Mill and Willy Lott's Cottage

Located off the A12, a half-hour's drive from the ports of Felixstowe and Harwich

£/$ A

Mallory Court

Less personalised than others of its ilk, but just as perfect, Mallory Court was built in the 1900s, though you could easily think it dated from an earlier period thanks to its chimneys and mullioned windows. Until Allan Holland and Jeremy Mort took over some 12 years ago, it was the home of the head of Standard Motors, who added some of the luxury touches.

The restaurant has always been the mainstay — Allan's own province, producing award-winning dishes. Sunny yellow linen brightens the interconnecting rooms that comprise the restaurant here, and the wide selection of wines offers good value.

The 10 acres (4 ha) of gardens are delightful, with a water garden, rose garden, terraces and that original 1930s pool. It is all part of that faultlessly maintained, immaculate image which the rest of the hotel lives up to.

Harbury Lane, Tachbrook, Mallory, Leamington Spa, Warwickshire CV33 9QB. ✆ (0926) 30214

10 (Including four-poster; each with en suite bathroom and colour TV.) No children under 12. Breaks available. Rates includes continental breakfast

Year round

✕ 5-course dinner; table d'hôte and à la carte lunch. Sample starter: warm salad of langoustines and smoked duck. Jacket and tie necessary

✻ Immaculate

Swimming pool, squash, croquet, tennis; nearby golf, riding

♫ No

★ Kenilworth Castle, Stratford-upon-Avon, Upton House, Farnbrough Hall, Charlecote Park, Oxford

2 miles (3 km) south of Leamington Spa off the A452

£/$ B

The Manor House

This century's developments have not detracted from the Manor's 15th–16th century character. The front hall's panelling dates from 1664, and the carved stone mantelpiece above the fire shows the shields of Scrope (the Barons Scrope were former owners) impaling Gore and Gorges. A scroll showing the heraldic lineage of the families who have owned the Manor since the Norman Conquest until 1947, when it became a hotel, hangs in the bar.

Many of the antiques were collected in Victorian times and some Victoriana has been re-installed, like the cast-iron bath footed as was the fashion and fitted with brass, which stands resplendent in the middle of the bathroom of the Lower Thompsons Suite.

The Manor House has 26 acres (10½ ha) of garden and parkland in which to relax. To the south, lawns sweep down to the trout-stocked River Bybrook.

Castle Combe, Chippenham, Wiltshire SN14 7HR.
✆ (0249) 782206

33 (Including half-tester and four-poster beds, suites and cottage accommodation; each individually furnished and with en suite bathroom and colour TV.) Rates include early-morning tea, newspaper and full English breakfast

Open: Year round

✕ Table d'hôte and à la carte, English and Continental

✻ Friendly, easy-going gentility

Heated outdoor pool, hard tennis court, fishing; golf, riding, shooting may be arranged

♫ No

★ Roman Cirencester and Bath, Wells and Gloucester Cathedrals

🚗 Between the M4 and A420 just off the B4039, 6 miles (10 km) from Chippenham, 12 miles (19 km) from Bath, 20 miles (32 km) from Bristol. From London leave M4 at Junction 17 or 18

£/$ C

The Manor House

The Manor house is a Georgian private residence built around 1800 but fully restored by local craftsmen in 1980. It is the home of Mrs Lesley Berry, an antique dealer by trade, who now accepts paying guests in her two rooms. She has revived the craft of Gansey knitting — intricate but practical fisherman's sweaters — which you'll find on sale together with antiques in a converted stable block here.

In line with usual Wolsey Lodge policy, a fixed-price dinner is offered by arrangement; the bedrooms are comfortably furnished and well appointed; and guests have their own sitting room complete with log fire.

Flamborough Head itself is one of the most prominent features on England's east coast, and a manor has been recorded here in the Domesday Book.

Flamborough, Bridlington, East Yorkshire YO15 1PD.
✆ (0262) 850943

2 — (1 with en suite bathroom.) No children under 8. Rates include breakfast

Year round, except Xmas

✕ Fixed-price dinner on request

✻ Getaway Yorkshire

No

♫ No

★ North York Moors National Park on whose fringes are the ruins of Rievaulx, Byland and Whitby Abbeys. Also nearby are Castle Howard, Helmsley Castle and Kirkham Priory

From Bridlington take the B1255 to Flamborough and follow signs to the lighthouse, past St Oswald's Church on the right. The manor house is on the next corner

£/$ E

Manor House Hotel

It was King Henry VIII who granted the Manor to the Dean and Chapter of Westminster in 1539, who subsequently leased it to the Creswykes. The house itself is thought to have been built by a Lord Saye in 1545.

One of the Creswyke daughters married into the Grinstead family — a direct line can be traced to Lady Elizabeth Bowes Lyon (the Queen Mother) who married King George VI. Of interest in the house today is the priest's hiding hole and a secret passage.

As a hotel, it is comfortable in a family-run type of way, with a snug bar, log fires in the lounges and a restaurant whose emphasis is on English cuisine.

The main pride of Manor House, though, is its garden, a large one with lawns and an orchard. Meals and drinks are served outside in warm weather and keen gardeners may find the greenhouse plants of interest.

Moreton-in-Marsh, Gloucestershire GL56 0LJ.
✆ (0608) 50501

38 (Modern and traditional in décor, including four-posters and a 3-room cottage in the grounds; each room with en suite bathroom and colour TV.) Rates include full English breakfast

Year round

✕ English food, with emphasis on fresh vegetables

✻ Cheerful

Putting in the grounds, indoor heated pool; nearby golf and riding

♫ No

★ Oxford colleges, Stratford, Tewkesbury's Norman Abbey, Hidcote Gardens, Batsford Arboretum, Sudeley Castle, Sulgrave Manor; many pretty Cotswold villages

Located in the heart of Moreton-in-Marsh on the A44, 17 miles (27 km) from Stratford-upon-Avon, 21 miles (34 km) from Banbury

£/$ C

Michael's Nook

An attractive example of a Lakeland stone-built house (1859) used as a summer residence by Lancashire textile industrialists the Smalley family, who were responsible for many of its best features including the plaster mouldings in the hall and drawing room, and the beautiful Honduras mahogany woodwork.

Michael's Nook is still very much a private home, so although concessions have, of course, been made to the times, at the owner's insistence there are no individual room keys, admittance is by ringing the doorbell, and meal times are at set hours.

The 3 acres (1¼ ha) of landscaped gardens surrounding the hotel owe much to the foresight of the predecessors, and are a particular pleasure in spring and early summer when the terrace is a romantic spot for sunset drinks.

Grasmere, nr Ambleside, Cumbria. ✆ (09665) 496

11 (9 double, 2 suites; each with en suite bathroom, colour TV, flowers, fruit, mineral water, hair dryer, bathrobes, toiletries.) Room service. Rates include breakfast and dinner

Year round

✕ Fixed-price, 5-course dinners offer a different selection each day. Sample dishes: guinea fowl and leek terrine, game consommé with pheasant quenelles, breast of wild mallard in champagne sauce, chocolate marquise. No-smoking dining room

❋ Slightly 'eccentric home' rather than showplace

Croquet on the lawn. Guests may also use the heated indoor pool, sauna and solarium of the nearby Wordsworth Hotel in Grasmere

♫ No

★ Lake Windermere and all the Lake District scenery

In a secluded position overlooking the Grasmere Valley, reached via the A591 from Ambleside

£/$ A but half board

Middlethorpe Hall

Had you viewed Middlethorpe at the start of renovation, before it opened as a hotel in 1984 on the outskirts of York, you would appreciate the excellent job that was executed to bring this perfect William and Mary house back into gem-like condition. Built in red brick in 1699 for Thomas Barlow, a prosperous master cutler, its Queen Anne façade was inspired by Christopher Wren's architecture. Note the white sash windows, stone quoins and window surrounds, the north entrance front of seven bays, surmounted by a stone eagle — the Barlow family crest. Note also that the Flemish-bond brickwork is tuck pointed, a technique popular in expensive houses of the time. The south front or main façade looks more impressive because of the flanking wings added mid-18th century by Francis Barlow, High Sheriff of Yorkshire.

The front door leads into the stone-flagged entrance hall, which in turn leads to the staircase hall whose finely carved oak staircase is one of the main architectural features of the interior. The quality of woodwork throughout the house is exceptionally high, no more so than in the dining room, which is perhaps the most ornate room in the hotel with panelling that incorporates round-headed panels flanked by ionic pilasters and dates from the original period.

What was the ballroom has now become a handsome sitting room in the west wing. It was altered in the 19th century when bronze glazing bars and Adam style plasterwork was added. Now it is a comfortable place to relax with a book or magazine, surrounded by antique furniture and decorative portraits. In addition to this main drawing room, Middlethorpe offers a library/sitting room adorned with architectural engravings, and a small panelled sitting room.

Before Historic House Hotels purchased the property, the Hall had been the family home of famous diarist, Lady Mary Wortley Montagu (her portrait still hangs here), a girls' school and even a nightclub. No dorms or laser lights now — instead a charm and elegance carried to the bedrooms above, decorated with country house wallpapers and original prints or watercolours. Where possible, the original chimneypieces have been kept or re-installed, and to help the traditional look, bathrooms feature brass taps and fitments. Former brick-built 18th-century stables have been converted into further bedrooms and a conference centre.

The same care given to renovating the house has been given to the grounds, which have been replanted. A ha-ha was constructed, the 17th-century dovecote restored, a lake formed and the kitchen garden reconditioned. The whole estate overlooks York Racecourse so is ideally suited to racing enthusiasts.

Bishopthorpe Road, York YO2 1QP. ✆ (0904) 641241

18 (12 in main house, 6 in converted stables; individually decorated, including four-posters, with Edwardian-styled bathrooms, all en suite, each with colour TV and electric trouser press.) Rates include newspaper and early-morning tea. Special breaks available. No children under 8

Year round

✕ Choice of 2 restaurants à la carte. Both imaginative dishes or grills

✳ Gracious

No

♫ No

★ York itself, with the exciting Jorvik Centre; the ruins of Fountains Abbey, also Rievaulx and Jervaulx; stately homes like Castle Howard and interesting towns like Whitby and Scarborough. The beauty of the dales and moors within easy reach

Overlooking York racecourse, 1½ miles (2 km) from the city. By road, take the A64 off the A1 near Tadcaster and follow the signs for York West, then follow the smaller signs to Bishopthorpe. 71 miles (114 km) from Manchester, 128 miles (206 km) from Birmingham

£/$ A

The Mill House

Wolsey Lodge members like Mill House are constantly pointing out they are not a hotel, but a private house/home, so I must do the same. This property is a Georgian residence owned by Capt. and Mrs John Stewart with only three rooms for let, but it is such a charming house, it seems a shame not to mention it.

For many years it was a miller's home — the original mill was sited further down the River Ouse and today the mill stream flows through the garden here. The present site was developed in the 16th century and has been used for milling grain until 1965. At one time, I'm told, Henry VIII owned this land though it is doubtful he ever visited it. Before the present couple purchased it, the Earls of Dartmouth owned it.

John and Eileen are life members of the International Wine and Food Society so they are well equipped to cater for dinners (if booked in advance) fully inclusive of pre-dinner drinks, four-course with wine, liqueurs and coffee. Visitors have their own sitting room with a TV.

Church Street, Olney, Buckinghamshire MK46 4AD.
✆ (0234) 711381

3 (double or twin, 2 with en suite bathrooms) Rates include breakfast

Year round, except Xmas and New Year

✕ Fixed-price dinner inclusive of drinks by arrangement

✻ Personal

No

♫ No

★ Olney, a market town made famous by poet William Cowper. Oxford, Cambridge and Stratford are within an hour's drive

Olney is reached from the M1, leaving at Junction 14 via A509, or from the east via A428. The Mill House is at the far end of Church Street, adjacent to the church

£/$ E

Mill House Hotel

In the pastoral setting of the Cotswolds, Mill House Hotel is noted for its friendly staff and convivial atmosphere. Originally, this was an old Lanfall flour mill in the 17th century and is still bordered by the mill stream of that bygone age. Built of Cotswold stone, it has been gradually added to over the years.

Social centre is the comfortable lounge, where one is encouraged to relax with a drink in front of the log fire. A step away, the 60-seater restaurant features daily-changing table d'hôte menus. Fresh flowers decorate all the public and guest rooms and potpourri made from an old secret recipe scents the whole establishment. A curiosity at Mill House is the private collection of dolls from years gone by.

The hotel is surrounded by fields and a fast-flowing trout stream, set well back from a minor road in peace and tranquillity.

Kingham, Oxfordshire OX7 6UH. ✆ (060871) 8188

20 (Double or twin, including a four-poster; each with en suite bathroom, colour TV, coffee/tea facility.) Rates include English breakfast. No children under 5. Breaks available

Year round

✕ Table d'hôte and à la carte; 180 wines

✱ Convivial

No

♫ No

★ Traditional Cotswold villages like Chipping Camden and Winchcombe. Blenheim Palace, Hidcote Gardens. Stratford, Oxford and Cheltenham all within easy reach

Kingham is about 1 hour 25 minutes by train from London. From the M5 Motorway, leave at Junction 9 (Tewkesbury) and take the A438 to Stow-on-the-Wold, then the A436 signposted to Chipping Norton. About 1½ miles (2½ km) out of Stow, fork right signed Bledington and Kingham. Go through the village of Bledington, past the Kingham station on the left. Take the next turning left

£/$ C

The Millstream Hotel

What was quite a small hotel in the heart of a small sailing village has almost doubled its number of rooms in the last decade, but reports say that the food is remarkably good and the staff unfailingly courteous.

Originally in 1701 this was a worker's cottage built alongside the Malt House, but there have since been many additions. The village is one of the most photographable in England, and the hotel stands back from the main road in front of a small millstream with ducks and little bridges that lead across the water into a charming garden.

It's not a fancy place, though it's cheerfully smart and recommended as a touring base.

Bosham Lane, Old Bosham, nr Chichester, West Sussex PO18 8HL. ✆ (0243) 573234

29 (Including suite but mostly double; each with en suite bathroom, radio, colour TV, tea/coffee facility.) Rates include breakfast

Year round

Table d'hôte and à la carte

Unfancy

Nearby fishing, sailing and golf

♫ No

★ Roman-walled Chichester, Goodwood House, Arundel Castle, Petworth and Parham Houses

14 miles (23 km) from Portsmouth, 28 miles (45 km) from Southampton. 4 miles (6 km) west of Chichester, turn off the A27 to Old Bosham, follow road to T junction, turn right. The hotel is 200 yards (183 m) on right

£/$ C

Mortons House Hotel

An E-shaped Elizabethan manor built of Purbeck stone, Mortons House is linked by underground tunnel to Corfe Castle, blown up by Cromwell in 1645. The manor was first erected in 1600 and extended in 1666 with the stones from the ruined castle. At the time of writing there is talk of a ten-room extension and an additional restaurant to seat 40, which will also be constructed of Purbeck stone.

The hall's stone fireplace where logs are burnt in winter, is the original, and one of the reception rooms features magnificently carved and decorated oak panelling with an elm frieze. Not, unfortunately, the dining room, though food is of prime importance to the owners. Unusually, the chef (or should I say chefesse) is a lady by the name of Janice Timothy, who was not only trained by the Roux Brothers, but for two years before moving here was Andrew Lloyd Webber's personal chef. It is still early days for this recent conversion, but since Janice is also partial owner, we reckon style will be perfected, and we know that her ideas are good and the wine list good value for money.

Food is enough of an emphasis that the dining rooms and terrace are licensed to serve non-residents for lunch and dinner any day of the week, including Sunday, and people are just as welcome to enjoy the views over a cup of afternoon tea even if they do not stay. But of course, overnighting is also comfortable, perhaps in the Mortons Suite, which features a four-poster bed, spa bath and a dressing room, or the double-bedded Garrett Suite which has a living room, too.

Corfe Castle village itself is ancient (home of the first king of all England) and has often been used in its natural totality as a film set for movies like 'Far from the Madding Crowd'.

East Street, Corfe Castle, Dorset BH20 5EE.
✆ (0929) 480988

7 but additional 10 planned (Each twin or double, including 2 suites, one with four-poster; en suite bathroom and colour TV.) Rates include morning tea, newspaper and English breakfast. Special breaks available

Year round

✕ Referred to as 'Modern British' table d'hôte and à la carte, 7 days a week. Sample dishes: quiche on a bed of leeks with port sauce, pork fillet stuffed with blue cheese and apple; pan-fried venison with aubergine. Good value, if small, wine list

✻ Manor house

Not on site but close to many facilities; shooting and salmon fishing may be arranged

♫ No

★ The ruins of Corfe Castle and the Purbeck Hills. Lulworth Cove and scenes used in 'The French Lieutenant's Woman' close by

Located on the Isle of Purbeck, so called because it is a peninsula bordered by the River Frome at Wareham. By ferry from Bournemouth — it is 10 miles (16 km), 20 miles (32 km) by road. Wareham is 5 miles (8 km) away, Poole 15 miles (24 km) and Southampton, 50 miles (80 km)

£/$ C

Nanny Brow

White-painted, creeper-clad Nanny Brow is an attractive house designed and built in 1908 by a London architect. With quality furnishings and restful décor, it has been converted well from private home to hotel with a tasteful drawing room and intimate dining room.

Most of the pretty chintz bedrooms enjoy views of the surrounding fells, and those in the garden wing (more latterly added to the original house) are extremely luxurious. In the same wing is a fully equipped billiard room, a spa bath and solarium. The suites have a separate sitting room and some also have a kitchen and dining area.

Relaxation is the key to the Lakeland. Here at Nanny Brow there are 5 acres (2 ha) of gardens and woodland with pleasant pathways and terraces; views are of the Brathay Valley towards Wetherlam, Wrynose Pass and the famous Langdale Pikes.

Ambleside, Cumbria LA22 9NF. ✆ (05394) 32036

19 (Including suites; each with en suite bathroom, colour TV, tea/coffee facility.) Rates include full English breakfast. Breaks available

Year round

✕ Fixed-price and à la carte

✻ Lakeland tranquillity

No, but many sports nearby

♫ No

★ The fells, glens and lakes that comprise the Lake District

A short distance from Ambleside just beyond Clappersgate on the A593

£/$ C

Netherfield Place

When you know that the proprietor of a countryside hotel is also the chef, you have an idea where enthusiasm runs. Here at Netherfield fresh fruit and vegetables are picked daily in the one-acre (½ ha) walled, kitchen garden, and the menus prepared by Michael Collier are complemented by an outstanding wine list which is split into 'fine or unusual wines' and those which are 'value for money', and includes some from California.

The hotel itself is an attractive one with a panelled formal dining room, a large lounge with adjacent cocktail bar. In warm weather drinks or tea are served on the terrace. Built in 1924, the house stands in 30 acres (12 ha) of parkland — a tranquil haven near Battle, where William of Normandy defeated Harold in 1066. Bedrooms are tastefully decorated and have up-to-date amenities.

Battle, East Sussex TN33 9PP. ✆ (04246) 4455

11 (Double or twin, including one four-poster and one suite; each with en suite bathroom, colour TV.) Rates include early-morning tea, newspaper and full English breakfast

Year round, except Xmas period

✕ Table d'hôte and à la carte. Sample dishes: poached quails eggs on mushroom purée in puff pastry; thin slices of wild rabbit in Calvados sauce

✻ Elegant

No, but facilities nearby

♫ No

★ Seaside resorts of Brighton and Eastbourne, Canterbury Cathedral, Glyndebourne's Opera House. Bodiam, Hastings, Pevensey, Leeds, Chiddingham and Rye Castles are all within easy reach

Heathrow and Gatwick are both within a two-hour drive. Brighton is 35 miles (56 km) away, Eastbourne, 17 miles (27 km). The hotel may be reached via the A2100 from Hastings or the A21 from Tunbridge Wells

£/$ C

New Park Manor

It may not immediately seem evident that New Park was once the favourite hunting lodge of King Charles II and Nell Gwyn, for the manor does look surprisingly modern. But the acorns and oak leaves on the doors and fireplaces, commemmorate the debt owed by Charles to the oak tree which hid him from Cromwell's men in 1651. He used the lodge when he returned from his exile in France in 1666.

The king founded the Buckhound Kennels, and the New Forest fallow deer seen in the grounds were bred from a pair which he brought back from France. His stables, also found in the 260 acres (105 ha) of grounds, were later adapted to house the horses, carriages and grooms of the Manor and are these days the New Park Stables and Equitation Centre — a major feature for the hotel.

Brockenhurst, New Forest, Hampshire SO42 7QH.
✆ (0590) 23467

30 (Each with en suite bathroom, colour TV, coffee/tea facility. The newer Forest Rooms each has hair dryer and trouser press; the older Park Rooms are cosier. Include four-posters and no-smoking rooms.) Dogs welcome. Rates include English breakfast. Breaks available

Year round

Table d'hôte Modern English

Riding orientated

Stables in grounds for riding, instruction etc. Outdoor heated pool, tennis court, croquet. Polo from April to Sept; game shoots/clay pigeon shooting can be arranged

♫ No

★ Beaulieu Motor Museum, Lyndhurst. Bournemouth beach not far away

In the heart of the New Forest, ½ mile (800 m) off the A337 Lyndhurst to Brockenhurst Road in 6 acres (2½ ha) of gardens. 5 miles (8 km) from the M27, 9 miles (14 km) from Southampton and 20 miles (32 km) from Bournemouth

£/$ C

Northcote Manor

It's more than possible you've never heard of Northcote Manor, but then perhaps you've never been to Lancashire. Craig Bancroft, part owner of this former textile magnate's mansion, is Lancashire born and it shows in his ready smile and youthful enthusiasm when he talks to you — which he always does.

He is especially enthusiastic when it comes to food, and so he should be, for the restaurant is *the* feature and his young chef has made it a gem in the north. Nigel Howarth's menus are a combination of classical cooking with his own interpretation of nouvelle cuisine — one which doesn't mean stinted portions — the local market gets hungry. Presentation is attractive without being fussy, and if you're not into wild duckling marinaded with passion fruit and rosemary, or roulade of salmon and pike on a chervil butter sauce, there's always plain grilled sole or steak.

At Northcote I talk about convivial, happy atmosphere, especially in the small bar — bar, not cocktail lounge — friendly young staff and genuine northern hospitality. Don't come if you're looking for antiquey décor or a place where one whispers.

Northcote Road, Langho, Blackburn, Lancashire BB6 8BE.
✆ (0254) 40555

6 (Each with en suite bathroom.) Rates include full English breakfast. Breaks available

Year round

✕ Fixed-price menus featuring fresh fish and game

✻ Friendly and foodie

No

♫ No

★ Clitheroe Castle and museum, Roman Ribchester, Houghton Tower, the Trough of Bowland

Leave the M6 at Junction 31 and turn right onto the A59 following signs to Clitheroe. At the first set of traffic lights at the end of the dual carriageway, bear left onto the Skipton/Clitheroe road for 8 miles (13 km). Before the roundabout, turn left into Northcote Road

£/$ E

The Oak House

The Oak House is an unpretentious 14th-century inn situated in the market square of medieval Axbridge. Don't expect it to be something it's not, and you'll find it cosily charming, worth its BTA commendation. Indeed, it was an old coaching inn, reflected by the décor in the bar and restaurant area where ceilings are low beamed and walls are of cobbled brick, and a period fireplace adds to the intimate atmosphere.

This is not a de luxe hotel reeking of chintz and schmaltz, but is more down to earth so don't anticipate sizeable bedrooms or specialised extras. The restaurant is open seven days a week all year round, but then the location isn't an isolated one by any means. Recommendation is for overnight while touring the area.

Axbridge, Somerset BS26 2AP. ✆ (0934) 732444

9 (7 have en suite bathrooms, each has colour TV and tea/coffee facility.) Rates include breakfast

Year round

✕ A la carte English. Local produce includes Blagdon trout, Wye Valley salmon, venison, quail, home-smoked hams

✻ Cosy inn

No, but sports nearby

♫ No

★ Cheddar Gorge, Wookey Hole, the Mendips, Exmoor, Sedgemoor (site of the 1695 rebellion)

A few minutes drive off the M4 and M5. On the A38 south of Bristol.

£/$ D

Oaksmere

A Grade II listed building dating in part to 1550 but more substantially Victorian, Oaksmere is a delightful, small country house hotel which comes well recommended. Historically, it was the Dower House to Brome Hall, the ancestral home of the illustrious Cornwallis family — it was General Lord Cornwallis who surrendered the American colonies to George Washington at Yorktown, Virginia, ending the American War of Independence.

Neither grand and daunting nor exactly casual, beamed and panelled Oaksmere promises comfort and relaxation in its various lounges, large Tudor bar and Victorian dining rooms, all scattered with antique furniture.

Guest bedrooms are not full of ruched curtains and Laura Ashley designs, but they do have the good fluffy towels and reading material that have become accepted features of first-class country hotels. There are 20 acres (8 ha) of grounds to explore including the hotel's own cricket ground.

Brome, Eye, Suffolk IP23 8AJ. ✆ (0379) 870326

5	(Including four-poster, each with colour TV and coffee/tea facility.) Rates include full English breakfast
🏨	Year round, except Xmas
✕	Modern English table d'hôte and à la carte, e.g. venison pan fried with cranberry and orange sauce
✳	Olde worlde
🎾	Cricket ground, day yacht charter available
♫	No
★	Melford Hall, Cliff Plantation beauty spot
🚗	2 miles (3 km) from the centre of Brome. At junction of A140 (Ipswich to Norwich) and B1077 (Diss to Eye)
£/$	D

Ockenden Manor

There is a homely feeling about this independently owned old house, first recorded in 1520 when it belonged to the Michel family. Perhaps because the staff is young, English, and fresh, and the energetic manager is as likely to be seen taking meal orders or pouring wine as he is dealing with administration. Perhaps because it has been a family home and all the guest rooms are named for the children who grew up here. Perhaps because its wood-panelled bar, lounge and dining room are all small and cosy.

In 1658 ironmaster Walter Burrell lived here, adding the stone south wing to the original Tudor building. His son Timothy (for whom one of the smaller rooms is named) wrote about Cuckfield life at the time, and his granddaughter became the Duchess of Marlborough. One of my favourite rooms is Master, a heavily wood-panelled twin room with its own small 'snug' or sitting room. Thomas is another room with a separate sitting room, but guests will have to remember to duck their heads to avoid the beams!

The square, oak-walled dining room with its painted ceiling and stained-glass windows, is a handsome stylish one, but family groups will feel just as comfortable here, especially for Sunday lunch. Lack of ash trays on the tables is merely to discourage, not compel diners not to smoke. Table d'hôte lunches and evening meals (table d'hôte and à la carte) are popular enough with non-residents for overnighters to be asked to make advance bookings for tables.

Food presentation is important here, so that cheesecake sits on patterned chocolate sauce and fruit-mousse-filled buns are on a strawberry coulis. English breakfasts are cooked to order so expect a wait that's worth it. For such a small hotel, Ockenden boasts a particularly fine wine cellar, emphasising the Bordeaux and including pricey vintages.

In the early 19th century the house was called 'Cluttons', for William Clutton the churchwarden whose family lived here until 1862 — you can see the church spire across the gardens from some of the windows. Others look out over the Sussex Downs or the courtyard.

Ockenden Lane, Cuckfield, Sussex RH17 5LD.
✆ (0444) 416111

14	(Mostly twin or double, one four-poster; each with en suite bathroom, colour TV, hair dryer, coffee/tea-making facility). Rates include continental breakfast	♫	No
		★	Bluebell Railway
		🚗	A 10-minute drive from Haywards Heath railway station and 13 miles (21 km) from Gatwick Airport
🏨	Year round	£/$	C
✕	What the chef calls 'Modern English'; big on presentation. Excellent wine cellar — 300 bins		
✻	Cosily comfortable		
🎾	No		

Ye Olde Bell

This is reputedly the oldest inn in England, founded as a guest house of a Benedictine monastery in 1135.

The oldest part of the main house is certainly the tiny oak-beamed bar, truly a piece of 'olde England' the way you'd expect it to be. The Norman entrance to the inn is part of the original structure and the first-floor landing, medieval. Try an 'Old Bell Special' or your favourite tipple in either the Hogarth Bar or the adjacent oak-beamed lounge, where a coal fire roars in winter.

As for the restaurant, it's a delight — half panelled, candle-lit at night, and by day with a view of the rose arbour, ornamental gardens and patio. Traditional fare is served at an unhurried pace.

Take a short walk to the bottom of the lane where the inn is sited, through the ancient village of Hurley, and you'll reach the banks of the Thames. On the way, you'll pass the 12th-century flintstone church with its unusual bell turret and Norman west door.

Hurley, nr Maidenhead, Berkshire SL6 5LX.
✆ (062882) 5881

38 (Most twins or doubles, including suites; each with en suite bathroom, mini bar, coffee/tea facility, hair dryer, trouser press)

Year round

✕ Table d'hôte and à la carte traditional English

✻ Quaint charm

Fishing, boating can be arranged; riding and golf within easy reach

♫ No

★ Henley, Windsor, Eton, Ascot, Marlow, Runnymede. Nearby stately homes include Cliveden, Stoner and West Wycombe Park

On the A423, 4 miles (6 km) from Henley; 3 miles (5 km) from the M4, 4 miles (6 km) from the M40 and 16 miles (26 km) from Heathrow Airport. Nearest railway station is Maidenhead, 6 miles (10 km) away

£/$ C

The Old Hall

A softly coloured stone house, this one used to be the servants' quarters of the local manor house in the 16th century. Set in almost 4 acres (1½ ha) of land and courtyards with stabling and grazing sheep, it is the perfect picture of a Yorkshire home. Home owners are Ian and Angela Close, who have collected period pieces for the interior.

The house features an antique, carved pine staircase, a plaster frieze plus tiles and stones from Jervaulx Abbey itself. There are flowers everywhere — Angela demonstrates flower-arranging as well as decorating china with her flower paintings.

In addition to the three bedrooms in the main house, further former servants' quarters have been restored above the old stables and coach house, adjacent to The Old Hall. Abbey Cottage comprises two double rooms en suite; Witton Cottage, three double rooms and a bathroom. Each has a lounge/dining area with wood-burning stove and colour TV, plus a kitchen. Guests at the cottages may dine at the Old Hall, which also provides the linen.

Jervaulx Abbey, Ripon, North Yorkshire HG4 4PH.
✆ (0677) 60313

3 (Each with en suite bathroom, coffee/tea facility) plus 2 cottages self-contained. Rates include breakfast. No children under 11

Year round

✕ Fixed-price meal by request

✻ Antiquey

No

♫ No

★ Herriot Country

15 miles (24 km) west of Ripon on the A6108, half-way between Masham and Leyburn, 12 miles (19 km) west of the A1.

£/$ E

The Old Rectory

The Old Rectory is a private home accepting paying guests. The main house dates from the 15th century and has great character — one of its fascinating features is a unique pendulum clock which swings through a hole in the floor.

A glass-enclosed corridor links the newly converted stable rooms to the main house, and they are certainly very comfortable. Decorated with oak beams and old stable doors, complete with latches, they conveniently have en suite bathrooms and telephones.

There's a guest lounge with a TV and help-yourself bar; a small sitting room and a conservatory where meals are served — all in the main house. Jill prides herself in using seasonal produce from her garden whenever possible. Portions are certainly not skimped, whether for the massive English breakfast or the three-course dinner, which must be ordered by lunchtime from a fixed menu. The conservatory looks out onto the gardens and the fish ponds.

Ipsley Lane, Ipsley, Redditch, Worcestershire B98 0AP. ✆ (0527) 23000

10 (5 double, 3 twin, 2 single; each with private bathroom and phone)

Year round

✕ Home cooked. Jill often uses her own recipes

✻ Relaxing, informal home

No

♫ No

★ Cheltenham, Broadway and the Cotswolds

Located 12 miles (19 km) from Stratford-upon-Avon, 14 miles (23 km) from Warwick and 19 (31 km) from Birmingham's airport. Telephone for specific instructions to reach the house

£/$ E

The Old Vicarage

The Old Vicarage is such a find that it has been found by many colleagues and competitive guides — and all of them rave about the place. Despite the fact there are only seven bedrooms in this Georgian vicarage, it is a proper country house hotel complete with cocktail lounge, licensed restaurant and room amenities like TVs and telephones.

The Old Vicarage is owned and operated by two couples whose aim it is to offer first-class accommodation to a small number of guests in a friendly atmosphere. There are two pleasant sitting rooms, one with French doors leading onto the garden — ideal for an aperitif in summer — and a small bar.

Accolades and commendations are particularly given for the cuisine. (Meals are served in a Victorian-styled dining room and emphasise freshly prepared food and presentation, even when vegetarian or for other dietary requirements.) Home-baked rolls and soups are practically a speciality, and though there is no choice in the five-course dinners (except for dessert, when guests are encouraged to try both the hot and cold), menus are carefully planned. Some say they're the best in Cumbria!

An interesting wine list boasts over 100 wines, including dessert varieties. The proprietors also propose cheese and port, offering some unusual varieties such as flavourful Cumberland Farmhouse, Coleford Blue Ewesmilk, Ribblesdale Goatsmilk and newly re-introduced, handmade Coverdale.

The hotel's selection of teas might well whet the appetite too — from the more familiar Earl Grey and Indian Assam, to herbal kinds like Jasmine and Lemon Balm, or Chinese Lapsang Souchong, a smoky-flavoured black tea.

Proprietors here express the hope that breakfast will be one of the day's pleasures. Everything's cooked to order from the free-range eggs and home-cured bacon, to kippers or kidneys or porridge made with whisky.

Though there's nothing flash about The Old Vicarage, furnishings are quality, with good use of pine and cane in the bedrooms and ample reading light.

The scenic attractions of the Lake District are, needless to say, well known, but this hotel in the Winster Valley is a more secluded, delightful retreat in 5 acres (2 ha) of gardens and woodland.

Witherslack, nr Grange-over-Sands, Cumbria LA11 6RS.
✆ (044852) 381

7 (Double or twin, each with en suite bathroom, colour TV, coffee/tea making facility, hair dryer.) Rates include breakfast. No children under 10

Year round

✕ Much praised, fixed-price menu, 6-course, e.g. fresh salmon, halibut and sole mousseline cooked in puff pastry served with Cumberland sauce. Lakeland lamb, apple and blackcurrant fool

✻ Intimate country elegance

No, but nearby walks and fishing

♫ No

★ The Lake District National Park

A 15-minute drive off the M6. Leave the motorway at Junction 36 and follow the signs to Barrow-in-Furness. Turn off the A590 into Witherslack and just past the telephone box, turn left. The Old Vicarage is ¾ mile (1¼ km) along this lane on the left

£/$ C

The Oxenham Arms

This inn is believed to have been built in the latter part of the 12th century by lay monks. After the dissolution it became the Dower House of the Burgoynes, whose heiress carried it to the Oxenham family after whom it is named.

First licensed in 1477, The Oxenham Arms is a unique and most traditional English country inn. One interesting part is the small lounge behind the bar where a monolith is set into a wall. Archeologists believe that the monks built their house around this prehistoric stone. In the main lounge the large granite fireplace is a notable feature, and the old dining room with a granite pillar to support the beam is also of much interest.

Not all the bedrooms have an en suite bathroom though they can all provide hot and cold water; and across the road there is a cottage in which there are two large bedrooms with private facilities and a sitting room, which could well suit a family.

South Zeal, Devon EX20 2JT. ✆ (0837) 840244

5	(Each with en suite bathroom, colour TV and coffee/tea facility.) Rates include breakfast. Dogs welcome for a small charge	♫	No
		★	Dartmoor is easy to explore — the hotel nestles at the base of the celebrated Cawsand Beacon
🏨	Year round	🚗	Located 17 miles (27 km) from Exeter. At Whiddon Down roundabout, bear left following signs to Sticklepath on the old A30. After 1½ miles (2½ km), turn right to South Zeal and you'll find the hotel in the village centre. Do not take the new by-pass
✕	Traditional English		
✻	Old traditional inn		
🎾	No, but fishing can be done on the rivers Taw, Torridge and Teign. Good riding is in vicinity; and golf courses are at nearby Okehampton and Moretonhampstead		
		£/$	E

Parkhill Hotel

Parkhill Hotel is a member of a consortium known as 'Relais du Silence', noted for their friendliness, good service and above all, quiet location. This is a glorious location — in the heart of the New Forest with 10 acres (4 ha) of its own parkland. In the 13th century there was a hunting lodge here on the site of an earlier Roman fort. In 1740 the Duke of Clarence bought the property and rebuilt it as you see it today, in some parts. However, there were more changes made in 1850 by Captain Morant, Master of the New Forest Hounds. By 1880 it was a famous boys' school, and it was only after World War II that it became a hotel.

Some of the guest rooms are in the main house and there are suites in the converted coach house, including a four-poster. Also a garden bungalow comprising twin-bedded room and conservatory plus a lounge. (Those bringing a dog must ask for a garden suite, where they are permitted.)

Beaulieu Road, Lyndhurst, Hampshire SO43 7FZ.
✆ (042128) 2944

22 (Including suites and a four-poster; each with en suite bathroom, colour TV, tea tray.) Rates include breakfast

Mid Jan to Dec

✕ Game dishes a speciality. A la carte and table d'hôte

✻ Suited to families who like tranquillity

Outdoor heated pool for summer use, croquet; New Forest walks

♫ No

★ Beaulieu Motor Museum, Rufus Stone and all the picturesque villages of the New Forest

1 mile (1½ km) southeast of Lyndhurst, off B3056 to Beaulieu

£/$ C

Pennyhill Park

Considering that central London is only 27 miles (43 km) away, Pennyhill Park is an oasis of unexpected calm. For whatever reason, Bagshot was one of the few hamlets allowed to exist in the otherwise wooded and wild heathland of the Windsor Great Forest, royal hunting grounds for the early Stuarts.

In the 18th century the hill upon which this hotel stands was used as a lookout point by highwaymen on the watch for the King's men. The present house was built in 1849 by pioneer Canadian bridge-builder James Hodge, who designed and built the first structure to span the St Lawrence River. It was modified several times during the Victorian and Edwardian eras — the last home owner was responsible for the superbly landscaped parkland that beautifies today's hotel.

With 112 acres (45 ha), it's not surprising that this hotel and country club suits most sporting needs. On the north side, tennis courts and a Roman-styled swimming pool; on the south side, a nine-hole golf course spanning down as far as the 3 acre (1¼ ha) trout lake. Horse riding and clay pigeon shooting are also available on the premises, with instruction if required.

A large attentive staff look after you well from the moment you step inside the entrance hall and up the sweep of a period staircase, to the moment you walk into the rustically beamed Latymer Restaurant. Cuisine is good, though perhaps not stunning, and the wine list includes many rare vintages.

Each of the guest rooms is named for a shrub or flower, except for the Hayward Suite, the namesake of the manor's last permanent occupant. Eighteen rooms are in the main house and the other 30 in a restored old coach house in the courtyard.

College Ride, Bagshot, Surrey GU19 5ET.
✆ (0276) 71774

48 (All individually designed and named for trees or flowers, like 'Oak' or 'Walnut', 18 in the main house, 30 in restored coach house, including suites. Each with en suite bathroom, colour TV, radio.)

Year round

Cuisine moderne, English style

Somewhat business orientated

Tennis, swimming pool, nine-hole golf course, lake fishing, horse riding, clay pigeon shooting, sauna

♫ No

★ Windsor, Epsom Downs and London's attractions

Leave the M3 at exit 3, then through Bagshot village and High Street; turn left onto the A30, then first right into Church Road, leading to College Ride

£/$ A

The Plough at Clanfield

Deep in the heart of Cotswold hunting country, a few miles (km) from the Vale of the White Horse, The Plough is a prime example of Elizabethan architecture. The 16th-century hostelry, noted for good food under the supervision of general manager/chef de cuisine Paul Barnard, is a perfect country retreat — a house of character but with standards of modern comfort and service.

It is what you might call a realistic inn with a lounge to feel at home in and a rustic bar. The restaurants, the Knights Room and Tapestry Room, are impeccably set with silverware, crystal, Wedgwood and floral arrangements — cuisine is a matter of pride here.

You'll find most people's idea of a true English cottage garden at the back — a lawn bounded by a low wall, flower beds full of roses and hollyhocks.

Bourton Road, Clanfield, Oxfordshire OX8 2RB.
✆ (036781) 222

7 (Including suites and four-poster; some with jacuzzi bath. All individually designed and each with en suite facilities, colour TV, free in-house video, trouser press and hair dryer.) Rates include newspaper, early-morning tea and English breakfast. Special breaks available

Year round

✕ Celebrated desserts and good cheese selection, home-grown vegetables. Fixed-price menu; 150 wines

✳ Country cottage charm

♫ No

★ Bath, Shakespeare's birthplace, Stratford-upon-Avon and the Cotswolds

Sited on the A4095, easily reached from Cheltenham via the A40

£/$ C

Plumber Manor

In the middle of Hardy's Dorset, Plumber Manor has been the home of the Prideaux-Brune family since the 17th century. In 1973 Richard, Alison and Brian Prideaux-Brune turned the residence into what they term 'a restaurant with bedrooms'.

The house was built by Charles Brune in 1665 — a painting of how it used to look hangs above the staircase and has also been reproduced in the book *History of Dorset*. Nowadays a converted stone barn in the grounds has given six additional bedrooms, and the restaurant — a series of three dining rooms which are the mainstay of the business — is under the direction of Brian Prideaux-Brune, a talented chef. Lunches, however, are not available here.

Plumber Manor provides free stabling for those guests wishing to hunt, and will make other sporting arrangements, but don't expect the kind of hotel services to be found in a larger property.

Sturminster Newton, Dorset DT10 2AF.
✆ (0258) 72507

12 — (6 in the main house, 6 in a converted barn with window seats overlooking the stream and garden; each with en suite bathroom). Rates include English breakfast. No children under 12. Breaks available

Open: Mar to Jan

✕ Fixed-price dinner

✳ Restaurant the mainstay

Sports: Hard tennis court, croquet

♫ No

★ Picturesque villages like Milton and Cerne Abbas, the Piddle Valley and small coastal towns of Lyme Regis and Abbotsbury. Montacute, Stourhead and Wilton also nearby

Car: A resting place for those headed further west, 2 miles (3 km) southwest of Sturminster Newton on the Hazelbury Bryan road. The nearest railway station is Gillingham, in Dorset. London is 2½ hours by car

£/$ C

Polurrian Hotel

Polurrian may not be a country house hotel in the accepted sense for it is large, and has the facilities of a value-for-money family seaside hotel. It is a family-owned and run hotel with above-average food and reasonably priced wine. The Lizard Peninsula is Britain's most southerly point, and the white hotel, an Edwardian one, stands on the cliffs overlooking St. Michael's Mount and Polurrian Cove, one of the few surfing coves in the south with its own beach.

Surroundings are untamed but the hotel is most civilised. There is, for example, both a formal dining room and cocktail bar plus the Achilles Bar and restaurant for more informal meals.

Mullion, South Cornwall TR12 7EN. ✆ (0326) 240421

42 (Including four-poster suite; each with en suite bathroom, colour TV with video link, radio.) Rates are half board. Special breaks available

Mar to Oct

✕ Table d'hôte and à la carte in both dining room and Achilles Restaurant. Reasonably priced wine. Health food in Aqua Bar. High teas for children

✻ Family orientated

Leisure Centre with heated pool, snooker, squash, gym, sauna and solarium, beauty treatments and teenage centre. Outdoor heated pool, tennis courts, 18-hole putting green, croquet, badminton, children's playground

♫ Dancing several times a week

★ Cornish Seal Sanctuary at Gweek, British Telecom's Satellite Earth Station at Goonhilly, Flambards Theme Park at Helston, Lizard Point

1 hour from Newquay airport (driving time), ¾ hour from Penzance station. By road M5, then the A30 to Redruth. From there A393 to Helston; follow signs for A3083 to The Lizard, and after 6 miles (10 km), turn right onto the B3296 to Mullion. Follow signs to Mullion Cove, ½ mile (800 m) from village, take Polurrian Road, on the right

£/$ C half board

The Priory

The Priory's position is so discreetly tucked into a private garden it is hard to believe it is so near to Bath, yet indeed, this Gothic style Georgian house is sited in a residential district near Victoria Park.

The house was origially built of Bath stone in 1835 as a private residence, part of a row of elegant homes on the west side of the city. In the 1960s it was used as accommodation by a boys' school, and became a privately owned hotel in 1969 until late this decade (1980s) when it was sold to a group.

Under the new ownership it continues to be a tastefully decorated establishment designed for those who like deep, chintzy sofas, soft colours and nouvellish food.

The main dining room, shaded peach with fine paintings on the walls, leaves enough space between tables to ensure intimate dining. Lunch is taken in the Orangery and Garden Rooms.

Weston Road, Bath, Avon BA1 2XT. ✆ (0225) 331922

21 (including four-poster; each individually decorated and with en suite bathroom, colour TV.) Unsuitable for children under 10. Rates include continental breakfast. Breaks available

Year round

✕ Fixed-price and à la carte French style. Extensive wine list. No-smoking restaurant. Jacket and tie requested

✻ Sophisticated

Outdoor heated pool, croquet

♫ No

★ Bath, the cathedral cities of Salisbury and Wells, Stonehenge

From Bristol and Wells via the A4 and A39, turn left at Park Lane and left again at Weston Road. From London via the M4 and A46, follow the one-way system from the London road into Paragon, right at the traffic lights into Lansdown Road. Make a left turn at Julian Road which continues into Crescent Lane, then Weston Road

£/$ A

Priory Steps

An American guest at Priory Steps last year was so enamoured of the place, he made a line drawing of it for owners Diana Stockbridge and Carey Chapman. It certainly is an establishment with character — originally six 17th-century weavers' cottages, now converted to provide five individually furnished rooms overlooking the town of Bradford-on-Avon, an old weaving town built out of locally quarried stone on a hilly site.

Diana is a keen cook and offers a wide choice of breakfasts. As this is a private property she doesn't provide an à la carte choice for dinner, though give some notice and she'll cater for any special diet. Dinner is served at 7.30 p.m., usually round one large dining table in the elegant dining room, in front of a log fire on colder days, or on the terrace overlooking the town.

Newtown, Bradford-on-Avon, Wiltshire BA15 1NQ.
✆ (02216) 2230

5	(Each with en suite bathroom, tea/coffee facility, colour TV on request.) Rates include breakfast
🏨	Year round
✕	Fixed-price dinner at 7.30 p.m. Priory Steps is licensed with small, reasonable wine list
✻	Historically pleasant
🎾	No
♫	No
★	Longleat House and Safari Park, Lacock National Trust village, Bath, Bowood Stately Home, Cheddar Gorge
🚗	Bradford-on-Avon is on the A363, 8 miles (13 km) southeast of Bath. Take first left (Market Street) just north of the bridge; left again at the top of the street by thatched cottage and Priory Steps is 100 yards (92 m) on the left
£/$	E

Red Lion Hotel

A 13th-century coaching inn situated in the heart of Salisbury, The Red Lion is, if you like, a country house hotel in town. Inside the black and white Tudor frontage the rooms are cluttered with china and copper collections and famous clocks. If history is a draw, don't miss this hotel.

The south wing is original, as you'll see from the wealth of exposed beams and examples of wattle and daub. In one bedroom there is a good example of handpainted medieval plaster, while the signatures carved in the adjacent wall date to 1693. With the advent of the stagecoach, further wings were added to form the central courtyard, now adorned by a creeper known as 'Hanging Virginia', said to be one of the oldest specimens of its kind in Europe. It is, of course, a native of the USA, introduced to the British Isles around 1629, gloriously crimson in the autumn.

Among the unusual clocks in the hotel, the Skeleton Organ Clock is one of the most noticeable. Reputedly, it was carved by Spanish prisoners in the original Dartmoor Jail, following the defeat of the Armada in 1588. The casing and movement were probably constructed in the 1800s.

Two other fine clocks, known as Act of Parliament Clocks, are to be found in the Victoria Lounge and Dining Room. The Act, made in 1797, taxed anyone with a clock or watch, which naturally reduced the demand for them, depriving many people of a livelihood, so much so that only a year later the Act was repealed. In the meantime, however, tavern keepers anticipating a scarcity — and with an eye to business — installed several of these large mural-type timepieces.

The Red Lion features character bedrooms (all with modern amenities) and a much admired dining room where English dishes are specialities.

Milford Street, Salisbury, Wiltshire SP1 2AN.
✆ (0722) 23334

59 (Including four-posters, each with en suite bathroom, colour TV, radio, coffee/tea facility, mini bar.) Rates include breakfast

Year round

English fare a speciality including venison, jugged hare, oxtail, trout and roast beef. Collar and tie requested

Cosily historic

No

No

★ Salisbury Cathedral, Stonehenge only 10 miles (17 km) away, Old Sarum. Many historic houses including Broadlands (Earl Mountbatten's) and Wilton House (Earl of Pembroke's)

30 miles (48 km) from the M3, 20 (32 km) from the M27, 30 miles (48 km) to the M4. Located 10 miles (17 km) south of A303, 1 mile (1½ km) from Salisbury railway station

£/$ C

Riber Hall

When a four-poster bed is the ultimate, you might very well think about this hotel situated on the borders of the Peak District National Park, in the quiet backwater of Riber Village. They are a feature — in all 11 — handsomely furnished, half-timbered bedrooms.

The house itself, now a listed building, is an attractive Elizabethan manor in its own grounds, built in the 1400s by the Riberghs of Riber, passing by marriage to the Robothams and then to the Wolleys, who lived here for seven generations until 1668.

Period furniture, including some superb, carved-oak pieces and magnificent fireplaces, plus a dining room whose tables are left uncovered, all add to the charm of Riber Hall, which emphasises personalised service in a secluded setting in the foothills of the Pennines.

Matlock, Derbyshire DE4 5JU. ✆ (0629) 2795

11 (All individually designed, with antique four-poster beds; each with en suite bathroom, two with whirlpool baths, bar, colour TV and coffee/tea facility.) Rates include continental breakfast

Year round

Superb à la carte with game in season. Good wine list. Jacket and tie requested

Manor house style

All-weather tennis court; Riding and golf nearby

No

★ Chatsworth House, Haddon Hall, Hardwick Hall, Sudbury Hall, Kedleston Hall, Wingfield Manor and Calke Abbey. Crown Derby Pottery also within easy reach

20 minutes from the M1 (Junction 28) and ¾-hour from East Midlands Airport, 1½ hours from Manchester Airport. Conveniently located for easy access to Sheffield, Chesterfield, Nottingham and Derby

£/$ C

Riverside Country House Hotel

A charming little hotel in the middle of the Peak District National Park, with an acre (½ ha) of cottage garden that leads down to the River Wye. Although parts of the ivy-clad Riverside date to the mid-17th century, the house is essentially Georgian style. The hotel's original beams and polished-oak panelling found in the public areas have, however, been carefully maintained.

From the window of the main sitting room there are views over the garden towards the river. Two dining rooms both feature polished antique tables — the main one dominated by a Regency-style crystal chandelier. Each of the guest bedrooms has an antique bed, most draped with Nottingham lace, their bathrooms adorned by antique brass and gold fittings.

Fennel Street, Ashford-in-the-Water, Bakewell, Derbyshire DE4 1QF. ✆ (062981) 4275

7 (5 doubles, 2 twins, all individually styled, including four-posters and half-testers, each with en suite bathroom, colour TV.) Rates are half board — wine with dinner. Special breaks available

Year round

Fixed-price meals cooked nouvelle style

Personal service in serene setting

No, but golf, fishing, shooting and guided walks can be easily arranged

♫ No

★ Chatsworth House (the Duke and Duchess of Devonshire's home); Haddon Hall, Hardwick Hall. The cities of Nottingham and Derby only 40 miles (64 km) away

Located in a quiet Derbyshire village midst quaint cottages close to Bakewell. From the latter town, follow the A6 for about 2 miles (3 km) to Ashford-in-the-Water

£/$ D but half board, including wine with dinner

Rookery Hall

What strange architecture is this? Rookery Hall started off life as a Georgian mansion when it was built 200 or so years ago by William Hilton Cooke, but when Baron William von Schroder purchased it in 1867, he changed it to a Victorian manor house.

Now a listed building, Rookery Hall has long had a reputation for excellence, one which continues even after the Select Country Hotels took over its management. The welcome is always evident — they rarely miss seeing guests in, and off the premises — and are usually around to take dinner orders. And that Victorian dining room is splendid with its walnut wooden panelling and highly polished mahogany. Tables here don't need the benefit of cloths, but are highlighted by Aynsley china and Brierley crystal.

The whole of the interior befits a Victorian residence: well-proportioned reception rooms with a particularly elegant salon: much panelling and ceiling plaster work; a superb, oak main staircase. It is only just that such a house should sit in 28 acres (11½ ha) of gardens and wooded parkland fringing the River Weaver.

Many of the windows look onto the gardens, including those French ones of the luxury coach house bedrooms.

Worleston, nr Nantwich, Cheshire CW5 6DQ.
✆ (0270) 626866

13 (Each with en suite bathroom and colour TV; 1 four-poster suite, 2 suites in lakeside annexe.) No children under 10

Year round, except mid-Jan to mid-Feb

Excellent, beautifully presented 6-course fixed-price menu which changes seasonally. First-class wine list featuring a large selection of fine Burgundy, Bordeaux and vintage port

Victorian splendour

Hard tennis court, croquet, putting, clay pigeon shooting, coarse fishing in the River Weaver. Riding and golf nearby

No

★ Roman Chester, Royal Doulton china factory. North Wales and the Peak District within easy reach

On a hill overlooking the Cheshire plains, 15 minutes from the M6, 30 minutes from Manchester's airport and 10 minutes from Crewe station

£/$ B

Rothay Manor

Once the family home of a prosperous Liverpool merchant, this delightful Lakeland manor still permeates an unfussed warmth. Many of its original features remain intact, like the verandah with its cast-iron railings and the excellent woodwork.

The Nixons, who operate Rothay now, have given it an atmosphere of a private house ... staying with friends. In addition to the rooms in the manor itself, the lodge at the side of the Manor has been converted into two self-contained suites. A third independent lodge is ideal for family use — or for those who are disabled, since a ramp slopes from the large lounge to garden and the bathroom is fitted with a spacious shower.

Imaginatively prepared food is served in an attractive dining room and breakfast is the large, Cumberland variety. The lakeland setting, need we say, is incomparable.

Rothay Bridge, Ambleside, Cumbria LA22 0EH.
✆ (05394) 33605

15 plus 3 self-contained suites (each with colour TV and en suite bathroom; a couple with balconies.) Rates include Cumberland breakfast. Special packages available

Mid-Feb to early Jan

✕ Imaginative, rather rich fare; comprehensive wine list

✻ Unfussy

Croquet in the garden; nearby river and lake fishing sailing and watersking

♫ No

★ The National Park Centre at Brockhole and stately homes are within easy motoring distance. Motor launches operate down Lake Windermere, and from the southern tip a steam train operates to Haverthwaite and back

From the centre of Ambleside or Waterhead, follow the signs for Coniston on A593. The hotel is located on the Langdale outskirts of Ambleside

£/$ C

Rothley Court

For centuries Rothley Court was called Rothley Temple, for the manor was granted to the Knights Templar by Henry III in 1231, and their chapel built adjacent in 1240 still stands today, Britain's second best-preserved Templar chapel. When the Templars were abolished in the 14th century, this property passed to the Knights of St John of Jerusalem, who leased out the lands for farming.

A long line of Babingtons had their home here from 1565 to 1845. It was probably the only family estate to stay intact after the Babington Plot was discovered — a plan to overthrow Elizabeth I in favour of Mary Queen of Scots — and for which Antony Babington was executed. The room in which statesman, Thomas Babington Macaulay was born in 1800 is today The Macaulay Room, little changed with its floor-to-ceiling oak panelling, but used for private meetings.

Many a distinguished guest has stayed under this roof. It was here that William Wilberforce drafted his treaty for the abolition of slavery. The room now named for him, originally a Victorian, panelled billiard room, is also used as a function room. Lord Kitchener was summoned from here to his campaign in Egypt — the two 'Nubian slaves' you see in the coffee lounge and on the half-landing above are the remains of a magnificient fireplace and mantel Kitchener sent home.

The original dining room and butler's pantry have since become the Babington Restaurant and The Garden Room. Old stables have been turned into 20 modern bedrooms, and in the hotel's 18th-century wing the lounge bar and conservatory has a glazed porch leading on to the terrace overlooking the lawns and Rothley Brook, in 6 acres (2½ ha) of grounds.

Westfield Lane, Rothley, Leicester LE7 7LG. ✆ (0533) 374141

18 (Mostly double, including suites and four-posters; traditional rooms in main house, modern rooms in converted stables. Each with private bathroom, colour TV, video, radio alarm clock, hair dryer, electric trouser press, mini bar.) Rates include full English breakfast

Mid-Feb to early Jan

Rich and imaginative

For escapists

Riding and golf close by; tennis and squash may be arranged

No

Charnwood Forest, Bradgate Park with its wildfowl reserve, Belvoir Castle, Belton and Boughton Houses, Bosworth Battlefield

Midway between Leicester and Loughborough on the edge of Charnwood Forest. Off the main A6 road

£/$ A

Rowley Manor

It is almost incredible that England still boasts large numbers of Georgian houses. This one was once the rectory to St Peter's Church, said to have been built originally in 1621. In 1638 the rector at the time emigrated to the USA and founded Rowley in Massachusetts. Rowley here remained a rectory until 1928, when local shipping magnate T.A. Filmer Wilson (of the Ellerman Wilson Line) bought it and installed panelling in the study and the water temple in the garden.

Now a friendly hotel, its most famous feature is the panelled Pine Room with its paintings and antiques. Some of the food for the tables in the chandeliered and mirrored dining room is grown in the grounds — 34 acres (14 ha) of lawns, rose gardens and parkland.

Little Weighton, nr Hull, North Humberside HU20 3XR.
✆ (0482) 848248

? (Including four-posters; each with en suite bathroom, colour TV, radio clock.) Dogs accepted for small charge. Rates include full English breakfast. Breaks available

Year round

✕ Emphasis on fresh, local produce

✻ Business convenient, holiday quiet

Solarium, croquet

♫ No

★ York and the Wolds

A few minutes drive from Hull and Beverley. Convenient to the M62 and Humber Bridge

£/$ C

Sharrow Bay Country House Hotel

Sharrow Bay is almost a legend among country house hotels, maybe the first of the breed. There is no reception desk, no bar, and orders are taken without the use of pencil and paper. It is a house where the atmosphere is unhurried, the décor and furnishing pleasing and almost continental, built as it is with low low-angled roof ridges and wide eaves on its lakeside elevation.

In fact, the actual form of the hotel is interesting, and any difficulties it might have presented have certainly been overcome by the owners Francis Coulson and Brian Sack, who have been here for over 40 years. Accommodation, you see is scattered between the main house, a cottage a few yards (metres) away, another more distant, a gatehouse and a large converted 17th-century farmhouse called Bank House, a mile (km) or so down the road. So be careful when booking a room which one it is. Bank House actually offers a magnificent lake view and contains its own sitting rooms. Breakfast is served here, so it's more or less self-contained except for dining.

In the main house itself there are a comfortable lounge and two smallish dining rooms. From the picture window in the drawing room you can see across the lake to the Martindale Fells. Afternoon tea here is a tradition, with homemade scones and jam and local cream, all served on the finest English porcelain. It was the high standard of afternoon tea which first put Sharrow Bay on the map when it opened as a hotel in 1949.

Since then more than mere tea has won gourmet Brownie points. Food here has an emphasis on English ingredients — fish from Aberdeen, Martindale chickens and Alston geese. The sweet trolley is another long-standing tradition, mostly a cold selection with one hot pudding each day. A British member of Relais et Chateaux, Sharrow Bay lives up beautifully to the reputation.

Lake Ullswater, Howtown Road, nr Penrith, Cumbria CA10 2LZ. ✆ (08536) 301

36 (Including suites; 18 are in cottages and Bank House. 24 with en suite facility — each with colour TV, tea/coffee facility, hair dryer.) No children under 13. Rates are half board

Early Mar to early Dec

Rich cordon bleu. Especially notable desserts like fruit terrine with raspberry sauce or hearts of hazelnut shortbread layered with chocolate mousse, served with dariole of apple mousse, quenelle of apple sorbet on grated apple with calvados sauce. Also exceptional breakfasts and afternoon teas. No-smoking dining room. Jacket and tie requested

Food with a view

Lake swimming, trout fishing; golf nearby

No

★ Hadrian's Wall, Long Meg stone circle, Wordsworth's cottage and Museum at Grasmere, Martindale

7 miles (11 km) west of Penrith. Take the M6 to Junction 40

£/$ A but half board

Sir Christopher Wren's House Hotel

Beneath the ramparts of Windsor Castle is a quiet, dignified hotel which was once the home of Sir Christopher Wren. He designed and built it in 1676 as his family home, though in his earlier years, he lived in the Deanery in the castle grounds. Though additions have been made since 1900 and the house is now a 41-room hotel, it retains much of its original character. You may care to know, for instance, that when Wren became MP for Old Windsor he was responsible for the design and completion of Windsor Guildhall, which possesses identical ornate plaster to his house.

The hotel's drawing room is especially noteworthy, showing many alteration dates like the brick in the bay (1752) and the monogram over the door which is probably that of the family who lived here at the time. Main feature is the beautiful alabaster fireplace, attributed to Sir Thomas Fettiplace and dated 1442, but which was installed during Wren's residency. The full height, oak panelling above the fireplace in the Oak Room lounge is also of an early date and said to have been a gift to Wren.

By comparison, the Orangerie Restaurant and cocktail bar are not in period design but do overlook river and gardens. So too do the bedrooms, but proffer your request for an old one or a new one.

As an alternative to hotel dining (but under the same management) is The Hideaway, a five-minute walk towards the Castle, in the middle of Thames Street's gift shops, opposite the Curfew Tower. This bistro grill is open daily for morning coffees, lunch, afternoon teas and informal candlelit dinners.

Sir Christopher Wren's House Hotel is one of the most interesting in the Thames Valley. Windsor itself is an obviously popular sightseers' destination, being the home and burial place of English monarchs for 900 years and a personal favourite of the current Royal Family.

Thames Street, Windsor, Berkshire SL4 1PX. ✆ (0753) 861354

41 (Many with four-posters, most overlooking river, terraced gardens or castle; each with en suite bathroom and colour TV.) Rates include early-morning tea, newspaper and English breakfast. Breaks available

Year round

Table d'hôte and à la carte

Calm and historic

No

No

Windsor Castle, Theatre Royal, Eton

Located in the shadow of Windsor Castle, close to the M4 motorway (leave at Junction 6) and within easy reach of the M3/M25 motorway. 22 miles (35 km) from London, within 15 minutes drive of Heathrow. Direct train service links Windsor to Paddington and Waterloo

£/$ B

The Springs Hotel

In the heart of the Thames Valley, close to the river and overlooking 6 acres (2½ ha) of gardens, stands The Springs, which takes its name from the spring-fed lake in front of it. It was built in 1874 by Sir Albert Condie-Stephens, a diplomat in the service of Queen Victoria, who had it designed in the mock Tudor style fashionable in that era. At the turn of the century it was purchased by Sir John Wormold, who created the Wintergarden, now the restaurant that has a superb view of the lake, floodlit at night. He also panelled the library (today used for private functions).

The cocktail bar, period furnished, also enjoys good views of the lake and grounds — outdoor food service is possible in summer. Bedroom suites too overlook greenery. Set back from the road, The Springs is secluded enough yet within easy reach of many historic and cultural attractions.

North Stoke, Wallingford, Oxfordshire. ✆ (0491) 36687

34 (Individually furnished, each with en suite bathroom, colour TV; room safes in some.) Rates include full English breakfast

Year round

✕ International

✻ Lakeside retreat

Hard tennis court, heated pool, croquet lawn, pitch and putt, sauna

♫ No

★ Oxford, Windsor, Newbury, Ascot, Cheltenham

On the B4009 Goring to Wallingford road. From the M4 leave by Junction 8 or 9 through Henley to Crowmarsh and left onto the B4009. Reading is 14 miles (23 km) away, Henley, 7 (11 km)

£/$ A

Stapleford Park

American entrepreneur Bob Payton (best known for his Chicago Rib Shack restaurant chain) is clever at novelty, as well as astute in business. He may have fallen in love with this stately Grade I listed building that was until the 1850s the seat of six of the Earls of Harborough, enough to make it his own family home, but he also invited famous names to create 'Signature Bedrooms' for hotel use.

Choosing which to book is a matter of personality. I think, for example that the Turnbull & Asser Suite is fun, with its wall and bed covering made from shirting material; its silk and velour curtains held together by silk ties; and its wall illustrations hung on trouser braces. Someone else might prefer the Wedgwood designed Jasper Room (blue and white, naturally!) with its four-poster bed, china-based telephone, Jasper ware ornaments and Waterford crystal chandelier. Or there's the Crabtree and Evelyn Room, which is very ornate with lots of pictures on the walls and a bathroom that features mahogany, white marble and brass fittings, not to mention a generous selection of the company's toiletries.

The house itself is a very fine one, and set as it is in 500 acres (202 ha) of wooded parkland, reminiscent of a Victorian gentleman's favourite hunting lodge. Indeed, according to Bob, Edward Prince of Wales wished to buy it but his mother, Queen Victoria, forbade it for fear her son might be corrupted by the Leicestershire hunting society!

Equestrian links continue to be associated with this part of Britain, of course, but the Stapleford estate has its own stables where horses may be hired and instruction given. During the season a day's hunting can be arranged with the Belvoir, Cottesmore or Quorn Hunts (Sept to Mar). Less taxing is the croquet, miniature golf and horseshoes available in the hotel's walled garden. Anyone with more stamina is encouraged to try the basketball facilities (Payton Americana coming out), jog or walk around the grounds — wellies available for visitors who come without them.

American ownership of a historic property first mentioned in the Domesday Book, has undoubtedly lent a casual air, so while the dining room (whose wood carvings are attributed to master carver Grinling Gibbons) is certainly elegant, jackets and ties for dinner are not a must. Following the fashion of the decade, however, smokers have to wait for coffee in the drawing room to light up. The chef is English, but the occasional American dish pops up on the menu.

The library acts as a bar and the breakfast room is the old kitchen. Another Paytonism here: your kippers, kedgeree and blueberry muffins will be served up on Wedgwood Peter Rabbit china! At night, by the way, guests won't find a goodnight candy on their pillow, but a tin of Wendy Payton's chocolate chip cookies instead.

Stapleford Park and Sporting Estate opened only last year (1988) and was already planning to double the amount of accommodation as the first guests walked through.

Melton Mowbray, Leicestershire LE14 2EF. ✆ (057) 284 522

23 (De luxe king or twin, each individually designed and decorated, with en suite bathroom, colour TV.) No children under 10. Kennels in the grounds for pets. Rates include continental breakfast and newspaper

Year round

✕ Hot breakfasts include kippers and kedgeree served on Peter Rabbit china. Dinner menus change weekly — occasional American dishes. No-smoking dining room

✳ American casual in Victorian gentleman's hunting lodge setting

Riding in the grounds, two all-weather tennis courts, fishing in the lake in front of hotel. Basketball, croquet, miniature golf, and horseshoes in walled garden. Game shooting, trout fishing at Rutland Water; hunting may be arranged. Four nearby golf courses

♫ No

★ Belvoir Castle (seat of the Dukes of Rutland); Lincoln Castle; Rockingham Castle (built by William the Conquerer. Also historic houses like Belton and Chatsworth

Located near Melton Mowbray, famous for its pork pies, Stapleford can be reached by train from London — to Leicester or Grantham. By road, from the A1, take the B676 towards Melton Mowbray at the Colsterworth roundabout, for 9 miles (14 km). Turn left for the hotel 1 mile (1½ km) past Saxby. From the M1, leave at Junction 23. Drive through Melton Mowbray towards Bourne (B676). Stapleford is signposted 3 miles (5 km) east of Melton.

£/$ A

The Steppes

This striking, black and white 17th-century farmhouse has attracted enough attention to warrant it a country house hotel commendation from the BTA. It is a listed building certainly, though the current owners are not familiar with the history attached to it. Many of its original features remain like the beams, exposed throughout — modernisation has been achieved sympathetically.

You'll find period furniture throughout the house and both log fires and central heating to keep you warm in winter. You'll also find the hospitality more than generous. Service indeed is so personalised and The Steppes so tiny (only three guest rooms) that it can hardly be considered a hotel, yet nor is it exactly a guest house, nor a Wolsey Lodge or average B & B.

Hostess Mrs Tricia Howland makes candlelight dinner an occasion (ties for gentlemen, note). The dining room itself is probably the most charming room in the house, with its low-beamed ceiling, inglenook fireplace, pretty windows and original floor.

Ullingswick, nr Hereford HR1 3JG. ✆ (0432) 820424

3 (All double, each with en suite bathroom, colour TV, tea/coffee making facility) Rates half board. No children under 12

Mid-Jan to mid-Dec

✕ Hearty, full English breakfast. Four-course set-priced gourmet dinners using medieval or local recipes and home-grown produce. Also à la carte available

✻ Tranquil, personalised

No

♫ No

★ Daily tours are conducted round the Royal Worcester porcelain works. Plenty of crafts and festivals

In the Wye Valley, reached via the A465 from Hereford, the A417 from Leominster, the A465 from Worcester or the A417 from Gloucester

£/$ C

Ston Easton Park

A distinguished Grade I Palladian mansion, Ston Easton as you see it today was completed in 1791 but still retains the core of an earlier Tudor house and its Queen Anne additions within the present structure. It was the possession of the Hippisley family for 400 years following a Grant of Letters Patent to John Hippisley by Henry VIII in 1544.

The interior restoration is the work of Jean Monro, an acknowledged authority on 18th-century décor. Several of the bedrooms, for example, feature four-poster beds of the Chippendale and Heppelwhite periods, all overlooking romantic parklands created by Humphrey Repton in 1793.

Ston Easton guests are invited to look at the basement's early kitchens, a fine 18th-century linen room, a servant's hall, a billiard room and the wine cellar — now restocked to include rare wines and vintages.

Chewton Mendip, Bath, Somerset BA3 4DF. ✆ (076121) 631

21	(Including four-posters and suites, each with en suite bathroom, colour TV and radio.) No children under 12. Rates include early-morning tea, newspaper and continental breakfast	✻	Distinguished
			Croquet, bowls, archery, riding, ballooning
		♫	No
		★	Bath, Mendip Hills
			11 miles (18 km) south of Bath. On the A37 from Bristol to Shepton Mallet
	Year round		
✕	English and French à la carte	£/$	A

Stonehouse Court Hotel

Stonehouse Court is the type of mellow old building in the West Cotswolds that attracts potential purchasers. Indeed, it has done just that, having been recently acquired by a small hotel group under the label of 'Clipper Hotels'. Whether or not changes will be made by the new owners remains to be seen, but it is currently graded a three star by the RAC and AA and four crowns by the ETB.

It was originally built in the early 17th century as a Manor Court and is as mellow inside as it is out. The Arundel Bar, with its open fireplace, could be better decorated but is nevertheless a convivial rendezvous for a drink. Alternatively, in fine weather, the outdoor terrace is used.

Stonehouse Court benefits from its large, leaded windows (in the bedrooms too) with views onto 6 acres (2½ ha) of secluded park.

Bristol Road, Stonehouse, nr Stroud, Gloucestershire GL10 3RA. ✆ (045382) 5155

- 23 (Each with en suite bathroom, colour TV, tea/coffee facility). Rates include newspaper and English breakfast
- Year round
- ✗ Reasonably priced table d'hôte and à la carte.
- ✳ Straightforward comfort
- Croquet; nearby golf and riding
- ♫ No
- ★ Gloucester Cathedral, Bristol's dock area and museums, Cheltenham Spa. Stroud is 5-minutes drive away; Forest of Dean also nearby
- In the centre of the West Cotswolds but readily accessible from the A419 and 1 mile (1½ km) from Junction 13 on the M5 and the A38. A 15-minute drive from Cheltenham, 12 miles (19 km) from Gloucester
- £/$ C

Studley Priory

In the 12th century the Priory was a Benedictine nunnery, but with the dissolution of the monasteries under Henry VIII, it was purchased by the Croke family in whose hands it remained for 335 years. A private chapel was consecrated in 1639 and a north wing added in 1666, but otherwise the exterior has stayed as it was in the reign of Elizabeth I.

The entrance hall is panelled with early 18th-century pitch pine with coats-of-arms on the cornice. The Croke family coat-of-arms can be seen in the 16th to 17th-century stained glass windows here. Wood panelling is used abundantly at Studley Priory, especially in the bar, which was formerly a Victorian dining room, and in the Croke Restaurant. One of the most impressive guest bedrooms is the heavily panelled Elizabethan Suite, the original master bedroom, with its half-tester bed dating about 1700.

Horton-cum-Studley, Oxford OX9 1AZ. ✆ (086735) 203

19	(Each with en suite facilities; colour TV, tea/coffee facility.) Rates include full English breakfast
🏨	Year round
✕	Fixed-price and à la carte English and French cuisine
✻	Stately
🎾	Grass tennis court, croquet
♫	No
★	Oxford colleges, Blenheim Palace, Woodstock. Also Waddesdon Manor (home of the Rothschild family) and Milton Manor near Abingdon (home of the Mockler family)
🚗	7 miles (11 km) from Oxford
£/$	C

Swynford Paddocks

Swynford Paddocks was once the home of Col. George Leigh, as a gift from the Prince of Wales in 1809 as a 'thank you' for managing his horses at Newmarket. The Colonel's wife, Augusta, was half-sister to Lord Byron, with whom she had a passionate romance in 1813, althogh nobody knows for sure whether the daughter born to Augusta the following April was Byron's child.

Eventually the house became the property of Lord and Lady Halifax until 1976, when it was converted into today's luxury hotel. Today guests are free to roam the grounds and make use of the giant chess set, croquet lawn or putting course.

One of the features at Swynford Paddocks is afternoon tea served in style and English fashion: dainty cucumber sandwiches on delicate china, freshily baked scones with homemade strawberry jam and clotted cream, and a choice of Darjeeling, Earl Grey or scented tea.

Six Mile Bottom, Newmarket CB8 0UE. ✆ (163870) 234

15 (Including suite and four-poster, each individually decorated and with en suite bathroom, colour TV, clock radio alarm, tea/coffee facility and mini bar, trouser press and hair dryer.) Rates include early morning tea, newspaper and English breakfast. Breaks available

Year round except between Xmas and New Year

✕ Top quality fresh produce, cooked nouvelle style

✳ Genteel

Tennis, croquet, putting, giant outdoor chess

♫ No

★ Ely Cathedral, Cambridge colleges, Tattersalls Sales Paddocks, the Wickenfen Wild Fowl Trust and the Imperial War Museum at Duxford Aerodrome

On the A1304, 5 miles (8 km) south of Newmarket and 3/4 mile (1 1/4 km) north of the junction of the A1304 and A11 (M)

£/$ C

The Talbot Inn

Of all the English shires, Shropshire is perhaps the least known and the most unspoilt. So what better place to find an inn which has been caring for the weary traveller for six centuries? Dating from 1360, the Inn was once part of Wenlock Abbey and used to be known as the Abbot's Hall, perhaps was the Almoner's house.

Today's owners Tim and Meriel Lathe are just as keen on traditional hostelry hospitality, as you'll discover when you walk through the archway on Much Wenlock's historic High Street into a quiet courtyard garden. Inside the inn are exposed beams, open log fires and fresh flowers. Dishes are homemade and the wine list reflects the owners' preference for Italian varieties.

This setting, by the way, was used for some of the scenes with Jennifer Jones in the film adaptation of Mary Webb's novel *Gone to Earth*.

Much Wenlock, Shropshire TF13 6AA. ✆ (0952) 727077

- 5 — (Doubles, and with en suite bathroom) in the 18th-century malthouse. Rates include full English breakfast
- Year round
- ✕ Lunches and dinners available at the inn, homemade from fresh produce. Speciality is bread-and-butter pudding and traditional Sunday lunch roasts
- ✻ Old-fashioned inn appeal
- No
- ♫ No
- ★ Medieval market towns like Ludlow and Shrewsbury. Severn Gorge with its Ironbridge Museum, Wroxeter Roman City and National Trust properties like Benthall Hall
- On the A458, 12 miles (19 km) southeast of Shrewsbury and 9 miles (14 km) northwest of Bridgnorth. Convenient for the M54, exit at Wellington for Eaton Constantine and Cressage
- £/$ E

Teignworthy

On the edge of Dartmoor National Park in the tiny hamlet of Frenchbeer, Teignworthy is built in Lutyens style of local stone. Staying here is almost like visiting friends in the country. That, anyway, is the impression that John and Gillian Newell wish to convey for their lovely little country property in the midst of some of Britain's most unspoilt terrain.

Dartmoor granite and Delabole slate were used to build this former forester's home in the 1920s, whose interior is comfy rather than ostentatious. The oak-panelled hall and huge granite fireplaces are the most notable architectural features, but it is the food and unrushed ambience which are the attraction. Soothe away bad weather with a good book borrowed from the selection in the sitting room, or a jazz or classical recording. Enjoy good weather and explore the moor on foot with a Teignworthy packed lunch to hand, or wander the 14 acres (5 ha) of gardens and woodland that are part of the hotel grounds.

Frenchbeer, Chagford, Devon TQ13 8EX. ✆ (06473) 3355

9 (Individually decorated: 6 in main house, 3 in the converted hay loft; each with en suite bathroom and colour TV.) Rates include English breakfast. Special packages available

Year round

✕ Beef and lamb from the Hatherleighs butcher; fresh red mullet and John Dory from coastal waters; free range poultry; cheese from Sharpam, Curworthy etc. Table d'hôte.

✻ Tranquilly intimate

Grass tennis court, walled croquet lawn; golf nearby at Mortonhampstead; horse riding on the moor and fishing on the Dart and Teign Rivers and at Pernworthy Reservoir. Hotel has own sauna and sunbed plus 14 acres (5½ ha) of garden

♫ No

★ Near the cathedral city of Exeter and historic Plymouth. A short drive from the north and south Devon beaches, cliffs and harbours

🚗 Within a few miles (km) of the fast motorway network to London and the Midlands and within easy reach of local airports. 2½ miles (4 km) south west of Chagford — follow the signposts to Fernworthy and then Kestor Rock

£/$ C

Tillmouth Park Hotel

There's a lot to be said for Border country, especially when 1,000 acres (405 ha) of it surround an imposing Victorian, listed country mansion and overlook the River Till.

One of the main features inside the hotel is the Galleried Lounge, which has a magnificent, massive stone fireplace. Among the guest bedrooms, the Sir Walter Scott Room is of particular note, decorated with antiques, oil portraits and framed tapestries and unusually featuring twin four-poster beds. The other notable accommodation is the honeymoon bungalow or Garden Suite.

This hotel could well be the rural choice of a fisherman, for Tillmouth has fishing licence for 9 miles (14 km) of water on the Rivers Tweed and Till: for the sport of fresh-run salmon and sea trout, for brown trout or coarse fishing.

Cornhill-on-Tweed, Northumberland TD12 4UU.
✆ (0890) 2255

---

12 (Each with en suite bathroom, colour TV, tea/coffee making facility, hair dryer and trouser press.) Rates include full English breakfast. Special breaks available.

🏨 Year round

✕ Specialities include local produce and estate game, salmon and sea trout

✻ Gentle quiet

🎣 Fishing for salmon, sea trout or brown trout — boats and ghillies provided. Nearby golfing at Coldstream, Goswick, North Berwick and Muirfield

♫ No

★ Barnburgh Castle and Lindisfarne Island are within easy reach; so are Flodden Field and nearby Kelso, Melrose and Galashiels (where knitwear is made). Stately homes include Floors Castle, Mellerstain and Manderston

🚗 On the A698 Berwick to Coldstream road, set in its own estate

£/$ A

Tylney Hall

By way of contrast to most other properties featured in this book, magnificent, Grade II listed Tylney Hall is very large (90 rooms) for a country house hotel. But there — it is a *hall* with large public rooms and ornate furnishings and 66 acres (27 ha) of grounds to its name.

A mansion house has existed on the site since 1561, though the first Tylney Hall *per se* was not built until 1700, and what you see today was architected for Lionel Phillips between 1899 and 1902. Its conservative style is due to the conservative tastes of the man commissioned to design it — Seldon Wornum. The more interesting details and decoration were added by another architect, Robert Weir Schultz, whose principles are nost visible in the garden buildings.

During World War I the Hall was used as a hospital. Its last private owner was Major Cayzer, later to become Lord Rotherwick, who used the Hall as headquarters for his successful shipping line Clan during World War II. Tylney became a school from 1953 until 1984, when it was closed for extensive refurbishment for a year until opening as a hotel.

You'll find the reception rooms extremely opulent, particularly the Great Hall (now a lounge), partially panelled with Italian walnut and with a gilded and intricately carved oak ceiling that was brought over in sections from the Grimatian Palace in Florence to adorn Sir Lionel's new mansion. Another spacious lounge is the Grey Room, decoratively plastered but more restful. Pre-dinner drinks are suggested in the oak-panelled library prior to a sampling of *haute cuisine* in the glass-domed restaurant, also oak panelled and featuring superb carved leather panelling.

No two rooms are alike in the main house though all are furnished to luxury standards, some with four-posters, some with jacuzzi baths. Fifty-five new bedrooms were opened just last year (1988) as part of the Courtyard Wing, which also houses health and leisure facilities.

The acreage surrounding the hotel alone gives it prestigious countrified appeal and is of significant historic interest. (Both gardens and park are listed on the English Heritage Register.) By the time this is in print the water garden designed by Schultz and Gertrude Jekyll should be officially reopened. Two water courses join two pools here, surrounded by a number of unusual trees. A new bridge has been built across the main lake and the Italian Garden has been restored.

Rotherwick, nr Hook, Hampshire RG27 9AJ. ✆ (025672) 4881

90 (Including suites, all luxuriously decorated, some with four-posters, some with jacuzzi baths; each with en suite facilities, colour TV, trouser press.) Rates include newspaper and English breakfast. Special packages available

Year round

New French and traditional English, table d'hôte and à la carte. Jacket and tie for dinner. No children under 8 in dining room

Impressive, grand hall

Snooker, health studio with indoor heated pool, gym, sauna and jacuzzi. Outdoor pool, croquet, 2 tennis courts; 18-hole golf course adjacent. Archery and clay pigeon shooting may be arranged in the grounds

No

★ Winchester, The New Forest, Beaulieu Motor Museum, Stratfield Saye House, Wellington Country Park; also Stonehenge and Salisbury Cathedral, Windsor Castle and Ascot

In Rotherwick Village, 6½ miles (10 km) from Basingstoke via the A30 with easy access to the M3 and M4 motorways. London is less than an hour's drive away. Nearest train stations are Reading, Hook or Basingstoke. Heathrow is 35 miles (56 km), Gatwick, 62 (100 km) — chauffeur pickup can be arranged. Helipad

£/$ A

Upton House

Upton House is a part Tudor, part Georgian farmhouse that is Grade II listed. Believed to date back to Norman times, today it is the home of Hugh and Angela Jefferson, one of those tiny off-the-beaten-track places that can only accommodate very few.

There are three, pretty colour-themed bedrooms with exposed beams, English chintzes and floral prints. The Pink Bedroom is a king-size double overlooking the croquet lawn and rose garden. The Peach Bedroom is also a king-size double with an additional small dressing room area and more or less the same outlook. the Blue Bedroom overlooks the courtyard and drive and has twin beds. All are en suite. Angela believes in 'frills' so each room is provided with a trouser press, hair dryer, notepaper, fresh flowers, pot pourri and a range of toiletries.

As this is a private home, dinner is a home-cooked family affair round one table — a four-course no choice meal that must be booked in advance if required. Advise on any dislikes and bring in your own wine as Upton House is unlicensed.

The house is naturally filled with the Jeffersons' own possessions as well as an array of guidebooks and maps to help tourists, but because of the uneven floors and small flights of steps, it is considered unsuitable for small children.

Set in 2 acres (¾ ha) of well-kept lawns and gardens, Upton House lies to the west of the 13th-century church, and has an almost perfectly preserved cider mill attached to it plus a listed cottage in the grounds.

Upton Snodsbury, Worcester WR7 4NR. ✆ (090) 560 226

3 (Double or twin; each with en suite bathroom, coffee/tea facility, trouser press, hair dryer, toiletries) Rates include breakfast

Year round, except Xmas

4-course meal with coffee and chocolates; no choice, fixed price, must be booked in advance

Warm and personal

No

No

Ragley Hall and Warwick Castle, Royal Brierley Crystal factory, Hidcote Gardens and Spetchley Park, Burford Wild Life Park. Also Worcester Cathedral and Royal Worcester porcelain factory

Upton Snodsbury is situated 6 miles (10 km) east of Worcester just off the A422. Leave M5 at Junctions 6 or 7

£/$ E

Whitehall

Exuding an air of peace and *bonhomie*, the 15th-century manor house that is the Whitehall Hotel sits on a hillside overlooking the rolling northwest Essex countryside. The estate has in the past been owned by the Countess of Warwick, a noted Edwardian society hostess, and more recently by the late Lord (Rab) Butler. Broxted itself was referred to in the Domesday Book — the earliest mention of a manor was in 1151, when Alured de Bendaville gave it to the hospital of St John of Jerusalem.

Whitehall is a cheerful country house hotel with light and airy décor both in the lounges and the reception hall, where a log fire burns in winter. The vaulted and timbered dining room, whose prominent colour is deep pink, is the setting for fine table d'hôte or à la carte lunches and à la carte dinners. All the bedrooms are pastel shaded and prettily furnished.

Church End, Broxted, Essex CM6 2BZ.
✆ (0279) 850603

10	(Double or twin; each with en suite bathroom.) Rates include English breakfast
🏨	Year round
✕	Table d'hôte lunch Tues to Sat and à la carte. A la carte dinner. Also-fixed price Sun lunch
✻	Refined, country charm
⚲	Outdoor pool, 2 tennis courts; golf, fishing, clay pigeon shooting nearby
♫	No
★	Historic Cambridge, Tudor towns and villages like Thaxted, Saffron Walden and Finchingfield
🚗	Midway between London and Cambridge, ten minutes from Junction 8 exit (Bishop's Stortford) of the M1. Less than 1-hour's drive from London, 30 minutes from Cambridge, and very near Stanstead Airport
£/$	C

The White Hart Hotel

The White Hart's major asset is its setting, a beautiful riverside one in one of the loveliest villages on the Thames, which has retained its centuries-old character. From the 11th to 16th centuries the Bishops and Deans of Salisbury had residences in the village of Sonning, and the hotel stands in the grounds of the Bishop's Palace.

An ale-house has stood on the site since 1200, when a ferry provided a river crossing until Sonning Bridge was built in 1790. The name comes from the white hart of Richard II's coat-of-arms. Carvery luncheons are available daily in the bistro along with à la carte suggestions.

The Riverside Terrace Restaurant looks out onto the gardens and river with an open air terrace utilised in summer for pre- and post-dinner drinks. Most of the accommodation is in the main hotel, but there are also two cottages located around the courtyard and wishing well.

Sonning-on-Thames, Berkshire RG4 0UT.
✆ (0734) 692277

25 (Including four-posters; each with en suite bathroom, colour TV, trouser press, fresh flowers, tea/coffee facility.) Rates include English breakfast and newspaper. Breaks available

Year round

✕ A la carte lunch and dinner menus in the Riverside Restaurant, English and continental cuisine. Carvery lunches and evening grills in Hideaway Bistro

✳ Riverside attraction

No

♫ No

★ Close to Henley, Ascot and Windsor; also the stately homes of Stratfield Saye, Stonor and Mapledurham

4 miles (6 km) east of Reading with easy access to the M4

£/$ C

The White House Hotel

Until recently this whitewashed Regency house was the family home of the Prince and Princess de Rohan, whose ancestors were connected with the French Royal family — Marie Antoinette helped them flee France. Some of its architectural features include unique curved walls and bow doors in the main rooms, and the current owners have decorated the house in period style.

Country house appeal is added by log fires, a cosy cocktail bar and crystal and silver table settings in the Regency Restaurant. As well as offering rooms in the main hotel, The White House offers accommodation in a cottage adjacent.

2 Hillside, Charmouth, Bridport, Dorset.
✆ (0297) 60411

10 (All individually decorated, and each with en suite bathroom, colour TV, tea/coffee facility); also 3 rooms in the adjacent White House Cottage, each with en suite shower or bathroom. Rates include English breakfast

Mid-Jan to mid-Dec

✕ Set menus emphasise fresh fish and the wine list includes a number of fine varieties. Patio Restaurant open for lunch

✻ Peaceful

Not on site, but arrangements can be made for fishing, riding, sailing etc

♫ No

★ The sub-tropical gardens and swannery at Abbotsbury along Chesil Beach are worth visiting; also the stately homes of Montacute, Barrington Court, Forde Abbey and Kingston Lacey

The small coastal village of Charmouth lies in the folds of Blackdown Vale not far from Lyme Regis on the main A35 road

£/$ D

Whitwell Hall

This hotel is a member of Relais du Silence, a consortium which emphasises the quiet country aspects; in fact Lt-Commander Milner and his wife do not accept any guests under 18.

The village of Whitwell-on-the-Hill leads into a woodland drive, which opens out to a terrace overlooking the Vale of York with a southern view to York Minster and the Pennine range of hills to the west. The neo-Gothic style house itself was built in 1830 though the present owners have added the Orangery Garden Restaurant. The hall's name derives from a source of clear water, and the site was originally part of the Manor of Whitwell once owned by Count Robert Waltheof in the 11th century.

These days, Whitwell Hall is very much a mixture of old traditional, like the impressive entrance hall and the antique studded drawing room, with the new, like the coach house bedrooms and games room. A well-kept country house garden lies behind the hall, part of 18 acres (7¼ ha) of surrounding lawns and woodland, criss-crossed by walking paths.

Whitwell-on-the-Hill, York YO6 7JJ. ✆ (065381) 551

20 (16 twin/double, including four-posters, four single; each with en suite facilities, colour TV, coffee/tea tray.) Rates include English breakfast. Not suitable for children. Breaks available

Year round

✕ Table d'hôte dinners in traditional dining room. Light lunches in Orangery

✻ Yorkshire quantity and quality

Croquet, tennis, games room, sauna, indoor pool, putting green, cycles

♫ No

★ Castle Howard, Fountains Abbey, Newby Hall, Rievaulx Abbey, Ripon Cathedral, Bolton Abbey, Ryedale Folk Museum

In the centre of North Yorkshire, ¼ mile (400 m) from the main A64 trunk road and 12 miles (19 km) from York

£/$ C

Wood Hall

Wood Hall is so new at time of writing that I have no genuine reports on it, but to find what looks to be a superb country house hotel in the North warrants its inclusion.

Though the house was built in 1750, you'll note a Jacobean wing and a new six-bedroom extension built in Jacobean style, of old stone. The grounds are tremendous — over 100 acres (40 ha) of park and woodland, approached by a private drive.

Wood Hall certainly appears to be comfortably relaxing, with a light and spacious drawing room, dining room and bar and an Italian garden, perfect on a sunny day for a spot of afternoon tea. Food is said to be a major feature, created by a young English chef headhunted from other respected country house hotels.

Linton, nr Wetherby, West Yorkshire LS22 4JA.
✆ (0937) 67271

22 (All individually decorated, including four-poster; each with en suite bathroom, colour TV, mini bar, hair dryer. Some suites.)

Year round

✕ Two fixed-price dinners plus small à la carte selection. Menu Gastronomique available for two or more given 48 hours notice. Choice of 280 wines

✳ Peacefully gracious

Indoor heated pool, sauna, sunbed, billiard room. Croquet, jogging paths, coarse fishing on a mile (1½ km) of the Wharfe, shooting over 800 acres (324 ha), hot air ballooning, archery

♫ No

★ Harrogate Spa, York Cathedral, Yorkshire Dales

9 miles (14 km) from Harrogate, 11 (18 km) from Leeds and 14 (23 km) from York. Take the Harrogate road north for about ½ mile (800 m), turn left to Sicklinghall and Linton. Cross the bridge, turn left again, signed to Linton and Wood Hall. Turn right in the middle of Linton, opposite the Windmill pub

£/$ C

Woodlands Manor

A late Victorian manor, Woodlands is a peaceful hotel yet within a few minutes drive of Bedford's commerce and industry. You can expect comfort without frills in this owner-managed establishment, which has retained the personalised approach of a country house.

Deep-seat armchairs and sofas covered in floral fabrics are to be found in the lounge. The original manor drawing room has since become the hotel's well-proportioned dining room, with enough space between the tables to allow mealtimes to be relaxing and agreeable. It is open for all meals all week except for Saturday lunch and, says management, it's always proud to include roast beef and Yorkshire whatever else the chef dreams up.

Guest rooms overlook the grounds and include a three-roomed suite.

Green Lane, Clapham, Bedfordshire MK41 6EP.
✆ (0234) 63281

21 (Each with en suite bathroom, colour TV, radio, refrigerator bar.) No children under 7. Rates include continental breakfast. Breaks available

Year round

✕ From the slightly adventurous to downright traditional; table d'hôte and à la carte

✻ Pleasant

No

♫ No

★ Woburn Abbey, Cambridge

15 miles (24 km) from Milton Keynes, 2 miles (3 km) from Bedford. Bedford can be reached from London in an hour via the M1 or ¾ hour by train

£/$ D

Le Fregate

A long-time Channel Island favourite, Le Fregate was originally an 18th-century manor house. It fits into the country house category since it is tucked away on a garden hillside overlooking the harbour of St Peter Port and the off-shore islands of Herm, Jethou and Sark. Nevertheless, it is only a five-minute walk from the main part of town.

Guests enjoy the views from the bedrooms, some of which have double-glazed patio windows leading onto private balconies. But the panorama may also be surveyed from Le Fregate's terraced lawns, perhaps over an apertitif or after-dinner coffee.

Décor throughout is of a high standard. One of the hotel's main claims to fame is its French restaurant, which has acquired a reputation for excellence over the years both locally and internationally.

Les Cotils, St Peter Port, Guernsey, Channel Islands.
✆ (0481) 24624

13 (All overlooking the harbour, some with private balcony; all with en suite bathrooms.)

Year round

✕ French

✻ Pleasant island retreat

No, but easy access to island beaches and harbour for fishing and 10 minutes to indoor leisure centre

♫ No

★ The whole of Guernsey (beaches, gardens, shops museums) is on the doorstep

Overlooking St Peter Port harbour, near Candie Gardens, 5 minutes walk from town centre. It may be best to telephone the hotel upon arrival for specific routing instructions

£/$ C

Longueville Manor

Traces of the 13th-century manor house which once stood here are still visible at Longueville, where guests enter under a medieval arch. Its credentials as a very fine country-style hotel have been noted for years, for three generations of the Lewis family have continued to operate it. Malcolm and Hilda Lewis and Simon and Sue Duffy represent the third generation, since Malcolm and Sue's grandparents founded the hotel in 1948.

It is in my opinion the prettiest hotel in Jersey, a gem away from the bucket-and-spade holiday air of the rest of the island, with its own secluded swimming pool, and inside, an air of delicate refinement.

Both the library and dining room boast 17th-century oak panelling. The Jacobean heavy wood in the inner part of the restaurant is highlighted by primrose linen and fresh flowers, and opens onto a large sunny room facing the gardens. The chef takes advantage of Jersey's fresh fish and the vegetables and herbs from the manor's own garden to prepare fancy but light dishes, and Simon Duffy offers a daily selection of suggested wines. In summer, lunch and/or drinks may be taken on the terrace at poolside.

Polished antique furniture, Jersey prints and oriental rugs can be found in the public rooms — the Manor Bar is furnished with sofas and armchairs in soft, grey and plum-coloured velvet. In winter log fires add a cheering touch.

Guest rooms and suites, named after roses, are distinctive in décor, and will certainly appeal to the ladies. The Lewis family have always given attention to detail and colour schemes, and it shows.

St Saviour, Jersey, Channel Islands. ✆ (0534) 25501

34 (Including 2 suites; each individually furnished with en suite bathroom and thoughtful extras.) No children under 7. Rates include breakfast

Year round

5-course, degustation and vegetarian menus plus à la carte. Excellent farmhouse cheese selection, and plenty of fresh fish. Sample dishes: fillets of sole with warm crab gratin, wild mushroom soup, iced strawberry roulade

Refined style

Outdoor heated pool; nearby golf and beaches

No

Gerald's Durrell's Wildlife Preservation Trust and all the other attractions of Jersey are within easy reach

6 miles (10 km) from Jersey Airport. Take the B36 from here, then A12, then A1 to St Helier. Near the harbour follow the signs for the Tunnel and the East A17 to Georgetown, then A3 to Longueville and Gorey for ½ mile (800 m). The manor is on the left

£/$ A

SCOTLAND

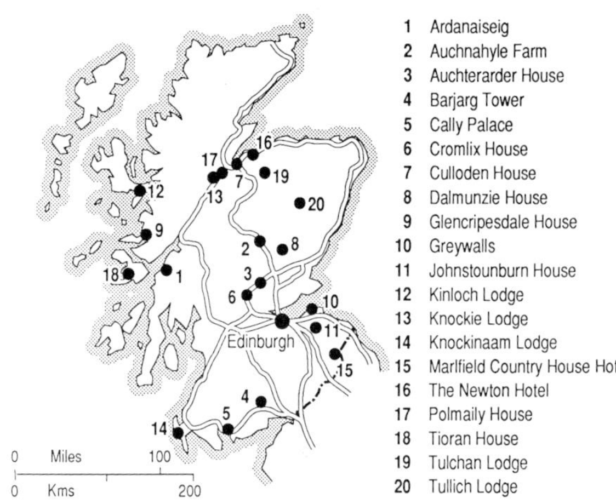

Scotland's country house hotels are a fine and variable breed. Many of the converted castles will be found in *Europe's Historic Castle and Palace Hotels*, but there are numerous other establishments that can certainly be recommended for overnight stops on tour or a longer restful break. When you do make a selection, be sure you have done some homework with a map first — a good proportion of Scottish hotels are tucked away in very rural and rugged corners, which may take a while to reach if travelling by road.

You can expect good value for money and hearty meals, especially from those hostelries which contribute to the 'Taste of Scotland' scheme. Because Scotland is so noted for its fishing and shooting, these facilities are also at hand in many cases, though you are less likely to find quite the number of swimming pools featured by English country house hotels.

Ardanaiseig

For a long time this gracious mansion, set in the heart of the mountainous region ruled by the Campbell Clan for centuries, has been a family home. It was built by Col. James Archibald Campbell in 1834, who was so enamoured of the setting on the shores of Loch Awe that he planted what was to become a great garden.

The walled garden, covering an acre (½ ha), was and still is used for fruit and vegetable-growing. Above, a network of paths lead through the woods — the main path leads past the side of the house and down to the Loch below the terraces.

Under Campbell hands the house was called 'New Inverawe', but the name was changed to Ardanaiseig (the Gaelic name for the point of land near which it was built) after Col. Campbell's death in 1879. The exterior of the Grade II listed building remains virtually unchanged, though the interior had to be modified when the house became a hotel.

You'll find the public rooms of good proportion and comfortably furnished with large chintzy chairs, polished tables and fresh flowers. Bedrooms are simply decorated and service is unobtrusive. A recommended centre for touring much of the west coast's dramatic scenery.

Kilchrenan, by Taynuilt, Argyll. ✆ (08663) 333

14 (Each with en suite bathroom.) No children under 8. Rates are half board

🏨 Easter to Oct

✕ Table d'hôte menu features Scottish fare. Jacket and tie requested

✻ Quietly scenic

⚲ Billiard room; highland croquet, tennis court, clay pigeon trap, fishing

♫ Do it yourself on the grand piano

★ From the port of Oban trips are possible to the Inner Hebrides

🚗 On the shores of Loch Awe. Take B845 from Taynuilt

£/$ C half board

Auchterarder House

A 'B' listed mansion in 17 acres (7 ha) that was built for Lt-Col. James Hunter in 1831, designed by famous Scottish architect William Burn (who was responsible for a drastic renovation of St Giles Cathedral in 1829). Burn's plans called for a two-storey building capped by crow-stepped gables in the Scottish Jacobean style, the oldest portion of what you see today.

In 1887, under the ownership of a James Reid, the south wing and terraces were added and the interior decorated in sumptuous Renaissance style. (His art collection however can be found in the Glasgow Art Galleries.) Today, this fancy Victorian house belongs to the Brown family. One of the most handsome public rooms is the old library, a baronial room no longer the domain of only the men! Dominated by a large billiard table, it features seating by a large fireplace at one end. Double doors at the other end open onto the croquet lawn, and a sideboard serves as the room's own cocktail bar.

Light, live music is offered each evening in the drawing room; alternatively the library with its collection of books is the place to sit and relax alone. The Winter Gardens Restaurant is the original marble and mosaic conservatory. The lovely centrepiece fountain gives it a summer setting even when nights draw in early. But there is also a formal dining room where Scottish specialities are served.

Of the eleven bedrooms here, five are spacious original Master Rooms. The Graham room, for example, is fitted with walnut furniture from 1900; similarly the Gordon Room is fitted with 1900 mahogany furniture in both bedroom and bathroom. In the Stuart Room there's a magnificent marble bathroom with the original shower dating from 1900. Bathrooms in the Cunningham Room, the Gordon Room and the Scott Room all have original fireplaces.

Auchterarder, nr Gleneagles, Perthshire PH3 1DZ.
✆ (0764) 62939

11 (All named and individually designed, including a suite; each with en suite bathroom and colour TV.) Rates include Scottish breakfast

Year round

✕ Fixed-price and à la carte. Sample starters: snail casserole or peppered avocado and nut terrine; sample main course: roast breast of grouse; sample dessert: chocolate chestnut terrine

✻ Splendid Victorian

Pitch and putt, croquet lawn; golf, shooting and fishing may be arranged

♫ Nightly music in the drawing room

★ Glenruthven Weaving Mill and Heritage Centre, Strathallan Air Museum, Glenturret Distillery

2 miles (3 km) from Gleneagles Golf Couse on the B8062 road

£/$ C

Auchnahyle Farm

If you're touring Scotland and want a cosy, family-style hostelry in which to overnight, I reckon this is quite a find. There has been a house at Auchnahyle since the 16th century when the land belonged to Dumfermline Abbey, though the buildings you see today are from a later period. The farmhouse itself is Penny and Alastair Howman's home, but there is also a stone cottage where visitors may stay, traditional stone barns and a circular horse mill built around a central courtyard.

Auchnahyle is a member of the Wolsey Lodge Scheme as well as 'Taste of Scotland', so you can be pretty sure that Penny's food is really good. Dinner by candlelight always includes a starter, main course, sweet, cheese and coffee.

The cottage accommodation is sufficient for five people, with its own dining room, sitting room and colour TV, kitchen, garden and pay phone.

Pitlochry, Perthshire PH16 5JA. ✆ (0796) 2318

3 in main house (2 twins with shared bathroom, coffee/tea making facility, third twin with en suite bathroom.) Rowan Tree Cottage has space for five with full facilities including colour TV, fridge, washing machine etc. No under 12s in main house

Easter to Sept

✕ Traditional Scottish breakfasts. Fixed-price dinners by advanced request — four courses using local fare. Picnic lunches also available

✻ Family friendly

No

♫ No

Between Moulin and Pitlochry, surrounded by farmland. Coming from the south, take the A9 to Pitlochry, under the railway bridge and turn right along the East Moulin road. Continue up the hill, take the fourth turning right — bearing right at the end to Auchnahyle

£/$ E

Barjarg Tower

At the time of writing Barjarg Tower (almost a castle) had been open only for a few months, so further comments about the property would be particularly welcome. If it lives up to its claims it could well be a find for the discerning traveller headed on tour of Scotland.

The name means 'The Red Hill Top Fort'. The original Peel Tower, forming the northeast corner of the house, was built by the Earl of Morton in the 16th century with walls several feet (over a metre) thick and an enclosed stone spiral stair. The house itself was added to in the early 19th century — much of the oak panelling to be seen in the public rooms was carved by Belgian refugees who came to the district during World War I.

The approach to the front door is via a long drive which runs uphill through a wooded portion of the 40-acre (16 ha) grounds before winding up to the balustraded gravel sweep in front of the entrance. Interior designer James Noble has used fabrics to complement the existing oak panelling, and there are four separate lounges for those who seek a degree of privacy.

In the oak-panelled dining room, where a dinner menu offers a small number of choices for each course, there is a feature fireplace reputed to be a copy of one in the old Scottish palace of Holyrood House. Within the carving over the mantel is the coat-of-arms of the Hunter Arundell family who lived here in 1825.

Auldgirth, Dumfriesshire DG2 OTN. ✆ (0848) 31545

10 (8 doubles, 2 singles, all doubles with private bathrooms. Each room has colour TV, trouser press and hair dryer.) Rates include full breakfast. Unsuitable for young children

Mid-Feb to mid-Jan

Cordon bleu French classic. Using salmon from the River Nith, Galloway beef, home-grown vegetables etc. Wine list has good selection of chateau-bottled claret

Attentive intimate

First-class fishing on the Nith and shooting in season at several local estates. Golf courses at Thornhill, Powfoot and Southerness

No

The Gardens at Threave, Drumlanrig Castle (ancestral home of the Dukes of Buccleuch), Maxwelton House (Annie Laurie's home), Ellisland Farm (where Robert Burns once lived)

In unspoilt Nithsdale, 11 miles (18 km) north of Dumfries, 35 miles (56 km) from the Scottish/English border. Travellers from the south should turn left off the main A76 at Auldgirth onto a road signposed to Dunscore and Penpont. Half a mile (800 m) up the hill, turn right signed to Penpont and Keir. From the north take the Moniaive road from Thornhill (A702) and turn left at Penpont

£/$ C

Cally Palace Hotel

Its looks match its name, with a frontage made impressive by massive granite pillars erected in 1835, the granite being quarried at Craigdeus, near Newton Stewart and conveyed here with great labour. The original entrance was on the other side of the house, up the balustraded flight of stone steps, leading to the French window of the bow-fronted middle portion of the house made of whitish, dressed Creetown granite finished with rose-pink sandstone around the windows. The site that former owner James Murray chose is still beautiful, overlooking the Galloway Hills. Many specimen trees may be seen in the grounds, which were initially laid out by William Dewar, who studied landscaping at Kew Gardens.

Gatehouse of Fleet, Dumfries and Galloway DG7 2DL.
✆ (05574) 341

60 (Each with en suite bathroom and colour TV; some suites.) Rates are half board. Breaks available

🏨 Year round

✕ Traditional Scottish. Collar and tie requested

✳ Sport orientated

🎾 Outdoor heated pool, sauna, sun bed. Fishing in the hotel's own loch. An agreement with 3 local golf courses allow guests to play: the Gatehouse of Fleet Golf Club's 9-hole course; Kirkcudbright's 18 holes and Newton Stewart's 9 holes. Pony-trekking also nearby

♫ No

★ The Solway Coast, Cardoness Castle, Carsluith Castle, the gardens of Threave House, Cairnsmore of Fleet nature reserve

🚗 From the M6 join the A74 highway just north of Carlisle. Cross the border at Gretna, then take the A75 to Cally. The hotel is 1 mile (1½ km) from the village of Gatehouse of Fleet

£/$ C but half board

Cromlix House

The Eden family has owned this Scottish baronial mansion and its 5,000-acre (2,024 ha) estate for four centuries, but it was only in 1980 they decided to convert it into a hotel. The present structure was built in 1880, considerably altered and extended in 1903, and has hosted many distinguished visitors including King Edward VII.

Much of the southwest wing remains in its original form with contents and furnishings, including fine prints, paintings, porcelain, silver and glassware, all acquired over several generations — dating from the 17th century to present times. Public rooms include a large, hunting-trophy-adorned entrance hall, handsomely panelled; a spacious refined drawing room; and dining room — all with open fires. The library is a peaceful reader's retreat when not being used for a board meeting.

Kinbuck, Dunblane, Perthshire FK15 9JT.
✆ (0786) 822125

14	(Including 8 suites; each with en suite bathroom and colour TV.) Rates include breakfast
🏨	Year round
✕	5-course, set menu using country house recipes, featuring locally caught salmon and estate game as well as Scottish beef and lamb
✻	Baronial
⚲	Hard tennis court, fishing in estate's 4 private lochs; riding and shooting may be arranged
♫	No
★	Stirling Castle, Wallace's Monument, Doune Castle, Stuart Crystal Factory, Kilmabog Woollen Mill
🚗	½ mile (800 m) north of Kinbuck, 3 miles (5 km) south of Braco. Take the A9 out of Dunblane, turn left onto B8033. Go through Kinbuck village and turn second left after the small bridge
£/$	A

Culloden House

A part of Scottish history, Culloden House was originally a Jacobean castle. Bonnie Prince Charlie made it his home and headquarters for three days before the tragic Battle of Culloden. He, of course, had not time to linger, but undoubtedly he would have approved of the facilities today's guests may enjoy.

Deep-cushioned comfort and warm colours soften the grandeur of the ornate ceilings and gleaming chandeliers in the public rooms. Bedrooms are delightful, as befits a member of the Prestige consortium — many with curtain-framed beds or four-posters. Today, the dungeons aren't for prisoners — instead, they house a sauna and solarium, and there's tennis in the 40 acres (16 ha) of parkland.

Inverness IV1 2NZ. ✆ (0463) 790461

20 (Include suite and four-posters; each with en suite bathroom and colour TV.) Rates include Scottish breakfast

Year round

Specialities include game, salmon and country house fare

Historic quality

Sauna, solarium, tennis, squash; nearby golf and riding

No

Culloden Battlefield

1 mile (1½ km) south off A96, adjacent to Culloden village

£/$ A

Dalmunzie House

Built in 1907 for summer use, it was converted into a hotel by the Winton family in 1946. Dalmunzie is tucked away in the hills in a Highland estate reached by private driveway. This mountain estate comprises 6,000 acres (2,428 ha), attracting those who like to fish and shoot, but the hotel also has its own golf course.

It is a restful place, where Simon and Alexandra Winton say they're happy to cater to requests for snacks and beverages at any time of day. There's no better place to relax than the Fire Lounge or Smoke Room, while the Scottish fare comes fresh from the surrounding hills and lochs.

Spittal O'Glenshee, Blairgowrie, Perthshire PH10 7QG.
✆ (025085) 224

20 (Most with en suite bathrooms.) Rates include Scottish breakfast

🏛 Jan to mid-Oct

✕ Typically Scottish, fresh from the lochs and hills

✻ Restful Scottish hideaway

🏌 Private golf course; nearby skiing

♫ No

★ Braemar, Balmoral, Pitlochry, Scone Palace

🚗 On the A93 from Aberdeen, close to Braemar and a few minutes drive from the Glenshee Ski Centre

£/$ D

Glencripesdale House

Some call it splendid isolation, for 18th-century Glencripesdale House lies at the end of an 8-mile (13 km) forest track, overlooking Loch Sunart, with not another building or telephone wire in sight. It therefore will not suit everybody: there is no village shop to pop in and there is no television.

You can take out the fibreglass dinghy on the loch to fish, or a sailboard if you have your own wetsuit. An inflatable dinghy with outboard motor may be rented for longer exploratory trips or for scuba diving. Sensible shoes are necessary for those who plan to enjoy walks in the surrounding moorland and hills.

We should point out that postal service is periodic as collection is by boat from over the loch, and that use of electrical appliances is by arrangement since the generator capacity is limited.

Loch Sunart, Acharacle, Argyll PH36 4JH.
✆ (096785) 263

4 (Each with en suite facility.) Rates are full board

Year round

✕ Down to earth Scottish fare; vegetarian menus on request. Limited hotel licence

✻ Solitude

Walking, bird watching, fishing the loch, sailboards

♫ No

★ Fauna and flora of the unspoilt peninsula of Morvern; strictly scenic and for nature-lovers

In Morvern on the south side of Loch Sunart. Visitors can be met at Fort William by arrangement for a small fee. Driving instructions on request

£/$ B Full board

Greywalls

This singularly attractive hotel close to Edinburgh was designed as a private residence for the Hon. Alfred Lyttleton by the famous architect Sir Edwin Lutyens. His imaginative partner, Gertrude Jekyll, laid out the gardens. When William James purchased Greywalls in 1905 he had the lodges built at the gate as staff accommodation, and late, in 1911, commissioned leading Scottish architect Sir Robert Lorimer to build-on the 'Nursery' wing.

Kind Edward VII frequently came here to visit Mrs James, but the only memorial left to him is hidden in the garden and known as the King's Loo — which it was, but now is staff accommodation.

Much praise goes to the reception rooms in the main house, particularly the panelled library with its open fire, but the older guest bedrooms are more pleasing than the newer ones.

Muirfield, Gullane, East Lothian EH31 2EG.
✆ (062084) 2144

23 (Mostly double, each with private bathroom and colour TV.) Rates include breakfast

Mid-Apr to end Oct

✕ Table d'hôte and à la carte, including Scottish specialities

✻ Leading country hotel elegance

Tennis and croquet in the grounds; 10 golf courses with easy reach. Shooting and fishing also nearby

♫ No

★ Edinburgh Castle and other attractions; Tantallon Castle and the bird sanctuary at Bass Rock

19 miles (31 km) east of Edinburgh on the A198

£/$ B

Johnstounburn House Hotel

Since 1625 Johnstounburn House has been in private hands, a charming historic house. Twentieth-century touches have been added discreetly, and the friendly, helpful service befits a country mansion.

The oldest part of the house is still the main part. The panelled dining room with its fine moulded ceiling dates from 1740. Given sufficient notice the chef here will cater to any special needs or preferences, but if you seek a lighter meal, say for lunch, there's a less substantial choice in the Garden Room or on the terrace overlooking the Lammermuir Hills.

Johnstounburn's dovecote is listed as an 18th-century Historic Monument — the house itself completed as it looks today in 1840 with the addition of the main tower. The Burn flows through the encircling parkland, which features old walled gardens.

Humbie, East Lothian EH36 5PL. ✆ (087533) 696

11 (Each with en suite bathroom, colour TV, radio.) Rates include continental breakfast

Year round

× Table d'hôte and à la carte, featuring local fresh seafood and game. Small, careful wine list

✻ Helpfully friendly

Fishing can be arranged; golf courses easily reached

♫ No

★ Edinburgh, 14th-century Tantallon Castle, Sir Walter Scott's home at Abbotsford, Traquair House

On the edge of the Lammermuir Hills, 15 miles (24 km) south of Edinburgh. From the latter take the A68 through Dalkeith and Pathhead to Fala. Turn left onto B6457. After 1½ miles (2½ km), turn right at T junction

£/$ C

Kinloch Lodge Hotel

A white-painted shooting lodge that has long been personally supervised by Lord and Lady Macdonald — titled but genial hosts. Sir Alexander Macdonald (late to become a Lord) built it in 1730 at the head of the beautiful wooded Sleat peninsula, from where there are panoramic views across the Loch na Dal to the dramatic mountains of Knoydart on the mainland and Skye's famous Cuillin Ridge to the west.

Guests who have stayed here before say the weather doesn't matter — the log fires and Lord Macdonald's impressive collection of malts is cheering and warming. Assisted by a kitchen team, Lady Macdonald thrives on food preparation (she is herself an enthusiastic cookbook writer). You won't be offered an extensive à la carte choice, but what there is proves good and imaginative. Almost all the items are homemade, from the coarse, brown bread and breakfast scones to the unusual soups and patés, not to mention the exotic ice creams and after-dinner fudge.

Guest rooms are on the small side, but children and pets are surprisingly welcome.

Sleat, Isle of Skye IV43 8QY. ✆ (04713) 214

10 (Mostly with baths; each with tea/coffee facility, hair dryer and electric blanket.) Rates include breakfast

Year round, except for Xmas and New Year

✕ Fixed-price meal with local food and prawns from the Minch, grouse from the moors

✻ Cosy

Nearby golf, sailing, fishing, rough shooting

♫ No

★ The island itself, also a starting point for a visit to the Outer Hebrides

1 mile (1½ km) off A851, 6 miles (10 km) south of Broadford, 10 miles (17 km) north of Armadale ferry. Four flights weekly from Glasgow

£/$ C

Knockie Lodge

In a privileged position overlooking Loch Nan Lann and the rugged slopes of Beinn A'Bhacaidh, stands Knockie Lodge, built as a hunting lodge in 1789 for the Chief of the Clan Fraser. Protected by forested hills where larch, pine and birch grow, this hotel's situation is one of exceptional beauty and repose without being isolated.

This is sport country, as fish and game records to be seen in the entrance hall will attest to.

Knockie isn't a noisy or lively place but it is a friendly one — the Milwards who live here enjoy sharing their antique furniture and family belongings with guests, who are expected to treat the hotel as their home. Dinner is an unhurried five-course, no-choice affair by candlelight at polished antique tables, and the bedrooms are simply but comfortably furnished in a typical lodge style.

Recommended for those who plan to tour the Northern Highlands.

Whitebridge, Inverness-shire IV1 2UO. ✆ (04563) 276

10 (7 twins, 1 double, 2 singles; each with en suite bathroom.) Rates are half board. No children under 10

Apr to Oct

✕ Simple Scottish fare in five-course, no-choice menus; dinner is at 8 p.m.

✻ Peaceful seclusion

Free trout fishing in hotel's lochs; nearby golf

♫ No

★ The gardens at Inverewe, Cawdor, Brodie, Dunrobin and Urquhart castles; the Speyside whisky trail and the Culloden battlefields

A 20-minute walk from Loch Ness off the B862 road from Fort Augustus

£/$ D

Knockinaam Lodge Hotel

It may seem odd to find a British country house hotel run by a French couple, but this is precisely so at Knockinaam Lodge where Marcel and Corinna Frichot are the resident owners. It was Marcel, himself a chef, who converted this property into a 'restaurant with rooms' in 1971, soon establishing an excellent reputation for fine fare. His food is good, and so is the view from the dining room with the sea breaking over the rocks at the end of the lawn.

Knockinaam was built for Lady Hunter Blair in 1869 as a holiday home set in a secluded position at the food of a wooded glen, surrounded on three sides by cliffs.

Today, with 10 rooms, it is a quietly romantic base from which to explore an unspoiled corner of Scotland that benefits from the mild climate engendered by the Gulf Stream. The garden itself runs down to a private sandy beach from which you can see the Irish coastline in the distance.

Portpatrick, Wigtownshire DG9 9AD. ✆ (077681) 471

10	(Including half-testers; each with en suite bathroom and colour TV.) Rates are half board
🏨	Easter to Dec
✕	French flair. 4-course, set-price menu. No children under 11 in dining room. Jacket and tie requested
✱	Pleasant isolation
🏸	Croquet, fishing nearby
♫	No
★	Gardens like Logan, Castle Kennedy and Ardwell are the main atraction
🚗	Off the A77 from Glasgow (a 2-hour drive). From the M6 to Carlisle take the A75.
£/$	C

Marlefield Country House Hotel

It is thought that Marlefield (now a listed historic building) was originally a 13th-century Peel Tower; however, detailed records stem only from the 17th century, when it was the property of the Bennet family. Sir William Bennet was said to be a man of great taste and achievement, and many of the trees he planted are features of the garden today.

Converted to a hotel in 1984, this is a tranquil place to stay mid its own 4 acres (1½ ha) of gardens and surrounded by thousands of acres (ha) of carefully tended farmland and the rolling Cheviot Hills. Magnificent fireplaces are key features in the public rooms — log fires are lit during most of the year. Views from the windows are superb; guest bedrooms are pleasant and comfortable, and the restaurant is of particular note. As the Willoughbys, who run Marlefield today, say: 'Our philosophy is simple — to provide comfortable, peaceful and beautiful surroundings with standards of cuisine that exceed our customer's expectations.'

Eckford, nr Kelso, Roxburghshire TD5 8ED. ✆ (05734) 561

7 (6 double or twin, 1 suite; each with en suite bathroom, colour TV, coffee/tea facility.) Rates include English breakfast. Special breaks available

Year round

✕ Table d'hôte and à la carte Scottish fare

✻ Border-country peace

Shooting, fishing can be arranged

♫ No

★ Edinburgh, Berwick, Carlisle and Newcastle are all within one hour's drive

Midway between Jedburgh and Kelso

£/$ C

The Newton Hotel

The Newton Hotel is a combination of both castle and Georgian mansion, imposingly Scottish baronial in 27 acres (11 ha) of secluded grounds overlooking the Moray Firth and the Ross-shire hills.

The panelled hall leads to a peaceful library and writing room and other reception rooms with period furniture, often upholstered in velvet. Some of the ceiling cornices are Victorian works of art themselves.

A tree-lined drive leads from the main road to The Newton's entrance door — steps away are the hotel's tennis court and putting green. The former granary sheltered by tall trees a few yards (metres) from the main door has been converted into a quadrangle with 14 bedrooms known as Newton Court, a complex which also houses a sauna, solarium and exercise room.

Nairn 12 4RX. ✆ (0667) 53144

42	(Each with en suite bathroom, colour TV.)	♫	No
🏨	Year round	★	Loch Ness, Glen Affric, Cawdor Castle and Culloden Battlefield
✕	Table d'hôte and à la carte; fresh local fish emphasised	🚗	20-minute drive from Inverness. Take the A82 road to Nairn or from Aberdeen the A96
✻	Baronial, but not offputting	£/$	C
⚲	Sauna, solarium, exercise room, tennis court, 9-hole putting green; squash, fishing, golf can be arranged locally		

Polmaily House

This rambling Edwardian house owned by Alison and Nick Parsons doesn't have a hotel feel about it, but its homely comforts are its virtues. For example, the Parsons don't call the room where you might sit and read, a library, but a 'book room', and the drawing room with its chintz covered chairs is the place to sit with a drink after the day's activities. The restaurant offers short à la carte menus which Alison prepares.

Most of the guest rooms have a private bathroom and some are suitable for family use. The 18 acres (7¼ ha) of grounds include a pool and tennis court for guests' use, and there are plenty of deckchairs for the less energetic. This is a good-value stopover for anyone touring the Scottish Highlands who doesn't want a baronial resting place.

Drumnadrochit, Inverness-shire IV3 6XT. ✆ (04562) 343

9 (7 with en suite bathrooms, some with double and single beds, including four-poster.) Rates include breakfast

Easter to mid-Oct

✕ Short à la carte menus include fresh seafood and game

✻ Homely

Outdoor swimming pool and hard tennis court; fishing, shooting and pony-trekking can be arranged locally

♫ No

★ Glen Affric beauty spot, Culloden Battlefield, Cawdor and Brodie Castles, Fort George; Skye is within a day's trip

3 miles (5 km) west of Drumnadrochit on the A831 Cannich road, 1 mile (1½ km) beyond the tiny village of Milton on the slopes of Glen Urquhart

£/$ C

Tiroran House

Tiroran House stands in a gloriously isolated position facing south across the waters of Loch Scridain. Originally a sporting lodge, it is now the home of the Blockeys, who have furnished it with their own family antiques and silver and accept guests only between May and October.

The 13 acres (5 ha) of gardens and woodlands sweep right down to the loch where the hotel has its own dinghies and boat for day trips. Tiroran's position on the Ardmeanach Peninsula gives immediate access to some of Mull's wildest and most splendid scenery, and the National Trust Reserve 5 miles away is accessible only on foot or by boat.

Pre-dinner drinks are served in the gracious drawing room and dinner is served promptly at 7.45 p.m. You won't find a TV, room phones, musak or even a newspaper in this ultra quiet and rural lodge, so it's not the place for everyone. It is, on the other hand, a wonderful place to see red deer and other wildlife, and enjoy unsullied open air.

Tiroran, Isle of Mull, Argyllshire PA69 6ES. ✆ (06815) 232

9	(Each with en suite bathroom, radio, tea/coffee facility.) Rates include breakfast. No children under 10
🏨	May to early Oct
✕	Table d'hôte; packed lunches commended
✻	Somewhat remote
⚲	Swimming, sailing and boating on the loch
♫	No
★	Picturesque Tobermory, Torosay Castle, Duart Castle, Old Byre Museum
🚗	45 minutes from the Oban-Craignure car ferry. By car, head for Stirling, then the A84/85 via Callandar and Crianlarich to Oban
£/$	C

Tulchan Lodge

For many fishing and shooting enthusiasts, Tulchan Lodge is a dream of a Scottish baronial estate in its commanding position overlooking the Spey Valley. It was originally built in 1906 — apart from the justly famous salmon and sea-trout fishing on the Tulchan Water, the Tulchan and Cromdale grouse moors were also known as some of the best in the UK, attracting much Royal patronage. King Edward VII came here on numerous occasions, both as prince and as king; so did King George V and King George VI (when he was Duke of York). A reminder of those royal days still exists in the tall flagstaff from which the Royal Standard was flown when the king was present, clearly seen from the Lodge looking west. Other reminders are 'King Edward's Hut' on 'A' beat and the 'batterys' which enabled the Prince of Wales to 'Spey Cast' without having to wade the river.

Today the Lodge is a splendid sportsman's base, with a noteworthy interior hung with paintings and firearms and further adorned with fine porcelain and objets d'art. A handsome panelled hall and library, discreet drawing room and a billiards room with full-sized table are all for guests' use, along with two dining rooms gleaming with silver candelabra and crystal.

The estate provides all fishing and shooting necessities, for purchase or hire — you'll find a well-equipped fly room, gun room and a strong room (for firearms storage). Some of the UK's best pheasant shooting is available here, with drives designed to provide visiting game shots with high birds and testing shooting. Also good duck-flighting and carefully controlled roe deer-stalking. By arrangement, guests may use the 300-metre rifle range or opt for clay pigeon shooting.

Recently refurbished, this house in the midst of the Highland malt whisky distilling country, a setting of mountain rivers, pine forests and open moorland, may also be the choice for non-sporting guests who just wish to relax. The garden cottage suite accommodation is excellent as a retreat. Tulchan is also an ideal touring base for northeast Scotland, an area steeped in history.

Advie, Grantown-on-Spey, Morayshire PH26 3PW.
✆ (08075) 200

11 (Individually decorated and sized; and with en suite bathroom.) Rates are half board

Apr to Jan

Set menus concentrate on prime Scottish beef and lamb, game from the estate, fresh local seafood, vegetables from the garden. Good wine cellar. Jacket and tie necessary

Outdoor-sport orientated

On the 22,000-acre (8,903 ha) estate salmon and sea-trout fishing, in-season grouse, duck and pheasant shooting. Also roe-buck stalking

No

★ Cawdor Castle (immortalised in Shakespeare's *Macbeth*), Culloden Moor (where Bonnie Prince Charlie was defeated in 1746). The dramatic Moray Firth coastline lies to the north, Balmoral to the south

On the north bank of the River Spey, opposite the village of Advie, 9 miles (14½ km) from the centre of Grantown on the B9102 and 10 miles (16 km) southwest of Aberlour on the A95. The main A9 Perth to Inverness trunk road is some 10 miles (16 km) southwest of Grantown

£/$ A but half board

Tullich Lodge

In many ways the sign of a good country house hotel is a long-standing proprietor — it shows the guests keep returning and therefore the product is good. So I am delighted to find Neil Bannister and Hector Macdonald still running Tullich Lodge, which they bought in 1968, so smoothly. It is not everyone's idea of total bliss (bedrooms are somewhat small and there's no choice of menu), but the connoisseur who treats it as a private home and uses it as a base for more than one night, will appreciate the Lodge's refined homeliness.

The lodge, built of pink granite from a local quarry, was first begun in 1897 for Aberdeen lawyer William Reid, sited on a wooded knoll overlooking the River Dee. It was later enlarged by another Scot who made his fortune in India. Little remains of the village of Tullich, from which the house took its name, but at one time it was the oldest Royal Burgh on Deeside, a settlement since Pictish times.

Though Tullich is crenellated and turreted with a tower whose bedroom is only suited to the fit, the Lodge is neither imposing nor foreboding. Inside, the elegant drawing room is furnished in keeping to the period of the house, with fine views from its first floor windows over the Coyles of Muick to Lochnagar, immortalised by Byron — once a volcano, whose crater is now a deep loch. Across the landing a pretty sitting room featuring lots of chintz, contains books for guests to browse through.

A friendly little bar with its peat fire is, I can promise, the most popular gathering place for drinks and conversation pre-or post-dinner. Very informal, most convivial. It is here guests gather to ponder menu and wine list before moving into a handsomely appointed dining room, panelled in mahogany and appropriately proportioned, where tables are set with crisp linen, silver and fine crystal. Back in the 1970s I argued with Neil about the concept of a no-choice menu, but his ideas haven't changed so you're still in for a nightly surprise. However, all food is freshly prepared and variety is provided by the seasons themselves. Most vegetables come from the property's kitchen garden; fish from Aberdeen and Buckie; meat from the local butcher. Given warning, vegetarian and diet requirements can be catered for.

The Deeside roads, relatively traffic-free, continue to make motoring an enjoyable experience, and there is good hill-walking, climbing and golfing in the area.

By Ballater, Aberdeenshire AB3 5SB. ✆ (0338) 55406

10	(All with en suite facilities.) Rates include English breakfast	♫	No
	Apr to Nov	★	Balmoral Castle, Braemar
✕	No-choice, fixed-price menu featuring seasonal produce, e.g. county salmon, sea trout, grouse, pheasant and grouse. No-smoking dining room. Jacket and tie necessary		1 mile (1½ km) east of Ballater on the A93 Aberdeen to Braemar road; not far from the royal summer residence of Balmoral
✳	Friendly, private home style	£/$	A
	None on site but plenty nearby		

WALES

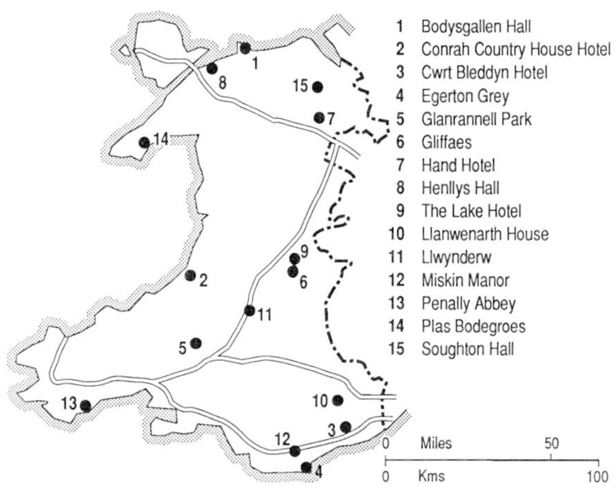

Only in recent years has Wales claimed country house hotels in the luxury category — now there are several well worth investigating. Tourists are now aware that Wales is not as inaccessible as they might have imagined; and while the local economy may not be so buoyant as in other parts of the country, the splendid scenery, the force of Welsh history and the genuinely warm welcome have encouraged visitors to see this part of Britain for themselves.

Some of the most charming and individualistic properties have been helped by the production of a brochure *Welsh Rarebits*, now in its fifth year. Some of these hotels (all small and privately owned) are mentioned here and may be booked through a central booking service: City Travel Ltd, 13 Duke St, Cardiff, tel: (0222) 395317 and in the US through the Wales Reservation Service, tel: 1-800-444-9988.

Don't expect gimmicks or discounts, though the better-known (and slightly larger) hotels like Bodysgallen Hall do feature special weekends on occasion.

Bodysgallen Hall

On the side of a hill looking down on the grandeur of Conwy Castle stands a country house hotel that is the ultimate for anyone visiting Wales.

Bodysgallen still has a 13th-century tower, splendid Elizabethan and Jacobean rooms with oak panelling and marvellous fireplaces, and mullioned windows. Two of the most notable rooms are the large, flagstoned entrance hall and the first floor drawing room, both oak panelled. The hotel also features two dining rooms, one generally used for private parties, a bar and a library.

There are 7 acres (3 ha) of formal gardens, which include a rare 17th-century Knot Garden of box hedges and scented herbs, a rockery with cascade and an 18th-century, walled rose garden. A further 40 acres (16 ha) of parkland surrounding the hotel have been purchased and is being replanted with oak and ash trees.

Llandudno, Gwynedd LL30 1RS. ✆ (0492) 84466

19 plus 9 cottage suites (including four-posters, individually decorated; each with en suite bathroom and colour TV; tea/coffee facilities in cottages.) No children under 8. Rates include early-morning tea, newspaper and continental breakfast. Special breaks available

Year round

✕ Bill of fare includes many traditional English and Welsh dishes. Jacket and tie requested

✻ Atmospheric and hospitable

Tennis and croquet in the grounds, sailing in Conwy Harbour

♫ No

★ Castles at Conwy, Caernarfon, Harlech and Beaumaris; National Trust properties at Plas Newydd on Anglesey, Penrhyn Castle and Bodnant Gardens

47 miles ($75\frac{1}{2}$ km) from Chester. The nearest station is Llandudno Junction. By road take the A55 to Llandudno and turn right on the B5115

£/$ A

Conrah Country House

Hidden away at the end of a tree and rhododendron-lined drive, Conrah Country Hotel is a country mansion with 18th-century origins. In 1753 it would have looked like a traditional Welsh farmhouse, but it was remodelled in the late 1860s to incorporate larger, more symmetrical rooms. The result was an imposing residence with a commanding view of the slopes of the Vale of Ystwyth. A 1911 fire considerably damaged the property, necessitating new construction. What is now the main banqueting area (the old billiard room), the outbuildings and gardens do remain from the old mansion, but the rest is 20th century.

Thirteen bedrooms are found in the main house, but there are also adjoining motel rooms in Magnolia Court annexe and a cottage suitable for families. Wherever you stay, you have use of the residents' lounges, cocktail bar and restaurant. The grounds comprise 22 acres (9 ha) — mansion window views look onto clipped lawns and sheep pasture.

Rhydgaled, Chancery, Aberystwyth, Dyfed SY23 4DF.
✆ (0970) 617941

13 in the main house (Most with en suite bathroom; each room has colour TV and tea/coffee facility.) Rates include breakfast

Year round

✕ Thoroughly Welsh fare

✻ Country comfort

Indoor heated pool and sauna in the grounds, table tennis in the summer house, lawn croquet

♫ No

★ Aberystwyth, the main resort on Cardigan Bay

3 miles (5 km) south of Aberystwyth, a few yards (metres) off the main A487 road

£/$ C

Cwrt Bleddyn Hotel

If you're looking for a reasonably sized country house hotel in Wales that isn't too grand but does have lots of facilities, Cwrt Bleddyn could be your answer. Originally it was a 17th-century manor, since extended of course. The Oak Room (now a function room) is in the oldest part of the house, as you can tell from its exquisite hand-carved oak panelling.

You will still find that this gabled house holds many treasures, including an old staircase that leads to nowhere and three period bedrooms, including a four-poster. There is also a self-contained cottage in the 17-acre (7 ha) grounds.

Recently the hotel opened a health and leisure complex for which its guests have temporary membership.

In its pastoral border country setting, this is a good base for exploring Wales.

Llangybi, nr Usk, Gwent NP5 1PG. ✆ (063349) 521

30 (Including period rooms with four-poster or half-tester beds, and modern suites with jacuzzi baths, each with en suite bathroom, hair dryer, trouser press, colour TV.) Rates include Welsh breakfast. Special breaks available

Year round

✕ A la carte menu

✻ Friendly old/new mix

Health and fitness centre features swimming pool, including children's paddling pool, 2 solariums, 2 saunas, steam room, pool tables, 2 outdoor tennis courts, 2 squash courts, weight-training area and children's play area

♫ No

★ Roman Caerleon

A few minutes from Junction 25 of the M4 and ½ hour from the Severn Bridge. Approaching from Cardiff or Bristol, take the road to Caerleon and follow the one-way system around the village, then take the road to Usk. The hotel is 3 miles (5 km) along on the left

£/$ C

Egerton Grey Country House

American owner Bart Zuzik and his wife fell in love with this splendid manor house the moment they saw it and have preserved much of its character, so you'll find a wealth of antiques, the old Victorian baths and brasswork, open fireplaces, ornate mouldings and some superb mahogany and oak panelling.

The call for drinks in the library is at 7.15 p.m. followed by a six-course dinner at 8 p.m. sharp, to be completed by coffee and petit fours in the drawing room. Dining tables are separate, but the menu is a no-choice one except for desserts and the Welsh cheese board.

Bart (who had previously run a successful Cardiff hotel for some time) is full of American enthusiasm, but as he's an anglophile (or is it Welshophile) he makes afternoon tea at Egerton Grey a speciality.

Porthkerry, South Glamorgan CF6 9BZ. ✆ (0446) 71166

11 (Including 1 single and 1 four-poster, each with en suite bathroom.) Rates include breakfast. No children under 12. Breaks available

Year round

✕ Fixed-price, no-choice menu

✻ Manor house atmosphere, American welcome

Croquet lawn, all-weather tennis court; riding, fishing and golf can be arranged

♫ No

★ The Welsh Folk Museum at St Fagans, Dyffryn House and gardens; historic Cowbridge, Caerphilly Castle

At Porthkerry, 10 miles (16 km) west of Cardiff. From London leave the M4 at Junction 33 and take the A4232 signed to Cardiff Wales Airport (A4050). Then the A4226 towards Porthkerry, and after about ⅕ mile (320 m) there are four thatched cottages — turn into the lane between the second and third

£/$ C

Glanrannell Park Hotel

This secluded hotel is popular with bird watchers since it is within easy reach of a range of reserves and habitats. The hotel's situation in the Cothi Valley is one of the most beautiful in Wales, with the Brecon Beacons and Black Mountains to the east and the wild Wales land to the north. It's all excellent country for walking and riding.

Glanrannell itself is surrounded by lawns in 23 acres (9¼ ha) of grounds and overlooks a private lake. It derives its name from the Annell, a trout stream which bounds one side of the estate. The simply furnished dining room also overlooks the lake, and guests are welcome to inspect the wine cellar.

This is an unpretentious, personally supervised hotel, suited to the outdoors enthusiast. A bar opens into the Paddock Room, one of two lounges; the other has a colour TV and small library. If you want a picnic lunch and a suggested touring itinerary, ask Dai and Bronwen Davies — they'll be happy to assist.

Crugybar, Llanwrda, Dyfed SA19 8SA. ✆ (05583) 230

12 (8 in main house, 5 with en suite bathrooms, each with tea/coffee facility.) Rates include breakfast

Apr to Oct

Traditional home cooking

Nature-lovers' retreat

Golfing and fishing can be arranged

♫ No

★ Carreg Cennen Castle, the lakeside ruins of Talley Abbey, the Dolaucothi Roman gold mines

In the Cothi Valley, a mile (1½ km) from the village of Crugybar. 20 miles (32 km) from Cardigan Bay, 35 miles (56 km) from Swansea

£/$ E

Gliffaes Country House Hotel

Gliffaes acquired its name from its position between the River Usk and Myarth Hill, for the word is a corruption of the Welsh *Gwlydd Faes*, 'dewy field'. (The river mists trapped by the hillside fall as heavy dew.)

For many centuries the site was one of a tenant farm, but the house as it is today was built in 1883 for a Rev. West. The latter had travelled extensively in Italy, which is perhaps why Gliffaes has that Italianate style with a campanile at each end. Some historians maintain it was a Lugar design, but since the Rev. West's brother was an architect it is equally possible he was responsible.

Inside the hotel you'll find a comfortable, panelled sitting room leading to a Regency-style drawing room. From here French windows open onto a glass-fronted sun room and then the terrace. The dining room and bar also open onto the terrace, from which there are splendid views of the surrounding hills and the River Usk below. A clubby atmosphere pervades the Billiard Room with its full-sized table.

The foundations of the 29 acres (12 ha) of gardens were laid out in the 19th century by William Henry West, an 'Ironmaster' with a great love of rare and beautiful trees. The care in maintaining the grounds and continuing the planting of rare shrubs is carried on by the present owners.

The main occupation for guests here is the fishing. The house overlooks one mile (1½ km) of left bank water of the Usk, and 2¼ miles (3½ km) further upstream is ¾ mile (1¼ km) including both banks, known as Llandetty. Fishermen will find every type of water from slow-flowing flats to little runs formed by rapids — waist waders are recommended. The Usk is most famous for its wild brown trout in a Mar. to Sept. season — some of the best sport is during March and April. Salmon are another possibility with a Jan. to Oct. season — annual catches have averaged 25–30 here over the past few years.

Crickhowell, Powys NP8 1RH. ✆ (0874) 730371

19	(All with individual décor and en suite facilities)	♫	No
🏨	Mid-Mar to Dec	★	Brecon Beacons and the Black Mountains for superb hill walking
✕	Good down to earth food, cold buffet lunches, homemade afternoon teas	🚗	Mid the scenery of Brecon Beacons National Park, one mile (1½ km) off the main A40 road
✻	Informal sporty	£/$	E
🎣	Fishing is the main attraction. In addition to the hotel's own waters there are 8 reservoirs within a 15-mile (24 km) radius. Llangorse Lake, 8 miles (13 km) away, holds pike, perch and other coarse fish. Flies and licences are available from the hotel; equipment (except waders) may be hired. In the grounds are lawns for putting, croquet and bowls; hard tennis court with practice board, also golf practice net. Many other sports in vicinity		

Hand Hotel

Olde Worlde charm and personal attention from owners Tim and Carolyn Alexander are what you'll find here in this former 16th-century farmhouse that has since become a three star, 14-room hotel. Many of the original features like beams and open fires have been retained, but you wouldn't recognise the cowshed — these days, it's an attractive restaurant.

The small hotel has fishing rights on the Ceiriog River, which runs through the village, and its own tennis court; and not surprisingly the surrounding area is excellent for walking and pony-trekking. The less energetic stick to the residents' TV lounge and licensed bar, both of which are cosy and low ceilinged.

Llanarmon Dyffryn Ceiriog, nr Llangollen, Clwyd LL20 7LD
✆ (069176) 666

14 (Each with en suite bathroom.) Rates include early-morning tea and breakfast

Mid-Mar to Jan

✕ Fixed-price menus of country cooking like roast lamb or duckling; homemade soups and desserts

✻ Personal

All-weather tennis court. Fishing on the Ceiriog River; nearby golf and pony-trekking

♫ No

★ Many scenic areas within easy driving distance. Notable National Trust properties, e.g. Erddig, Chirk and Powis Castles. Snowdonia, Caernarfon, Portmeirion and Bodnant Gardens are accessible for a day out

34 miles (55 km) from Chester and Shrewsbury, 82 (132 km) from Birmingham and 62 (100 km) from Liverpool. From the A5 in Chirk, take the B4500 for the 11 miles (18 km) to Llanarmon Dyffryn Ceiriog

£/$ C

Henllys Hall

A romantic hotel on a romantic island which has been the centre of Celtic culture since 150 BC. On Anglesey the Druids made their fiercest stand against the Romans, and the island's landscape derives from rugged, ancient rocks, the oldest in Wales.

Henllys Hall on the other hand wasn't built until 1852, on the site of the court of Llewelyn the Great, who was married to King John's daughter Princess Joan. When the Welsh rebelled in Anglesey in 1294, Edward I decided to build his castle at Beaumaris but ran out of money before he could complete it. He brought in English people to keep the Welsh down and made one family, the Hamptons, the officials of the castle. It was they who built a timber house here and it was Hansom of Hansom Cabs who designed Henllys as you see it.

The hotel is set in 50 acres (20 ha) with fantastic views of Snowdonia and the Menai Straits. In the grounds are two cottages, two bungalows and five apartments, a walled garden, tennis court and outdoor pool.

Beaumaris, Anglesey. ✆ (0248) 810412

22	(Each with en suite bathroom, including four-posters; plus 2 cottages, 2 bungalows and 5 apartments, each with colour TV, coffee/tea facility.) Rates include breakfast	♫	No
🏨	Year round	★	The island itself
✕	Traditional English table d'hôte and à la carte	🚗	Off the B5109
✻	Comfort and fun	£/$	C
🏸	Outdoor pool, jacuzzi, sauna and sunbeds, pool table, tennis court, table tennis		

The Lake Hotel

Jean-Pierre and Jan Mifsud regard their hotel as the Welsh equivalent of a Scottish country lodge. It is true it hides away in 50 acres (20 ha) of grounds — sweeping lawns, riverside walks, pathways lined with rhododendrons and a large trout-stocked lake. And it is true that anglers like it here for some of the best fishing in Wales.

The house, inside, stays true to its Victorian character in size and decoration of its public rooms. Bedrooms are also large, either with sitting area or as a suite. A host of country pursuits may be arranged, but the emphasis is on restful well-being.

Llangammarch Wells, Powys LD4 4BS. ✆ (05912) 202

19 (Including 9 suites, each with en suite bathroom and colour TV; some four-posters.) Rates include breakfast

Year round

✕ The emphasis is on game dishes and homemade desserts

✻ Restful

On the premises are a golf practice course, tennis court and billiard room; clay pigeon shooting may be arranged. 4 golf courses within vicinity and some of the best fishing on its doorstep — fishing also from the hotel's own lake. Pony treks can be arranged

♫ No

★ Brecon Beacons, Powis Castle is 1½ hours away

By rail to Swansea or Shrewsbury then on to Llangammarch Wells Station where guests are met. By car from London, leave the M4 at Junction 24, then the A449 to Raglan, the A40 to Abergavenny and follow the signs to Builth Wells up the Wye Valley. The A483 to Garth and follow the signs to the hotel

£/$ C

Llanwenarth House

The ancestral home of privateer Capt. Henry Morgan dates from the 16th century and is built of locally quarried, rosy-grey limestone. Located in the midst of Brecon Becons National Park, it remained in the hands of the Morgan family until 1955 but is now the family home of the Weatherills, who are happy to welcome guests.

It is quite probable that King Charles kept his reserve horses and armour here to assist the Royalist cause during the Civil War. (Harness and armour from that date were found when part of the attic was opened up in the 1950s.)

Because it is a family home attention is personalised. Amanda Weatherill is a cordon bleu cook and loves to cook the meals that are served by candlelight in the dining room. The Weatherills welcome children over 5 (they have some of their own).

Govilon, Abergavenny, Gwent NP7 9SF. ✆ (0873) 830289

5	(Each with en suite bathroom, colour TV and coffee/tea facility.) Children over 5 welcome. Rates include breakfast
🏛	Year round
✕	Fixed-price meal
✻	Welsh charm
⚲	Not on premises, but opportunities for walking, pony-trekking, climbing and rough shooting in vicinity; also golf on the Monmouthshire course and salmon fishing on the River Usk
♫	No
★	Chepstow, Raglan, Pembridge and numerous other castles. Hereford Cathedral, Offas Dyke, the superb Brecon Beacons and Black Mountains. The Brecon and Monmouthshire Canal, which the grounds border, is one of the best-preserved waterways in Britain
🚗	Govilon can be reached by leaving the M4 at Junction 26 to the A4042, then the B4269, then 3 miles (5 km) to Abergavenny
£/$	E

Llwynderw

If you fancy a hideaway place in the Welsh mountains — and I do mean hideaway — this could be it.

The house, an 18th-century Georgian-styled one, is built on land which once belonged to Cistercian monks in wild moorland some 1,000 ft (305 m) above sea-level, protected by beeches and oaks, with no other habitation in sight. It has its own spring water and its own peat fires. Proprietor Michael Yates sometimes takes charge of the cooking himself.

Llwynderw's charm is in its seclusion. Nature lovers will enjoy the walks possible from the hotel's front door — the beautiful landscape with its rare birds and flowers, the lakes that hold salmon and sea trout. It is a place to relax and unwind, of interest to painters, photographers, naturalists or those who wish to read in comfort. Because of its comparative isolation, a minimum two-night stay is requested.

Abergwesyn, Llanwrtyd Wells, Powys LD5 3TW.
✆ (05913) 238

12	(Each with en suite bathroom). Rates are half board. No children under 10
🏨	Easter to Xmas
✕	No-choice dinner menu varies to suit freshest produce; Welsh lamb, of course, a speciality. Jacket necessary
✻	Get away from it all — definitely not for ravers
⚲	No (but hotel has its own library)
♫	No
★	Powis Castle, Brecon Beacons
🚗	Located 67 miles (108 km) from Newport — the latter may be reached from London by express train in 1 hour 20 minutes. By road take the M4, the Severn bridge, Newport (leave at Junction 24 from the motorway)
£/$	C half board

Miskin Manor

There was a manor on this lovely Welsh site in 1092, when it was the home of the Prince of Glamorgan's daughter, but the present house was built in 1858 for David Williams whose family occupied it until it became a hotel in the 1980s. The manor is reached via a long, tree-lined drive through the grounds and gardens.

The interior is attractive without being stuffy. Drinks are served in the oak-panelled bar or comfortable lounge; meals are served in the pleasant oak-panelled restaurant with its views over the 20 acres (8 ha) of lawns and parkland. Well appointed guest rooms include one suite where the Prince of Wales (later King Edward VIII) stayed on one of his many trips to the manor in the 1920s.

A major feature at Miskin is Fredericks, a complete leisure-club complex that boasts its own bistro restaurant and bar whose menu specialises in salads and fondues.

Miskin, Mid Glamorgan CF7 8ND. ✆ (0443) 224204

32 (Individually furnished, including four-poster and suites; each with en suite bathroom, colour TV, hair dryer, trouser press.) Breaks available

Year round

✕ British à la carte; good range of wines, from the local Croffta to Château Petrus

✳ For the recreationally minded

Fredericks leisure complex features indoor heated pool, sauna, solarium, gym, billiards, aerobics classes, squash, badminton, table tennis etc

♫ No

★ Cardiff Castle, Caerphilly Castle

A few minutes drive from Junction 34 of the M4, 15 minutes from Cardiff Airport, just under two hours from Heathrow

£/$ C

Penally Abbey Hotel

A most attractive Pembrokeshire country house hotel in its own 5 acres (2 ha) of gardens and woodland with panoramic views across Carmarthen Bay, Caldey Island and Giltar Point. No one seems to know the building's history though religious connections are confirmed by the ruined chapel in the grounds. But in any case, the name conjures up the tranquillity that a stay here rewards you with.

No, you won't have to get up early — country breakfasts are served until 11 a.m., which makes a change — either on the terrace if the weather is good, or in the dining room. Marvellous views whichever one. At night the tables are lit by candlelight, and aperitifs may be taken in the Pillar Room Bar or Sun Lounge.

There are only 12 bedrooms, most with bathrooms and some with four-poster beds — ask for the converted coach house rooms. As a plus factor, Penally Abbey has its own small, indoor pool which may be heated to spa temperature.

Penally, nr Tenby, Pembroke, Dyfed. ✆ (0834) 3033

12 (Including four-poster rooms, 9 with en suite facilities, each with hair dryer, colour TV, coffee/tea tray.) Rates include country breakfast

Year round

Home made soups and patés, home-cured Abbey hams, Teifi salmon and Welsh lamb are all specialities

Most hospitable

Indoor pool; other sports nearby

No

St David's, St Bride's; many nature walks

From just outside Tenby, take the Pembroke–Penally coast road to the sign marked Penally. Follow the road for about 1 mile (1½ km) to the village green, where the hotel stands

£/$ E

Plas Bodegroes

This Welsh gem of a Georgian-styled country house is more of a 'restaurant with rooms', the term used by proprietors Chris Chown and Gunna Trodni. Chris does all the cooking, taking full advantage of the local produce which includes some of the best lamb and lobster in the world. Fresh seafood is prepared and enjoyed the very day the boat comes in, and the poultry and eggs used in the kitchen are all of the free-range variety.

Though the focus is on food, the house itself is furnished to a high standard in keeping with its 1780 date, and the limited accommodation is equally well decorated.

Bodegroes stands in 5 acres (2 ha) of grounds filled with ancient beeches, and on the doorstep is the Lleyn Peninsula's spectacular sea cliffs and sandy coves.

Pwllheli, Gwynedd, LL53 5TH. ✆ (0758) 612363

6 (All with en suite bathrooms, including four-posters.) Rates include breakfast

Year round

Specialities are fresh lobster, oysters, crab and turbot, also Welsh lamb and beef

Characteristically Welsh

Nearby fishing, riding, shooting, windsurfing, walking

No

Abersoch, Lloyd George Museum, the Llyn Peninsula

The northwest of the M56 connects with the A55, the main North Wales coast road to Bangor. From here take the A487 and A499 to Pwllheli

£/$ D

Soughton Hall

'Don't be afraid to ask for what you need', John and Rosemary Rodenhurst tell guests at this superb, Georgian mansion house hotel just outside Chester. They're pretty obliging whether requirements call for an exceptionally early breakfast or a late-night cold buffet, or whatever. Soughton Hall is a stately home but it's also a family one, restored with loving care — and good humour!

From the time it was built in 1714 until its purchase by the Rodenhursts, the Hall used to belong to the Wynne-Bankes family, a line which boasted many distinguished members including a bishop, two knights, a chaplain to Queen Victoria and a great traveller and collector, William John Bankes.

It was William John who added the roof pavilions, mullioned windows and Islamic turrets in the 1820s, inspired by his travels in the Middle East. His plans were drawn by Charles Barry, later to become a 'Sir', architect of the Houses of Parliament. The same William John inherited Kingston Lacy in Dorset, where he housed his gradually accumulated art treasure — now a pride of the National Trust.

As to Soughton Hall, after the World War II, its fortunes declined. When the Rodenhurst family bought it, the property was affected by dry rot and a leaking roof, and could only boast antiquated plumbing and electrics. Within a year, hard work and skilled local craftsmen turned the place around, reviving its original splendour in order to open as a hotel in 1987.

Impressive in appearance, Soughton's front door is reached via a grand avenue bordered by lime trees, surrounded by parkland. Among the curiosities in the grounds are a game larder, a mechanical stile and a coach house. On the more familiar side, there are tennis and croquet facilities.

The hotel's interior is equally impressive, featuring an 18th-century, carved and polished oak staircase giving access to public and guest rooms. French tapestries, Persian carpets and marble fireplaces add a stateliness to the 19th-century drawing room. In the elegant library, books may be borrowed for a peaceful read. Step through a hidden door in the bookcase and you're in the Justice Bar, once the courtroom of a Bankes family High Sheriff. Under a 19th-century French chandelier in the dining room, guests are served at polished wood tables gleaming with crystal and silver, and enjoy wine brought up from vaulted, stone-flagged cellars beneath the hall.

Bedrooms which have guested aristocrats and statesmen in the past have been decorated in romantic fashion, modernised to the extent that former dressing rooms have been converted into fully appointed — but period style — bathrooms, retaining their mullioned windows.

Northop, nr Mold, Clwyd C117 6AB. ✆ (035286) 207

11 (Twin or double, all individually decorated, including a four-poster and a 'character' Tower room. Each has colour TV, en suite bathroom, trouser press and personalised extras.) Rates include English breakfast. Breaks available

Year round

✕ Table d'hôte and à la carte, with the emphasis on fresh produce. Jacket and tie necessary

✻ Stately

Games room for billiards and darts; croquet and tennis in the grounds. Nearby riding, fishing, golf and clay pigeon shooting

♫ Resident harpist on Sat. night

★ The Roman and medieval walled city of Chester is very close by, as is the beautiful North Wales countryside. Visits may easily be made to Bodnant Gardens, Portmeirion, Snowdon Mountain Railway and Liverpool Maritime Museum

Located 6 minutes from Flint railway station and a 40-minute drive from Manchester International Airport, 15 minutes from Chester. Northop village is on the A55

£/$ A

SOUTHERN IRELAND (EIRE)

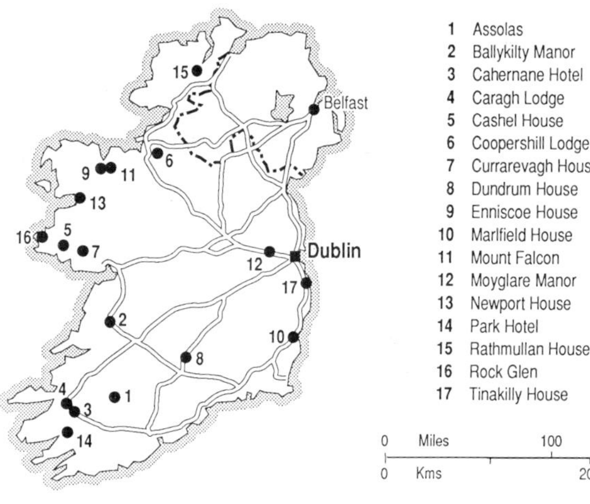

Eire's most celebrated castle hotels are featured in a companion volume, *Europe's Historic Castle and Palace Hotels* (Christopher Helm Ltd), but Southern Ireland is equally famous for its smaller country house hotels scattered throughout its most interesting holiday areas. They are not all of de luxe standard though Irish hospitality extends to excellent food not served in skimpy portions, and of course the traditional 'welcome mat'.

They certainly vary from the small and rural to the more glossy, used to receiving American tourists — and many of them offer bed and breakfast rates far below England's. The Irish Tourist Board itself publishes a booklet that lists an association of country house hotels and restaurants, though there is no central booking number. There is also a consortium of 'Manor House Hotels' in Southern Ireland with a central Dublin number: (01) 602955.

Assolas Country House

Hugh Bourke, whose family has owned Assolas House since 1915, is sure of its monastic origins, pointing out the 'Leper's Peep', a unique, still-visible feature which has been of great interest and controversy to this century's historians. The grey, ivy-clad central portion of the house is undeniably Jacobean — the shape of the windows, the deep walls and wood-panelled first floor rooms are all in keeping with this style. Later, Queen Anne wings and gables were added.

The name stems from the 18th century when Assolas belonged to a Rev. Francis Gore, a man who hung a lantern on his walls each night to guide travellers across a dangerous ford which used to span the river. It is reported he saved many a person from drowning, not to mention from highway gangs, and it is also true he held open house for any wounded travellers. The warm and friendly house, thus lit up, became so well known that it was called *Ata Solus* in Gaelic, meaning 'The Ford of the Light'. The abbreviated anglicised version is as we know it today — Assolas.

The Bourkes are quite a large family, with all members chipping in to the running of what is now a hotel: son Joe presides in the old flagstoned kitchen producing 'moderated nouvelle' cuisine; daughter Catherine contributes homemade terrines, chutneys and ice creams, while another daughter, Paula, arranges for fresh seafood. Hugh wife Eleanor creates the informal flower arrangements in every alcove, and the homely touches like log fires and hot water bottles.

Hugh Bourke grew up here and some of the room names (though they've changed their use) are reminders — The Schoolroom and The Nursery. His ancestors gaze from the gilt frames adorning the yellow wall of the drawing room.

Dinner is served at polished tables in the red dining room. Candles, flowers, sparkling glass and damask napkins are effective even though the menu offers a limited choice. And afterwards, to bed in a large, bright, spotless room.

Hugh Bourke is a passionate gardener, which is perhaps one main reason the grounds at Assolas are meticulously kept. Here, lawns, tennis court and gravel slope gently to the river with its weir, small boat and wooden bridge, and the Bourkes' much loved swans.

Kanturk, Co. Cork, Ireland. ✆ (029) 50015

14 (Including suites; mostly double with 3 de luxe rooms in Garden Court and mostly with private bathrooms.) Rates include full Irish breakfast

Easter to Oct

✕ Restricted menu choice, but well prepared

✻ Irish homely charm

Tennis, croquet, river with boating and fishing; nearby golf

♫ No

★ Killarney, Ring of Kerry, the Dingle Peninsula, Bantry Bay, Blarney Castle, Bunratty

1½ hours from Cork or Shannon Airport; northeast of Kanturk — turn off the road towards Buttevant

£/$ C

Ballykilty Manor House

Situated in 50 acres (20 ha) of rolling hills, woodland and trails, the Georgian manor of Ballykilty overlooks the famous 15th-century Quin Abbey. Until a few years ago the Blood family had lived here continually from 1614. (One of them stole the British Crown Jewels in the reign of Charles II.) Part of the original building is still used, while at the back are coach houses, stables and liveries.

The hotel has a spacious lounge bar in an old drawing room setting, a reading and TV room, and an Old Coach House bar. This is a comfortably informal base from which to tour the Clare countryside or indulge in nearby sporting facilities. The River Rine runs through the hotel's own estates, providing salmon and trout fishing, and there is also a par 3 nine-hole golf course in the grounds.

Quin, Co. Clare, Ireland. ✆ (065) 25627

- 11 — (Each with en suite bathroom.) Rates include breakfast
- Year round, except Xmas
- ✕ Table d'hôte and à la carte, featuring traditional Irish fare
- ✻ Casual
- 9-hole golf course, trout and salmon fishing in the grounds; nearby golf and beaches. Hunting within 30 miles (48 km) and local equestrian centres
- ♫ No, but medieval feasts at nearby Knappogue and Bunratty castles
- ★ Quin Abbey, Knappogue Castle, Craggaunowen, Bunratty's Castle & Folk Park
- 10 miles (16 km) from Shannon — take the N18 road
- £/$ C

Cahernane Hotel

A stately manor house, Cahernane was once the residence of the Herbert family, Earls of Pembroke. Today it is a 36-room comfortable, rather than overly ornate hotel, situated in a sylvan parkland setting that is a good starting point for touring the Ring of Kerry.

So far as the history is concerned, it was two brothers, members of the Pembroke family, whose ancestors fought on the Yorkist side during the War of the Roses, who came to Killarney in 1656. One brother was given the Muckross Estate, and the other got the smaller property of Currens and Cahernane, estates maintained by the Hebert family for five generations. The residence you see today was built by Henry Herbert as a more modest replacement of the original Queen Anne mansion.

The Herbert name lingers on in what is now the hotel restaurant, and management have adopted the motto: 'Every Man To His Taste' though I'm not quite sure whether they stick to Henry Herbert's theory that a salmon, to be worth eating, must be in the pot within 20 minutes of being alive in the lake!

Public and guest rooms are nicely appointed (with some feature fireplaces and woodenwork). Amenities include a tennis court and nine-hole golf course on the grounds as well as reserved fishing.

Muckross Road, Killarney, Co. Kerry, Ireland.
✆ (064) 31895

52 (Each with private bathroom.) Rates include breakfast

Easter to Dec

Traditional Irish fare; wine list 110-strong, amazingly includes the hotel's own Italian wine

Irish hospitable

Hard tennis court, 9-hole mini golf, croquet, private fishing; nearby golf and riding

Cellar bar with piano music

★ Ring of Kerry

Against a backdrop of lakes and mountains, ¾ mile (1 km) from Killarney town centre

£/$ C

Caragh Lodge

Michael and Ines Braasch own this pretty country hotel whose 9 acres (3½ ha) of gardens and parkland have in the past won a National Garden Award.

This is not an ornate country house, but the two lounges and dining room are full of good pieces of furniture and overlook that almost incomparable view. The Lodge grows its own vegetables and marinates its salmon — they turn up in well-prepared if not adventurous dishes.

Since the couple who run Caragh are of German origin, some guests may feel they will not experience the true 'Irish experience' by a stay here, as there are obviously some German overtones, but the hospitality offered is worthy of the Irish themselves, and the setting on the Ring of Kerry undeniably Eire personified.

Caragh Lake, Co. Kerry, Ireland. ✆ (066) 69115

10	(Each with en suite bathroom.) Rates include full Irish breakfast	♫	No
🏨	Mar to mid Oct	★	The Ring of Kerry is the biggest attraction
✕	Limited à la carte; fresh fish favoured	🚗	25 miles (40 km) northwest of Killarney, 1 mile (1½ km) off Ring of Kerry between Killorglin and Glenbeigh
✻	German overtones in superb Irish setting	£/$	E
🎾	All-weather tennis court, table tennis, sauna, fishing, boating and swimming on the lake; golf and riding nearby		

Cashel House Hotel

At the head of Cashel Bay is one of Connemara's most distinguished homes, a hotel since 1968 — one that has hosted de Gaulle among other personages, and one that has won the National Garden Award, praised for its attentive service, charm and good food.

A true oasis in the wilds of unspoilt Connemara, whose hundreds of lakes and streams provide the Cashel House kitchen with much of its fresh produce. The hosts supervise the cooking and serving in the pleasant dining room. There are several places within the hotel to sit and relax, including a choice of lounges, library and conservatory. But many guests are drawn to its 50 acres (20 ha) of garden. Exotic and familiar flowering shrubs include rhododendrons, azaleas, camellias and magnolias, bordering pathways. Hotel guests may walk along the seashore or head through the woods, eventually arriving at the summit of Cashel Hill.

Cashel, Connemara, Co. Galway, Ireland. ✆ (095) 31001

32 (Including 13 suites; all with en suite bathrooms — whirlpool baths in 4 garden suites)

Mar to Oct

× Fresh lobster, mussels, scallops etc. and choice Connemara lamb are the specialities

* Easy going, restful

Private beach for swimming, hard tennis court, horse riding and fishing; 18-hole golf course at Ballyconneely

♫ No

★ Connemara National Park; Aran Islands are nearby

In the small village of Cashel at the foot of Cashel Hill, on the edge of the Atlantic Ocean. From Galway take the N59. Turn left to village 1 mile (1½ km) after Recess

£/$ A

Coopershill House

Coopershill is a fine example of a Georgian mansion, home to seven generations of the O'Hara family. Since it was built in 1774 it has retained that spaciousness and elegance of that earlier era, but with added 20th-century comforts.

The house stands in 500 acres (202 ha) of woodland and farmland through which the Arrow River flows — the hotel makes a boat available for guests' use since the river contains pike and perch. There are also good trout waters nearby and many uncrowded beaches up and down the coast.

It is known for its outstanding Irish hospitality so you can anticipate a warm welcome when you stay here. Family silverware and crystal is used for dinner in a room overlooking the river. Unlike so many country house hotels, Coopershill welcomes children.

Riverstown, Co. Sligo, Ireland. ✆ (071) 65108

6 (Each with en suite bathroom, 5 with canopy or four-poster bed.) Children welcome. Rates include Irish breakfast

Apr to Oct

✕ Traditional Irish

✻ Good Irish hospitality

Fishing in the river; golfing 12 miles (19 km) away

♫ No

★ Donnegal and Connemara are an easy day's trip. This is Yeats country, and the poet himself is buried at Drumcliff not far away

12 miles (19 km) from Sligo via the N4

£/$ D

Currarevagh House

The name of this early Victorian manor is pronounced 'Curra reeva'. The house, situated in 150 acres (61 ha) of land about 100 yards (91 m) from Lough Corrib, hasn't much changed from its original layout and there is still an air of tranquillity and old-fashioned hospitality.

Lavish Edwardian breakfasts are still laid out each morning on the sideboard in the dining room. Full lunches are also laid on for those who don't wish to take advantage of the hotel's famous picnics, and dinners are five-course meals, after which coffee may be taken in one of the sitting rooms in front of an open peat fire if the weather warrants it. Afternoon tea is another ritual.

A long avenue flanked by chestnut, beech and pine trees leads to the mansion whose lawns overlook Lough Corrib and slope down to Currarevagh Bay. An earlier generation of Hodgesons brought back the rhododendrons from India, now growing in profusion everywhere. Very peaceful.

Oughterard, Connemara, Co. Galway, Ireland.
✆ (091) 82312

15	(All with en suite facilities.) Rates include breakfast	♫	No
🏨	Easter to Oct	★	Connemara National Park; Aran Islands nearby
✕	Quality and quantity based on fresh, local produce	🚗	4 miles (6 km) northwest of Oughterard. Take the N59 Galway–Flifden to Oughterard, turn right in the village square and follow the lakeshore road
✳	Old-fashioned hospitality in peaceful setting	£/$	C
🎾	All-weather tennis court, croquet, fishing (the hotel has its own boats and sporting rights over 5,000 acres (2024 ha)); 2 equestrian centres and 3 golf courses within easy reach		

Dundrum House Hotel

Dundrum is a fine 18th-century Georgian manor built by the Maude family in 1730, when it was surrounded by a 2,400 acre (971 ha) estate. This consolidated the family's possession of an estate which was once the property of Irish chieftains, the O'Dwyers of Kilnamanagh, dispossessed of their lands in Cromwell's time in the 17th century. The Maudes stayed owners until the beginning of this century, when a religious order acquired the property.

Austin and Mary Crowe bought Dundrum in 1978, making extensive renovation to revive its former graceful state. The quiet bar has feature stained-glass windows and the roomy, ornate lounges are never uninviting since huge open fires are lit during chilly evenings. Nowadays, this beautiful house is encircled by 100 acres (40 ha) studded with ancient trees and crossed by a trout-filled river.

Dundrum, Cashel, Co. Tipperary, Ireland.
✆ (062) 71116

55 (Each with en suite bathroom.) Rates include full Irish breakfast. Breaks available

Year round

✕ Fixed-price menu; favourite dish is fillet of beef in a whisky cream sauce

✻ Restored Georgian grandeur

Games room; fishing, golf, pony-trekking and tennis can be arranged

♫ No

★ Rock of Cashel, seat of Munster kings since 370 AD Glen of Aherlow, Cahir Castle and Holycross Abbey, both 12th century; also the Mitchelstown Caves

Located 6 miles (10 km) from Cashel, 31 (50 km) from Limerick and 60 (97 km) from Cork

£/$ C

Enniscoe House

Susan Kellett had the happy distinction of inheriting this Irish Georgian house from the original owners, and has worked very hard to ensure Enniscoe retains its elegance yet is accessible to the public. It is therefore open for tours at specified times of the year, and is open throughout the year as a guest house.

Surrounded by wooded parkland, the house has its own jetty on Lake Conn and two islets, one with a ruined 15th-century castle. The 300-acre (121 ha) estate is run as a working farm, but guests may fish for pike on a small lake within the estate.

The front part of the house, comprising two large reception rooms and an oval staircase hall was added in the 1790s to an earlier building. Considered the 'last great house of North Mayo', Enniscoe is noted for its delicate interior plasterwork and is filled with family portraits and antique furniture.

Castlehill, nr Crossmolina, Ballina, Co. Mayo, Ireland.
✆ (096) 31112

6 (Each with private but not en suite bathroom, with canopy or four-poster beds.) Rates include breakfast

Year round

✕ Local lamb and fresh fish are main features; fixed-price dinner

✻ Friendly, historic house

Fishing on Lake Conn for trout and salmon — boats and ghillies may be hired; or for pike in the estate's small lake. Also in the area the famous Moy River and deep-sea fishing at Killala and Belmullet. Riding, golf and beaches nearby

♫ No

★ The wild, rugged scenery of Co. Mayo

On Lough Conn, 2 miles (3 km) south of Crossmolina on the road to Pontoon and Castlebar, 12 miles (19 km) from Ballina

£/$ C

Marlfield House

Marlfield is a handsome example of a Regency house situated in 35 acres (14 ha) of woodland and gardens. It was the dower house on the Courtown Estate, former residence of the Earl of Courtown, and has been converted to a hotel 'for discerning guests' by Ray and Mary Bowe. The Regency elegance is notable in the well-proportioned drawing room, but other rooms recall the magnificence of Victorian, cast-iron, domed conservatories. This one was inspired by Richard Turner, the most important Irish conservatory builder in the 19th century, and the largest to be constructed this century using his principles.

The bar, more of a lounge, also reflects individuality in décor as do the bedrooms, several with original half-tester beds and some with fine antique furniture and fittings.

Built in 1820, the house was a private home until the present Earl sold it to Ray and Mary, whose aim is 'to make your stay as pleasurable as possible'.

Gorey, Co. Wexford, Ireland. ✆ (055) 21124

12 (All different, all with en suite bathroom, some with original half-tester beds.) No children under 6. Rates include breakfast

Jan 1 to Dec 23

✕ Highly acclaimed

✻ Stylish

Tennis court, croquet; golf, shooting, fishing, riding and hunting may be arranged. Good beaches nearby

♫ No

★ The waterfalls of Powerscourt Demesne, Russborough House, Mount Usher Gardens, the Devil's Glen and Glendalough

On the Gorey/Courtown road 1¼ miles (2 km) east of Gorey and 45 minutes drive from four of seven principal entry points into Ireland

£/$ C No credit cards

Mount Falcon Castle

Built in 1876 as the country mansion of John Fredrick Knox, Mount Falcon Castle is a fisherman's dream. It offers preserved salmon fishing on the River Moy, free salmon and trout fishing on Lough Conn and excellent estuary and sea fishing. The Moy is recognised as Ireland's best salmon river, with large numbers between April and September. The hotel's fishery has 7 miles (11 km) of double bank fishing on the lower reaches of the Moy, and maintains five private beats with ghillies and boats for guests' use. The hotel equally is the oldest established country house catering for the angler in Ireland — its proprietor and resident fishery manager are both experienced and knowledgeable anglers themselves.

The estate covers 100 acres (40 ha) with quiet walks through wood and parkland extending down to the river.

Ballina, Co. Mayo, Ireland. ✆ (096) 21172

11 (With period furniture and views of the estate; 8 with en suite bathrooms.) Rates include breakfast

Apr to Jan, but closed Xmas week

✕ Fresh salmon and trout the obvious speciality, home-grown produce

✻ Good fisherman's haunt

Fishing, all-weather tennis court, games room; in season, rough shooting for woodcock and snipe

♫ No

★ Deserted beaches, a rugged coastline, lakes, mountains and wild bogland form the surrounding area. Nearby Killala is where General Humbert's French army landed in 1798. Irish tweed weaving may be seen at Foxford Woollen Mills

Just off the N57 from Ballina

£/$ D

Moyglare Manor

A tree-lined avenue leads to this handsome Georgian house. Norah Devlin (who used to own Barberstown Castle and Ashbourne House) has furnished it to high standards and runs it with her family. There are several lounges, all restful, all with some period pieces — the lounge bar is especially well appointed and comfy — the convivial place to be for a drink and evening entertainment.

Antiques from the family collection enhance many of the bedrooms, some with four-posters, giving them all an air of nobility. Fresh flowers add the light touch, and all the windows afford views of hundreds of acres (hectares) of parkland and mountains in the background.

Good food (by candle light of an evening) and equally good wine list plus the traditional Irish hospitality make this country hotel worthy of mention.

Moyglare, Maynooth, Co. Kildare, Ireland.
✆ (01) 286351

13 (Including 2 garden suites and four-posters; individually furnished.) No children under 12. Rates include breakfast
Year round, except Xmas
✕ Good quality traditional Irish
✻ Peaceful, hospitable
Golf, fishing, riding can be arranged locally
♫ In lounge bar
★ Dublin, stud farms, Castletown House
18 miles (29 km) from Dublin, just outside the university town of Maynooth. Off the main Dublin–Galway road. Convenient to Dublin Airport and ferry ports of Dublin and Dun Laoghaire
£/$ B

Newport House

One of those beautiful Irish country houses full of character, Newport is a member of Relais & Chateaux and enjoys a charming location in West Mayo. For some 200 years it was the country estate and home of the O'Donel family, descendants of the fighting Earls of Tyrconnell and cousins of Ireland's famous 'Red Hugh'. It was Cromwell who transplanted them from Ulster to Mayo.

Built on earlier foundations, the house is Georgian in style, as you will see from the plasterwork in the small alcoves on the ground floor. One of the main features is the entrance hall with its graceful staircase surmounted by lantern and dome. Upstairs, the drawing room is decorated with Regency-style mirrors and chandelier, with windows that look out onto the garden.

The self-contained sections are particularly suited to families. The estate's own fishery and farm help provide fresh produce used by the kitchen.

Newport, Co. Mayo, Ireland. ✆ Newport 098 41222

18 (12 in the main house; six in the courtyard houses; all individually furnished.) Rates include breakfast

Mar to Oct

✕ Fresh products from the fishery, garden and farm are used, including home-smoked salmon

✻ Quality

Fishing in estate's private waters or nearby loughs; shooting and riding can be arranged. Nearby golf. Indoor billiard and snooker room

♫ No

★ Rockfleet and Kildonnet castles, the ruins of Castleaffy and the castle on Clare Island

Adjoining Newport, overlooking the river and quay, set between Achill Island and the mountains of Mayo

£/$ D

Park Hotel Kenmare

A vast Victorian mansion, custom-built of stone as a railway hotel at the turn of the century, the Park is a country hotel in grand style yet one with friendly, efficient service from a young staff. Fodor is impressed by it, so is Egon Ronay, who voted it Hotel of the Year last in 1988, so that may tell you something about this now privately-owned property in its own park overlooking Kenmare Bay. It is also a member of that luxury British consortium, Prestige.

If you love antiques, you'll be delighted by a stay here. In the Hall alone where peat fires blaze and 'Reception' is a mere desk tucked away near the grand staircase, there are magnificent paintings and tapestries vaguely lit by beautiful chandeliers. There are some exceptional pieces of furniture throughout the hotel restored to their old glory, including fine old antiques in the guest rooms.

In the elegant dining room where an open fire burns in cool weather, service is exemplary, and food a tempting mixture of local specialities and imaginative dishes, which have won the hotel coveted merits. The views are A1, too.

Kenmare, Co. Kerry, Ireland. ✆ (064) 41200

56 (Including 6 luxury suites; some with antiques, some more modern, several with four-posters. All with en suite bathrooms.) Rates are half board

Year round

Irish lamb and fresh fish are specialities: monkfish with tomato and garlic or baked turbot with crabmeat and apple perhaps. Unusual items like nettle soup, and desserts that might include chilled almond soufflé

Grand, but hospitable

The staff will recommend all kinds of walking and driving routes

No

★ Ring of Kerry

A stone's throw from the village of Kenmare on the Ring of Kerry route, the west coast's most striking region

£/$ C half board

Rathmullan House

An early 19th-century house, Rathmullan is distinguished enough to have been featured on television (though its own guest rooms do not have TVs), won a National Garden Award and is a member of the Relais & Chateaux group. Serene inside and out, the mansion stands on the shore of Lough Swilly, with a garden created by owner Bob Wheeler which slopes right down to a beach.

Furnishings are tasteful whether you're relaxing in front of a wood fire in the library or drawing room, watching the box in the TV room, or supping a glass or two down in the cellar bar. The dining room has a feature tent-style draping, and a menu which in the owner's capable hands manages to combine Irish simplicity with continental elegance.

County Donegal is sometimes 'overlooked', which at least has meant its beaches are uncrowded and its scenery left unspoilt by campsites.

Rathmullan, Letterkenny, Co. Donegal, Ireland.
✆ (074) 58188

19	(Of different sizes, most with en suite bathrooms.) Rates include full Irish breakfast	♫	No
	Easter to mid Oct	★	Glenveagh National Park and Derek Hill's Glebe Gallery
✕	Fixed-price meals with an emphasis on seafood		On the shores of Lough Swilly, 87 miles (140 km) from Sligo
✻	Informal elegance	£/$	C
	Table tennis and pool table, grass tennis court, croquet; golf and fishing nearby		

Rock Glen

John and Evangeline Roche emphasise traditional Irish hospitality at Rock Glen, a converted 18th-century shooting lodge. It's a homely rather than impressive place, though it's large enough to provide 30 bedrooms. Open turf fires and food which John prepares are among the attractions.

There is a cocktail bar and billiard room and all the bedrooms have private bath, but Rock Glen is not a glamorous place. On the contrary, it's a value-for-money, relaxing country hotel in the most westerly part of Ireland noted for its wildly beautiful land and seascapes. Suited to the more down-to-earth holidaymakers.

Clifden, Connemara, Co. Galway, Ireland. ✆ (095) 21035

30 (all with en suite bathrooms) Rates are for three days half board

🏨 April to Oct

✕ Table d'hôte 5-course, e.g. baked stuffed mussels, celery and stilton soup, roast stuffed Connemara lamb, homemade Bailey's ice cream gateau and coffee

✻ Down to earth

🎾 Golf, fishing, pony-trekking in the local area

♫ No

★ Alcock & Brown Museum; the scenic and sporting pleasures of Connemara on the doorstep

🚗 1½ miles from Clifden on the Roundstone road, and 4 miles (6 km) from Ballyconneely

£/$ A, but this is 3 days half board

Tinakilly House Hotel

Tinakilly was built in the 1870s for Captain Robert Halpin, the man who, as Commander of the *Great Eastern*, laid the first telegraph cable linking Europe to America. It was a 'thank you' for his contribution to world communications that the British government gave the money for the house's construction, and Halpin personally supervised the purchasing of the best timber to erect it.

The wonderful wooden doors, window shutters and staircase, augmented by Victorian architecture and furnishings, is shown off proudly these days by William and Bee Power, whose home it is. A lofty hall and spacious lounge bar, a comfortable drawing room and a restaurant comprising three dining rooms are among Tinakilly's facilities.

Bedrooms are a blend of Victorian good looks and modern comforts.

Rathnew, Co. Wicklow, Ireland. ✆ (0404) 69274

14 (Each with private facility, colour TV.) Rates include full Irish breakfast

🏨 Year round

✕ Typically Irish, home-baked brown bread

✳ Irish houseparty

Riding and beaches nearby

♫ No

★ Avondale (Charles Parnell's estate), Vale of Avoca beauty spot, Powerscourt Gardens, Russborough stately home, Mount Usher Gardens at Ashford

🚗 From Dublin take the N11 Dublin–Wexford road to Rathnew village. Continue on the R750 through it for about ⅓ mile (½ km). 30 miles (48 km) from Dublin City

£/$ C